BOURBON DEMOCRACY
OF THE
MIDDLE WEST

Nothing appears more surprising to those who consider human affairs with a philosophical eye than the easiness with which the many are governed by the few.

—DAVID HUME

THE SILVER KINGS' MILLENNIUM

WHEN YOUR WAGES WILL BUY JUST HALF WHAT THEY BUY NOW
In *Harpers' Weekly*, XL (August 15, 1896), 793.

Bourbon Democracy
of the
Middle West
1865-1896

HORACE SAMUEL MERRILL

LOUISIANA STATE UNIVERSITY PRESS

BATON ROUGE

MANUFACTURED IN THE UNITED STATES OF AMERICA
BY THE VAIL-BALLOU PRESS, INC., BINGHAMTON, N.Y.

TO

MARION GALBRAITH MERRILL

Preface

In preparing this study, the author enlisted the aid of many people. The tireless efforts of his wife were invaluable. Her success in creating the necessary environment for research and writing rivaled in importance her typing and editing services. The patient counsel and the encouragement that were constantly forthcoming from the mind and heart of Professor William B. Hesseltine of the University of Wisconsin were indispensable.

Professors Edward White, Scripps College, E. Bruce Thompson, Baylor University, and Clare L. Marquette, University of Mississippi, and Miss Alice Smith, State Historical Society of Wisconsin, furnished valuable material; Professors Hans Bernt, Elmira College, Herbert A. Crosman and David S. Sparks, University of Maryland, and T. Harry Williams, Louisiana State University, read the manuscript and gave pertinent suggestions; Professor John D. Hicks, University of California, aided me in the early research; Professor Selig Perlman, University of Wisconsin, went the second mile in providing encouragement; and Mrs. Thomas M. Smylie, Louisiana State University Press, edited with skill, patience, and good humor. Final decisions and final responsibility for the study, nevertheless, remain with the author.

The author employs the term Bourbon to identify and to characterize the dominant Democratic leadership in the Middle West and East. These post–Civil War Democratic leaders were Bourbons in the sense of being wealthy, self-esteemed, self-appointed guardians of an already fixed pattern for living and making a living. They were protectors of the existing, although accelerating, course of the industrial revolution. They jealously guarded this machinery of material progress against threats from restless farmers and wage earners. Often they referred to themselves, and were referred to by others, as Bourbons.

In the geographical sense, the Middle West of the Bourbons was an area on the move. During the three decades under consideration, people and their institutions gravitated westward. Especially notable in mid-America was the influx of industrial-financial enterprise and a corresponding westward expansion of agriculture. The continuous advance of industry into agricultural territory carried with it the Bourbon Democracy—giving aid and protection to industrial-financial entrepreneurs.

H. S. M.

University of Maryland
College Park, Maryland

Contents

Illustrations

Chapter One

A Thirty Years' War

The generation between 1865 and 1895 was already mortgaged to the railways, and no one knew it better than the generation itself.
                                        —HENRY ADAMS

MODERN WARS, being terrific volcanic eruptions of long-pent-up tensions, leave in their wake a twisted, distorted social structure. Victors acquire spoils to allocate, advantages to push forward and entrench. Conflict emerges among the victors; individuals and groups contend for the dominant role in rebuilding the social structure.

The most embracing post–Civil War cleavage within the victors' camp was the economic struggle between businessmen with bulging purses and farmers with slim purses. In terms of economic pursuits, the most conspicuous and dynamic element in the wealthy class was the industrialist and financier clan. With unprecedented speed and singleness of purpose, entrepreneurs swarmed out of the Civil War debris, carrying with them plans, inventions, and war-born fortunes to be used in turning the nation's natural resources and man power into instruments of unprecedented gain. Through the ensuing years, alert recruits found places in the parade of progress. Spearheading the opposition forces, made up of those less fortunate, was the discontented farmer. At times joining forces with the farmer was an army of unhappy wage earners.

The contending forces were in essential agreement on the desirability of industrial expansion, but they differed on the allocation of the profits. Various means were used by both sides to advance claims or retain a favorable place at the font of gains. The "haves" employed the devices of handouts, blandishments, intimidation, and politics; the "have-nots" tried supplication, threats, strikes, and politics. On both sides politics was the chief device employed.

One of the most influential political groups in America's madly surging industrial advance was the Bourbon Democracy of the Middle West. This was a cabal of industrialist-financier entrepreneurs operating within the Democratic party. Its task was to occupy the only really vulnerable outpost in the political-economic empire of big business, the discontented agrarian Middle West. This book is a record of the Bourbon Democracy's tactics, successes, and failures in carrying out its assignment to sit on the lid of farmer and wage-earner opposition. It is a record of embittering, frustrating defeats for those people who looked to the Democracy to distribute more equitably the fruits of the industrial-financial advance. It is the story of a thirty years' war between industrialist-financier large capitalists and farmer-laborer small capitalists.

The middle-western center of political recalcitrance was a slowly retreating caravan which crawled ever westward before the relentless infiltrations of industrialization. During the course of three decades, industrialist leaders crept into once predominantly agricultural Ohio, Indiana, and Michigan. Together with growing urban islands in other states, these bastions of industrialization became strong bases for political activity. But whatever the fluctuating size, shape, and strength of the Middle West, it remained a sizable area that was primarily agricultural, an ever-present core of discontent. At one time or another during the period, such states as Ohio, Indiana, Michigan, Minnesota, Illinois, Wisconsin, Iowa, and Nebraska embraced groups of embattled farmers and wage earners.

In the Middle West both tradition and circumstance dictated that a newly vigorous Bourbon Democracy should emerge to further big-business imperialism. Stephen A. Douglas had laid the political groundwork before the Civil War by emphasizing in his Democratic party a program of industrial expansion. The major difference between this older Bourbon Democracy of Douglas and the newer Bourbon Democracy was simply one of emphasis. While Douglas was the more susceptible to Potomac Fever, the postwar Bourbons were the more susceptible to Wall Street Fever. Douglas was a professional politician first and a businessman incidentally. The later Bourbons were business leaders first and politicians incidentally. Circumstances dictated this reversal in emphasis. Douglas had begun his career when politics was especially attractive, and not until much later did he discover and explore the potentialities of the industrial revolution. Most new Bourbon Democrats, on the other hand, had for their first love the fascinating pursuit of industrial-financial profits and entered politics only as an avocation or to protect their wealth against politically conscious farmers and laborers. These Bourbons received political aid from the powerful eastern Bourbon Democracy. After thirty years, though they had won but few elections, they could boast success in their main purpose—that of keeping farmers and wage earners from effective control of the Democratic party.

Many farmers likewise, in keeping with tradition and circumstance, turned to the Democracy. Fortunately these farmers had not entirely forgotten the great Thomas Jefferson, whose emphasis on individualism, equality, and agrarianism had been kept alive by Democratic party leaders. They had not completely forgotten Andrew Jackson, Thomas Hart Benton, and the Progressive Western Democracy of their own region. Part of their heritage was a common-sense hatred of monopoly and special privilege in all its forms. In the days of Andrew Jackson the antimonopoly sentiment had become deeply entrenched in the party. The eastern Locofoco wage-earner element provided some of its impetus, and some of it flowed from the indigenous middle-western frontier concept of equality and individualism. Many farmers realized that monopoly afforded opportunities for such things as high interest rates, high railroad rates, and high farm-implement prices. They perceived that big-business control of government gave monopolistic advantages in acquiring high tariffs, snatching the nation's natural resources, and maintaining a currency and a banking system suitable to the wealthy. Thus in the post–Civil War period many farmers looked hopefully to the Democracy.

Farmers, because of their numbers, could have maintained control of the Democratic machinery. They failed to recognize, however, that if the Democracy was to work *for* them, instead of for the Bourbons, it needed to be worked *by* them—worked with consistency and eternal vigilance. False signs of good times produced epidemics of political apathy that proved fatal. The farmers could have counteracted the power of the few. They could have refuted Samuel Johnson's dictum that "power is always gradually stealing away from the many to the few because the few are more vigilant and consistent." In this thirty years' war they did not exercise necessary vigilance and sustained action.

The result was a long-time dominance of the middle-western Democracy by the Bourbon element. This, combined with a similar situation in the southern region, left the nation without any effective political disciplining and moderating influence on the surging industrial revolution. Political unbalance and economic unbalance marched side by side.

Chapter Two

Backdrop to Bourbonism
1865-1867

> *There is a tide in the affairs of men,*
> *Which, taken at the flood, leads on to fortune;*
> *Omitted, all the voyage of their life*
> *Is bound in shallows and in miseries.*
> *On such a full sea are we now afloat;*
> *And we must take the current when it serves,*
> *Or lose our ventures.*
>
> —SHAKESPEARE

DURING THE initial years following the Civil War there existed no definable Bourbon Democracy. The Bourbons were too busy making money to dabble.in politics for pleasure or for prestige; nor did they see the Democracy as a threat to big-business enterprise and hence in need of Bourbon guardianship. The Democracy was so deep in the doldrums that it was little wonder that men failed to see in it either an opportunity for the excitement of politics or a threat to their particular economic class. Whatever was done with and by the Democracy came from the non-Bourbon element. It came from professional politicians, from sincere crusading politicians, and from never-say-die lovers of the party standard. For the Bourbon-Democracy-to-be it was a period of unconscious preparation, a period of laying the groundwork of issues to be fought over during the ensuing three decades.

The Democratic party, victim of countless misfortunes, was in serious need of large-scale rehabilitation. The slavery question had set off an explosion which had shattered Democratic unity. Party members had taken divergent paths, becoming Southern Democrats, Northern Democrats, Constitutional Unionists, and Republicans. Northern Democrats had split again into War Democrats, who supported the war, and Peace Democrats, who called the war a mistake and a failure. At the end of the war what was left of the Democratic party was without prestige, without purpose, and without honor. But despite its low status the Democracy was not devoid of opportunity. There was work to be done that called for application of traditional Democratic principles—work of representing the neglected "little man."

Greatest Democratic opportunity lay in the smoldering agrarian Middle West. Politicians with discernment perceived farmers restlessly waiting to collect larger profits from the newly accelerated industrial revolution. Before the Civil War the farmers had been told by Republican apostles of industrialization that farming would become more lucrative with the advent of the high protective tariff and with railroad construction. Republican free-land promises, actually fulfilled in the Homestead Act of 1862, seemed to evidence the party's sincere interest in the farmers' aspirations. But it became increasingly clear that a group of Republicans were successfully utilizing the machinery of government almost exclusively to divert the profits of the industrial revolution to the pockets of the industrialist and financier element.

Indeed, the business leaders could look with satisfaction upon the political situation. The politician friends of big business, key men in the Radical faction of the Republican party, already had demonstrated their worth to their patrons. Led by such able politicos as old Thad Stevens, the Radicals had taken the lead in fomenting hatred for the nonindustrial South; they had chalked up a record of wartime legislation and administration most favorable to industrialist-financier interests. To their credit was the high-rate Morrill tariff act, the sound National Bank Act and the subsidy-granting Pacific railway act. Then, too, after the war it was solace to businessmen to know that on financial matters the advice of Jay Cooke was closely followed by the government. And Jay Cooke, "financier of the Civil War," was the nation's foremost banker.[1] The assassination of President Lincoln in mid-April, 1865, seemed to remove a possibly serious obstacle to further entrenchment of industrialist-financier influence in the government. The new president, Andrew Johnson, was expected to be friendly to the Radical Republicans in Congress.[2]

In the situation of Radical–big business domination of the Republican party was opportunity for the badly mauled Democracy. Certainly it could become a strong party of opposition if it took up its old role as champion of the little man. But there were some ifs. It could play the role if it had a valuable program and if it had a leadership capable of selling that program to the farm voters and willing to do so.

For a pattern of antimonopoly, prodemocratic action, the Democracy could with logic look to its own Progressive Western Democracy of the 1840's and 1850's. That movement harbored a galaxy of aggressive spirits who looked to a future of liberal reform and conspicuous progress for the masses.[3] In it was Ohio's fiery Samuel Medary, who had wielded his facile pen to let it be known that "the true Democrat was earnestly against the existing state of society which is built upon the supposition that men are of less value than property." [4] In the group also was B. B. Taylor, who had

[1] Ellis P. Oberholtzer, *Jay Cooke, Financier of the Civil War* (Philadelphia, 1907), II, 2–6; Matthew Josephson, *The Politicos, 1865–1896* (New York, 1938), 40.

[2] See, for example, the Chicago *Tribune*, April 17, 20, 1865.

[3] Henry C. Hubbart, *The Older Middle West, 1840–1880* (New York, 1936), 4–12; Henry C. Hubbart, "Pro-Southern Influences in the Free West, 1840–1865," *Mississippi Valley Historical Review*, XX (June, 1933), 51.

[4] *Western Review*, 1846, p. 208, as cited in Hubbart, *Older Middle West*, 11.

been optimistic enough to "venture the prediction" in the *Democratic Monthly Journal* that from the West "is yet to go forth a spirit which shall rouse the nations, reform the civilization of the world." [5]

Some Progressives had doggedly carried their devotion to the movement throughout even the Civil War years. In 1861 one such persistent Progressive, Ohio's Clement L. Vallandigham, applied his philosophy to the causes of the Civil War. Addressing the House of Representatives, of which he was a member, this "King of the Copperheads" declared that "the great dividing line was always between capital and labor—between the few who had money and wanted to use the government to increase and 'protect' it, . . . and the many who had little but wanted to keep it and who only asked the government to let them alone." Out of this conflict, he declared, arose the issues of "a permanent public debt, a national bank, the public deposits, a protective tariff, internal improvements, and other questions of a similar character, all of them looking to the special interests of the money classes." For a long time only a combination of sectional interests, reasoned Vallandigham, had prevented the northern moneyed classes from forging a political party strong enough to obtain national dominance. But finally, in the Republican party, the "moneyed interest" discovered "an organization formed to their hand—an organization . . . founded on two of the most powerful passions of the human heart: sectionalism, which is only a narrow and localized patriotism, and anti-slavery, or love of freedom." [6] In 1863, Vallandigham's outstanding disapproval of the war prompted President Lincoln to banish him to the Confederacy. The next year he returned to the North, arriving in time to maneuver into the national Democratic platform of 1864 a resolution declaring the war a failure and demand-

[5] *Democratic Monthly Magazine*, June, 1844, p. 196, as cited *ibid.*, 3.
[6] Cited in Charles A. and Mary R. Beard, *The Rise of American Civilization* (New York, 1927), I, 677–78.

ing a cessation of fighting. With the coming of peace this intrepid figure was without public office, but was not retired from the political hustings.

Following the war others of the onetime Progressive Western Democracy kept alive the liberal heritage of the Democracy. In the House of Representatives was colorful Daniel Voorhees of Indiana, who early in 1866 took the floor to ask: "How long can the inequalities of our revenue system be borne? . . . We have two great interests in this country, one of which has prostrated the other." Agriculture, said he, "is driven to the counters of the most gigantic monopoly ever sanctioned by the law." And he told of the unfair position of bondholders through their freedom from taxation.[7] Still others who might have been expected to take up anew the political cudgels in the interest of the farmers were Senator Thomas A. Hendricks of Indiana and Allen G. Thurman, George H. Pendleton, and William Allen of Ohio. All were able, but none proved equal to the task of rehabilitating the party in the interest of the farmers. To varying degrees they were stigmatized with reputations of copperheadism. Failing to supply effective party leadership themselves, these Democratic politicos attached their uncertain future to the equally uncertain future of President Andrew Johnson. For lack of any other leadership, all other Democrats likewise looked to Andrew Johnson.

There was considerable logic in the postwar alliance between President Johnson and the Democrats. After all, Johnson, although placed on the 1864 Union party ticket with Lincoln, was a thoroughgoing Democrat. His philosophy was in keeping with that of the Progressive Western Democracy. His Tennessee environment and his devotion to the ideas of Thomas Jefferson had stamped him as a sincere champion of the yeoman class.[8] In the Congress of ante-

[7] *Congressional Globe*, 39 Congress, 1 Session, 115, 150–59; New York *World*, January 12, 1866.
[8] Howard K. Beale, *The Critical Year, A Study of Andrew Johnson*

bellum days he had often been heard pleading the cause of the farmer and the rural mechanic. "Mr. Jefferson never said a truer thing," said Johnson, "than when he declared that large cities are eye sores in the body-politic; in Democracies they are consuming cancers. . . . Build up your villages, build up your rural districts, and you will have men who rely upon their own . . . economy and application to business for support. . . . Our true policy is to build up the middle class; to sustain the villages, to populate the rural districts, and let the power of the Government remain with the middle class! I want no miserable city rabble on the one hand. I want no pampered, bloated, corrupted aristocracy on the other." [9]

Becoming president by accident, Johnson owed to no man or faction any specific political debt, nor did he head a political party having unfulfilled public commitments. The Union party had promised to win the Civil War, and that was accomplished.[10] Politically free and in a politically powerful office, President Johnson thus had the choice of returning to the Democratic fold, remaining with the Republicans, or constructing a new party out of factions from within the old. One could only guess which he would choose.

Soon Johnson made clear his stand on fundamental issues. His policy on southern Reconstruction echoed the moderate approach of Abraham Lincoln. Though possessed of an uncompromising hatred for the southern Bourbons, Andy Johnson did not believe that Radical-controlled Negroes should inherit the South. To him, the small farmers and mechanics deserved the right to govern the region. His economic program, aimed at northern monopolists and ex-

and Reconstruction (New York, 1930), 10–50; Josephson, *Politicos*, 24–25; George Fort Milton, *The Age of Hate* (New York, 1930), 59–159; Claude G. Bowers, *The Tragic Era: The Revolution after Lincoln* (New York, 1929), 24–44.

[9] Cited in Beard, *Rise of American Civilization*, I, 676–77.
[10] *Daily Milwaukee News*, April 26, 1865.

ploiters in general, called for payment of the war debt by taxing accumulated wealth, amending the Constitution to provide an income tax, and preventing corporations from procuring cheaply the best lands of the West.[11] The Tennessee tailor-statesman was being loyal to his Jeffersonian principles; he was refusing to bow before the glittering industrial Bourbonism of the North, just as he had refused to kowtow to the feudalistic plantation aristocracy of the South.

Johnson was staking his political future on the farmer and mechanic votes. He need not, and to fashion a national party he could not, neglect the growing labor vote of East and West; but the heart of his strength was the agrarian Middle West. This embraced the largest single segment of antimonopolist citizens outside the then politically sterile South, and hence the great preponderance of sentiment of the area was already in harmony with Johnson's principles. With the Civil War ended, there was in the Middle West no basic cleavage between the majority of Moderate Republicans and Democrats. Many of the Republicans were one-time Democrats, who had joined the Republican party because of the southern question. Now it remained for Andrew Johnson to spearhead the movement to unite the Moderates and the Democrats.

While it was soon made clear that President Johnson's sympathies lay with the yeoman class, it was far from clear that Johnson would be able to crystallize his following and potential following into an effective anti-Radical organization. The assignment was certainly not an easy one, for many prewar and war-born antagonisms, jealousies, and sus-

[11] Chicago *Tribune*, April 17, 1865; *Daily Milwaukee News*, May 20, 1865; Frank Moore, *Life and Speeches of Andrew Johnson* (Boston, 1865), 484; James D. Richardson, *A Compilation of the Messages and Papers of the Presidents, 1789–1897* (Washington, 1896–1897), VI, 365–66, 416, 426–27; Edward McPherson, *Political History of the United States During the Period of Reconstruction* (Washington, 1871), 51–52.

picions existed among his followers and would-be followers. To overcome this heritage it was necessary for the President to convince members of the heterogeneous anti-Radical element of their essential unity of purpose and of the practicability of their co-operation. But Johnson proved unequal to the task. Although he possessed a powerful mind, an excellent oratorical gift, and a trenchant pen, these were not enough for forming and sustaining party unity. His temper, while suited to the rough-and-tumble of Tennessee and congressional politics, was unsuited for the chore of healing breaches and preventing new ones. When composed, he acted with hesitancy; when angry, he was either recalcitrant or unrestrained. He thus was emotionally unprepared for his new political task, in which the premium was high on the ability to use discriminatingly the fine arts of compromise and firmness. In consequence he made many blunders in strategy as a party builder and leader. Nor was he emotionally well suited for sustaining popular support, for his public utterances too often reflected unrestrained, undignified anger. He accordingly never reached the point of formulating a definite new party or dominating one of the old parties.

During the summer and fall of 1865 the lines of battle between the Johnson forces and the Radicals took shape. In December, with the opening of the first session of the Thirty-ninth Congress, the antagonists moved into closer formation. Within two months both sides were maneuvering for a favorable position in the ensuing congressional elections.[12]

[12] On the unfolding factional cleavages, see R. P. L. Baber to Andrew Johnson, July 4, 1865; *id.* to *id.*, March 29, 1866; *id.* to William Seward, March 30, 1866; J. A. Williams to Hugh McCulloch, September 21, 1865; Lewis D. Campbell to D. P. Patterson, January 22, 1866; *id.* to *id.*, June 22, 1866; Joseph H. Geiger to James R. Doolittle, February 11, 1866; *id.* to Andrew Johnson, August 2, 1866; *id.* to *id.*, July 25, 1867; Ward H. Lamon to *id.*, February 26, 1866; R. B. Warden to *id.*, February 26, 1866;

A crisis came with the definite entrance of leading Democrats on the Johnson side. Events had been rapidly building up to this juncture. Early in the congressional session Radical Thad Stevens had vehemently and frankly warned the assembled House that southern members must be excluded from Congress if the Republican party hoped to retain control. In the Senate there already were 11 Democrats to 39 Republicans, and in the House, 63 Democrats to 140 Republicans. If the South were allowed to enter, argued Stevens, a combination of Democrats and wavering Republicans would place control in the hands of the prosouthern Johnson-Democratic forces.[13] Shortly thereafter the "Tall Sycamore of the Wabash," Democratic Daniel Voorhees, lashed out at Thad Stevens, endorsed President Johnson's Reconstruction program with praise, denied the charges that the Democracy was trying to steal the President, and pointed out the enormous wrongs shielded by the bloody shirt.[14]

Voorhees' outburst gladdened the hearts of the Radicals, who gloatingly visualized the discredited Democratic millstone on the necks of their Johnson–Moderate Republican rivals. They redoubled their efforts to make the millstone heavier. Radicals reiterated old accusations, calling their opponents rebels and exploiters of the Negro, in contrast to their own identification of Negro ascendency with championship of the common man. Many voters innocently accepted this contention. One sincere, albeit naïve, middlewestern citizen declared, ". . . the power of wealth is to combine against the masses of white and black, and struggle for the ownership of labor. Here, upon this proposition two

---

and W. S. Burnett to *id.*, March 24, 1866, in Andrew Johnson MSS., Library of Congress; Reginald C. McGrane, *William Allen, A Study in Western Democracy* (Columbus, 1925), 72–76.

[13] *Congressional Globe*, 39 Cong., 1 Sess., 73–74.

[14] *Congressional Globe*, 39 Cong., 1 Sess., 115, 150–59; New York *World*, January 12, 1866.

parties are to diverge." [15] Illinois' Congressman E. B. Washburne was one of the Radicals careful to "instruct" the voters that his faction was on the side of the masses. Washburne was friendly with Jay and Henry Cooke, but he did not say so when addressing the home folks. In fact, he told an Illinois farmers' convention that he knew "the power of individual, combined and corporate interests in Washington and how controlling their influences are there." He pointed out that these interests were "represented by the ablest, the sharpest, the keenest . . . men in the country. . . . The people at home on the farms . . . have nobody to urge their side of the case, and they are emphatically 'left out in the cold.' " [16] But it was through ranting claptrap about "rebels" that the masterful Radical rabble-rousers found the most effective means of camouflaging their real identity. Few voters understood that many of these skilled "revivalists" considered the ledger their Bible, the dollar their God, and the countinghouse their heaven. Few voters realized that the real exploiters of the masses were the Radical leaders.

To counteract this Radical bloody-shirt waving, Johnson needed to work fast and with firmness. The Democrats, by edging into the Johnson camp, forced upon the President the need of reconciling Moderate-Democratic differences and overcoming the stigma which the Copperhead Democrats brought to his political doorstep. This was not an easy assignment, and it was particularly complicated in Indiana, Ohio, and Illinois, where the Democrats felt strong enough to demand public offices and seats at the council table. If Johnson failed to assuage the jealous Moderates in those states, he could expect many of them to switch to the Radicals. Events moved rapidly.

Indiana's Oliver P. Morton always kept a watchful eye on

[15] J. C. Cover to Lucius Fairchild, June 10, 1865, in Lucius Fairchild MSS., Library of the State Historical Society of Wisconsin.
[16] Cited in Chicago *Industrial Age*, August 20, 1873.

his Democratic opponents and also was suspicious of the Thad Stevens Radicals. In September, 1865, this wartime governor endorsed Johnson's anti–Negro suffrage stand, urging that before granting the Negroes the franchise, they be given "time to acquire a little property, and get a little education, time to learn something about the simplest forms of business, and prepare themselves for the exercise of political power." Then, declared Morton, "at the end of ten, fifteen or twenty years, let them come into the enjoyment of their political rights. By that time these Southern states will have been so completely filled up by immigration from the North, and from Europe, that the negroes will be a permanent minority." But Morton carefully emphasized the right of Republicans, and not Democrats, to lead the anti-Radical forces. He feared the political strength of such fellow-Hoosiers as Senator Thomas A. Hendricks and Representative Daniel Voorhees. "This Democratic party," asserted Morton, "encouraged the rebellion by assuring rebels in the South that there would be no resistance offered on the part of the North to the work of secession. It opposed enlistment; it opposed taxation for the support of the Government; it depreciated the national currency; it encouraged foreign nations to intervene; it formed loose conspiracies in the North, and sought to introduce the horrors of civil war into our homes here, and as the great crowning act of wickedness, at Chicago, . . . that party there proclaimed, in its national convention, that the war was a failure, and called upon the Government and the nation to abandon it." [17]

In December Morton, apparently still loyal to Johnson, sailed for Europe and thereby escaped the emerging period of intensified political jitters. In the same month Ohio's James A. Garfield showed signs of nervousness that doubtless

[17] Oliver P. Morton, *Speech . . . at Richmond, Indiana, September 29, 1865* (pamphlet in Library of State Historical Society of Wisconsin, n.p., n.d.), 9, 19.

caused him to wish he were in Europe. This fence-sitting
Ohioan wrote his wife that he was "involved in one of the
strange fixes which have always beset my life." He explained:
"Radical friends want me to make a speech on reorganiza-
tion of the rebel states. . . . The President has appealed
to me to help him . . . and I find it difficult to steer between
Scylla and Charybdis." [18] Within three months he was in
the Radical camp. Lyman Trumbull, senator from Illinois,
likewise decided that it was expedient to abandon Johnson.
"I know," wrote a onetime editor of the Chicago *Tribune*,
C. H. Ray, "that Trumbull has no desire to quarrel with the
President; I *know* that his instincts and aspirations are for
a democratic policy and that he has been very unwillingly
forced into antagonism to Mr. Johnson by a party pressure
he could not resist." [19]

In April, 1866, after four months in Europe, Oliver P.
Morton returned to find that many Moderates had scamp-
ered into the Radical fold. He found such to be the case
in his own Indiana bailiwick—and that the Democrats were
leading the Johnson forces. Morton immediately joined the
Radicals and soon became the Middle West's prize Demo-
crat-baiter. He proclaimed that "every unregenerate rebel
. . . calls himself a Democrat. Every bounty jumper, every
deserter, every sneak who ran away from the draft. . . .
Every man . . . who murdered Union prisoners . . .
every wolf in sheep's clothing . . . every one who shoots
down negroes in the streets, burns negro schoolhouses and
meeting-houses, and murders women and children by the
light of their flaming dwellings, calls himself a Democrat.
. . . In short," he declared, "the Democratic party may be
described as a common sewer and loathsome receptacle, into
which is emptied every element of treason North and South,

[18] Theodore C. Smith, *Life and Letters of James A. Garfield* (New
Haven, 1925), I, 392.
[19] C. H. Ray to Montgomery Blair, April 10, 1866, as cited in Beale,
Critical Year, 111; *ibid.*, 106–107.

and every element of inhumanity and barbarism which has dishonored the age." [20]

Even in the states where the Democratic threat of stealing political control was less acute than in Indiana, Ohio, and Illinois, there developed a marked exodus from the Johnson camp. Wisconsin's Senator Timothy Howe switched to the Radicals and warned his colleagues that restoring the political functions of the South would dangerously impair the Republican numerical advantage in national politics.[21] Republican James R. Doolittle, Wisconsin's other senator, followed the opposite course, remaining loyal to Johnson; but events demonstrated that he was rowing against the tide. Doolittle had once been a Democratic state leader, but in the 1850's he joined the Republican movement. When Johnson became president, the Wisconsin senator immediately made common cause with this other onetime Democrat.[22] In September, 1865, he steered through his state's Republican convention a resolution against Negro suffrage. Exultingly he reported to Johnson that it "was carried triumphantly." [23] But within a month his pro-Johnson speeches were raising a "storm about his ears." Radicals had been doing effective work, and declared that it was Doolittle, and not themselves, who "was dividing and distracting the party." In December Doolittle showed uneasiness about the future but declared that he would "stand by the Administration to save the country." Later the loyal senator added action to these words, for when the Wisconsin legislature instructed him to

[20] W. D. Foulke, *Life of Oliver P. Morton* (Indianapolis, 1899), I, 474–75; Josephson, *Politicos*, 36–37.

[21] *Congressional Globe*, 39 Cong., 1 Sess., 165–66.

[22] Doolittle to Lucius Fairchild, December 5, 1865, in Fairchild MSS.; James L. Sellers, "James R. Doolittle," *Wisconsin Magazine of History*, XVII (March, 1934), 277–78.

[23] Doolittle to Andrew Johnson, September 9, 1865, in James R. Doolittle MSS., Library of the State Historical Society of Wisconsin. Other middle-western state Republican conventions also declared against Negro suffrage. See *Nation*, I (August 24, September 28, 1865), and III (August 2, 1866); St. Paul *Press*, September 9, 10, 16, 1865.

vote for the civil rights bill over the President's veto, Doolittle flatly refused.[24]

Clearly the Radicals were having their way, and just as
clearly they were receiving great help from Johnson himself. Tennessee's Johnson had proved to be a rank amateur
at directing large-scale political moves. His failure to make
effective use of the federal patronage was a conspicuous error.[25] Lincoln had masterfully handled the patronage; Johnson awkwardly fumbled its use. Properly handled, it could be
brandished as both a disciplinary whip and a tantalizing reward, but when wielded by Johnson it usually landed too
lightly, too late. Early and decisive use of the patronage
would have helped Johnson to force a decision on the antagonism between his Moderate Republican and Democratic
supporters by disciplining or repudiating all followers who
harped upon the Copperhead bugaboo. He could have
earned political prestige and effected an early showdown
with fence-sitter Republicans—they were practical politicians who had a firm respect for purposeful party discipline.

But before the President got around even to gesturing
with the patronage whip, the Radicals had convinced the
majority of practical-minded politicos wherein lay the safest
leadership. Following Johnson's December, 1865, message
to Congress, vote-wise Oliver P. Morton had warned Johnson of pitfalls ahead. While assuring the President that his
policy would be endorsed by the great body of the people,

[24] Lucius Fairchild to C. Fairchild, October 8, 1865; Wm. E. Smith to
Lucius Fairchild, October 9, 1865; and Doolittle to Lucius Fairchild,
December 5, 1865, in Fairchild MSS.; *Appletons' Annual Cyclopaedia and
Register of Important Events* (New York, 1862–1903), VI (1866), 769.

[25] On patronage, see Samuel Barlow to Blair, September 11, 1865; Oscar
Stephenson to Andrew Johnson, February 24, 1866; Burnett to *id.*, March
24, 1866; Baber to *id.*, March 29, 1866; *id.* to Seward, March 30, 1866;
Lewis D. Campbell to Andrew Johnson, June 22, 1866; Geiger to *id.*,
August 2, 1866 and William Allen to *id.*, September 21, 1866, in Johnson
MSS.

he had urged him to wield unsparingly the patronage whip upon the unruly in Congress.[26]

But the politically inept Johnson failed to follow this advice. In consequence the putty-minded members of Congress looked upon Johnson with less fear and less respect. The next month Senator D. P. Patterson received word from an experienced Ohio politico that President Johnson, by failing to use the patronage whip, was letting slip a great opportunity. "The President can be, as he is now, the leader of a vast unorganized party of the people, . . . which will with management prove more potent even than that of General Jackson." But he feared that the President was being "too forbearing," that "the very power which he can control is being used to embarrass him and break him down. Even in his cabinet there are men who are either too timid to speak out for him or are secretly at work strengthening the Radicals. The vast internal revenue patronage organization of Mr. [Salmon P.] Chase is daily at work directly among the people in every state—every county and at every crossroads stealthily impregnating the popular mind with prejudices against Johnson and changing them from friends to enemies." The Ohioan emphasized his indignation by adding, "I know these things." And why, therefore, he asked, will not Johnson "raise his battle-ax in defense of himself, his friends and the Union?" [27] In the spring Ohio's loyal Johnson supporter Joseph Geiger reported pessimistically to Senator Doolittle, "We have plenty of Johnson men here but they all whine and say that all the federal office holders that were at our late convention opposed the President and worked for his foes"; they complained that "it is no use in being sacrificed if enemies are to be kept in power." The Ohioan felt that if the Johnson group "had a good energetic body

[26] William A. Dunning, "More Light on Andrew Johnson," *American Historical Review*, XI (April, 1906), 576.
[27] Lewis D. Campbell to Patterson, January 20, 1866, in Johnson MSS.

of appointments of the right stamp, we would be feared and felt. As it is, we are despised by both sides." [28] Late in August Gideon Welles, secretary of the navy, gloomily recorded in his diary that the Radicals were entrenched too strongly and that Johnson should have "acted six or eight months earlier." [29]

The President threatened to dismiss Radical officeholders and did remove a few, but these halfway measures merely invited Radical complaints that he "persecuted" those not agreeing with his course. His unfulfilled gesture to dismiss Ohio's General Roeliff Brinkerhoff was an example of Johnson's feeble wielding of the axe. Brinkerhoff related: "Thieves and politicians . . . brought various influences to bear upon President Johnson to have me removed. Secretary Stanton, however, stood by me like a rock, and I was left undisturbed. . . . The only charge . . . was that I was using my position to further the election of Congressmen hostile to the policy of President Johnson. It was true I did not approve the political vagaries of the President. . . ." Twice Johnson moved to dismiss Brinkerhoff, but both times Stanton blocked the attempt.[30]

The President showed lack of political realism in handling the Copperheads. He made no pointed attempt to defend the Copperheads against the Radicals' flubdubbery; nor did he issue a forthright repudiation of Copperhead support. The Radicals consequently were left amazingly free to condition the public mind in the belief that the Johnson-Moderate-Democratic camp was dangerously infested with unregenerate champions of slavery and with loathsome rebels.

When President Johnson made no forthright move to repudiate the Copperhead following, his War Democrat and Moderate Republican supporters became much concerned.

[28] Geiger to Doolittle, June 25, 1866, in Doolittle MSS.
[29] Gideon Welles, *Diary of Gideon Welles* (Boston, 1911), II, 587.
[30] Roeliff Brinkerhoff, *Recollections of a Lifetime* (Cincinnati, 1900), 179. See also Burnett to Andrew Johnson, March 24, 1866, in Johnson MSS.

In July, 1866, General John A. Dix, New York Democrat, warned that "our danger is that the men whom we do not want get in to cover up their past sins. This would be a most serious injury, and might imperil the whole movement." [31] A few weeks later Ohio's Joseph Geiger declared that the anti-Radicals were "hurt more by the prominence given Vallandigham than by all other causes." He asserted that "our people shrink from contact with him." Geiger felt that "the fellow's doctrines *now* are not so bad, but his name is damnation." [32] Finally, late in the summer of 1866, the President delivered a backhanded repudiation to the extremists by refusing to see Vallandigham when he was making a call at the White House. The Moderates and the War Democrats were relieved and delighted, but this move came too late to eliminate the Copperhead stigma from the Moderate-Democratic reputation.

By meeting the Radicals' southern Reconstruction policy head on, the President committed his greatest blunder. Inexpedient to the extreme, he thereby forfeited the best vote-catching features of his program.[33] He should have realized that fundamentally the war-weary, financially discouraged voters were more interested in their own economic aspirations and plight than in franchising the Negro and chastising the rebel. The farmers' aspirations were not being fulfilled, and even gains previously made were beginning to slip away. Certainly Andrew Johnson, experienced in public life and aware of the perennial threat of monopoly, should have perceived the political potentialities inherent on the agrarian front. That is, Johnson could have been aware of farmer restlessness if he had not become angrily blinded by the Radicals' bloody-shirt waving in Congress and through the press.

[31] John A. Dix to Doolittle, July 10, 1866, in Doolittle MSS.
[32] Geiger to Andrew Johnson, August 2, 1866, in Johnson MSS.
[33] Beale, *Critical Year*, 144–55; Howard K. Beale, "Reconstruction," *Encyclopedia of Social Sciences* (New York, 1930–1935), XIII, 170.

Considerable agrarian resentment revolved around the greenback-currency question. The greenbacks, notes issued during the Civil War, were backed, not by gold or interest-paying government bonds, but simply by the government's designation of them as legal tender. The extreme sound-money interests, conspicuous among whom were financier Jay Cooke, his friend Secretary of the Treasury Hugh McCulloch, and directors of the national banks, all earnestly desired rapid retirement of the greenbacks.[34] This would increase the value of money and consequently augment the wealth of the already-rich. It would benefit the holders of government bonds who had made their purchases with the Civil War cheap money. At variance with the sound-money policy were moderates and extremists from all walks of life.[35] Many so-called extremists, especially in the Middle West, not only opposed retirement of the greenbacks but advocated further issuance of these notes. With these the government could retire the interest-paying, tax-exempt Civil War bonds. This would relieve the taxpayers and at the same time supply them with cheaper currency. The attitude was understandable from the point of view of the Middle West, where money was not available to meet debts and taxes or to make property improvements, and where bondholders were few. Commenting on the financial situation of 1866, the *Daily Milwaukee News* drew an East-West comparison on investment-capital distribution. In the entire West, it reported, there was little more than fifty million dollars invested in national banks, while in Massachusetts alone sixty million dollars was so invested.[36]

In December, 1865, Secretary McCulloch, after consulting with Jay Cooke, recommended legislation implement-

[34] Oberholtzer, *Jay Cooke*, II, 6.
[35] The 1865 party platforms of both the Republicans and the Democrats in Minnesota had called for lower interest rates on United States bonds. St. Paul *Press*, September 9, 16, 1865.
[36] *Daily Milwaukee News*, January 1, 1867.

ing the sound-money position, and soon the program was before Congress for consideration. It called for retirements of the greenbacks with new issues of interest-paying, tax-exempt bonds. And upon these new bonds national-bank notes could be issued.[37] Politicians, however, were too busily engaged in refighting the Civil War to concentrate attention on the proposal. A majority of the citizens remained uninformed on the subject, and the enlightened portion lacked sufficient organization. From some quarters, nevertheless, came heated protest against this and other sound-money schemes. In February, 1866, the secretary of an Illinois farm group wrote to Johnson that the farmers of the country "are suffering from onerous taxation and they are beginning to inquire into the cause—and they find one . . . to be an unjustly constituted money power." He then added his opinion of the consequences of having national-bank notes replace greenbacks. "The interest upon the Bonds standing behind the circulation," he said, "wd be about $60,-000,000 annually, which the producing interests (for they at last bear all this burden) have to pay into the coffers of these so constituted National Banks, and for what? . . . These very banks are today making . . . from 15 to 40% upon the capital invested." He asked if that was not a "centralizing power to be dreaded." [38] Some middle-western newspapers attacked the policy. "We seek in vain," said the Chicago *Republican*, "for an argument to show why the volume of greenbacks ought to be reduced, while that of national bank notes should be maintained in its present magnitude." [39] The Cincinnati *Daily Gazette* expressed apprehension over the currency-contraction scheme and favored instead a program of paying in greenbacks the war debt which had been contracted in depreciated currency. It

[37] Oberholtzer, *Jay Cooke*, II, 6.
[38] G. H. Locy to Andrew Johnson, February 25, 1866, in Johnson MSS.
[39] Chicago *Republican*, March 24, 1866.

considered twenty years ample time to achieve a return to gold payments.[40]

The President and Congress, however, continued to give the matter relatively slight attention, as compared with the southern question. The measure passed the House without much fanfare. In the Senate Ohio's John Sherman was one of the few showing real interest. During the debate Sherman attacked the measure, but in his plea the Ohioan sidestepped the real issues involved, simply stating that the bill conferred on the Secretary "greater powers than have ever been conferred since the foundation of the government upon any Secretary of the Treasury." [41] Most senators paid him little heed; only six voted with him against the bill. On April 12, 1866, it became a law.

The tariff was another economic question upon which Johnson and his friends could have capitalized in the Middle West. Not long after the passing of the 1857 moderate tariff the government had become increasingly solicitous of industrialists. The result was a series of measures which, starting with the wartime Morrill tariff of 1861, rapidly scaled upward those duties which meant greater profits for manufacturers; and following the war these insatiable entrepreneurs pressed forward requests for still higher rates. They knew what they wanted, and the eastern Radicals were their aggressive spokesmen. The opposition, meanwhile, was mostly defensive in nature. Middle-western opponents showed some strength; but after checking the industrialists' demands, most of the opposition leaders slipped back into the audience. They demonstrated energy in preventing increased industrial rates but took no positive steps to reduce the palpably unfair existing schedules. This negative approach sprang in part from the politicians' fear of the pro-

[40] Chester McA. Destler, "The Origin and Character of the Pendleton Plan," *Mississippi Valley Historical Review*, XXIV (September, 1937), 173.
[41] Oberholtzer, *Jay Cooke*, II, 7-8.

tectionists' effective arguments and great influence in party councils.

Andrew Johnson and his cohorts could have contributed toward a union of the West and the South against the eastern protectionists, had he and his followers taken a positive middle-ground course—a campaign to scale down to a reasonable level the high Civil War rates. Such a program would have met very slight opposition in the Middle West, because in that area there was only scattered interest in protecting the manufacturers. There was not even a cleavage on that ground between the farmers and the area's railroad interests, because neither wanted high-cost iron. But the Johnson forces failed to espouse boldly a moderate tariff program, and thus they left room for public confusion on the issue and the growth of small but effective protectionist pressure groups.

One middle-western special-interest group especially persistent and insistent in demanding protection was the woolgrowers.[42] In Ohio and Michigan, and to a lesser degree in Indiana and Illinois, woolgrowers organized associations to agitate for higher duties on wool. The Chicago *Tribune*, although opposed to the eastern tariff demands, urged Illinois' woolgrowers to organize and join forces with the Wool Growers Association of neighboring Indiana.[43] In 1865 the sheep-raisers obtained a substantially increased duty on wool. The next year lobbyist John L. Hayes, secretary of the National Association of Wool Manufacturers, persuaded that newly created eastern organization to foster an alliance with the middle-western woolgrowers. He saw in this plan an opportunity to drive an eastern protectionist wedge into the agrarian area. In the fall of the same year, addressing the first annual meeting of the Wool Growers

[42] William F. Switzler, *Special Report on Wool and Manufactures of Wool* (Bureau of Statistics, Treasury Department, Document No. 1025 [Washington, 1888]), 60.
[43] Chicago *Tribune*, February 22, 1866.

Association, Hayes bid for co-operation between the two groups. "There can be no reliance," said the shrewd Hayes, "upon a permanent friendly legislation for both interests unless the wool growers are satisfied. Our object is . . . to convince the farmers of the West, who will inevitably control the legislation of this country, of the absolute identity of our interests." In December a joint meeting of the woolen manufacturers and the woolgrowers resulted in the formation of a well-organized lobby, which incorporated higher wool and woolens duties into the tariff bill that passed the House of Representatives in 1866.[44]

A few middle-westerners had visions of industrializing the region through high tariffs. There was as much sense, contended a Wisconsin editor, in sending wool and flax to New England to be manufactured and then having the fabric returned as there would be in sending wheat there to be ground and the flour shipped back.[45] Ohio's Senator Benjamin Wade believed that the absence of a foreign market for farm products and the prohibitive cost of shipping to the East called for a higher tariff as a solution.[46] This, supposedly, would result in middle-western industrial development and a consequent home market for farm crops. Protectionist arguments, when utilized by such skillful campaigners, were good for many votes. Minnesota's Ignatius Donnelly gave the protectionist approach a try. In 1866 he was re-elected to Congress from an agrarian district on a platform emphasizing above all else the advantages of protectionism.[47]

In the spring of 1866 middle-westerners, despite the absence of organized party championship and despite the

[44] Howard K. Beale, "The Tariff and Reconstruction," *American Historical Review*, XXXV (January, 1930), 283.

[45] Friendship (Wis.) *Adams County Press*, February 2, 1866.

[46] *Congressional Globe*, 39 Cong., 1 Sess., 3756.

[47] Paul Sydney Smith, "Party Politics in Minnesota, 1865–1871" (unpublished master's thesis, University of Minnesota, 1918), 26.

scattered but well-organized protectionists, came near to a general attack on the discriminatory eastern-protectionist tariff schemes. Eastern Radicals started a drive for increased tariff rates and thereby started a wave of protest. When the measure was before the House, Iowa's Representative James F. Wilson warned the eastern protectionists of a potential storm from the West.[48] Eastern commercial interests, opposed to high tariffs because they restricted trade, joined the protest. The New York *Commercial and Financial Chronicle* warned the manufacturers of the perils which they certainly would incur if their representatives pushed the principle of protection "beyond the limits at which it has been fixed for some years past." The journal warned of a reunion of the agrarian South and West and believed that in any case the West's own potential strength was reason enough for avoiding antagonism. "A brief retrospect of the part played by the Western States in the late civil war," the paper suggested, "must satisfy every dispassionate observer that the practical control of our political affairs is destined at no distant date to pass into the hands of the Western people." [49] The New York Chamber of Commerce added its voice, asserting that the proposal "would mar the prosperity of agriculture, by increasing the cost of its supplies without enhancing the price of its products." [50]

The loudness of the thunder resulted in eastern Radical abandonment of the plan to increase the pig-iron rate six dollars a ton. The measure, still highly protectionist, passed the House, although Thad Stevens, who was personally interested in iron, was so disgusted with its devitalization that he refused to vote. The bitterest fighting occurred in the Senate. Middle-western Republicans led the attack while the Democrats sat back and watched. Democrats could be

---

[48] *Congressional Globe,* 39 Cong., 1 Sess., 3497.
[49] New York *Commercial and Financial Chronicle,* July 7, 1866, as cited in Beale, "Tariff and Reconstruction," *loc. cit.,* 280.
[50] Cited in Bowers, *Tragic Era,* 117.

counted upon to vote against any eastern-protectionist measure; but because they were doctrinaire free traders at that
time, they were out of place in a debate between industrial
protectionists and agricultural protectionists. They seemed
to prefer watching the entire protectionist crowd stewing
in its own juice. In the boiling cauldron, Senator John B.
Henderson, Missouri Republican, hotly argued that the
farmers needed a market and not a tariff and said that Mis-
sourians were burning their corn for want of a market.[51]
Iowa's incensed Senator James W. Grimes was especially
devastating in his attacks upon the measure and thereby became the center of eastern-protectionist reprisals. The Bir-
mingham *Iron Age* printed scurrilous attacks on his personal
integrity; the New York *Tribune*, seeking to ruin Grimes,
sent free copies of its weekly edition to important middle-
westerners.[52]

The Chicago *Tribune*, although an exponent of Radical
Reconstruction, became increasingly angry at the eastern
Radicals' protectionist attitude. "We tell these gentlemen,"
warned the *Tribune*, "that they are traveling to destruction
as fast as they can go. They are cutting open the goose to get
all the golden eggs at once. They are legislating the government funds into their pockets too rapidly for the permanence of the system." [53] Four days later the paper declared,
"The increased rates of duties (except possibly on wool) are
wholly unnessary and unjustifiable, and if adopted will work
injury to revenue and to public interest." [54] In two more
days the *Tribune*'s anger had reached a pitch high enough to
bring forth the charge that the measure "is a financial mon-
strosity, the like of which is rarely seen in any age or
clime." [55] The canny Radicals soon decided to postpone

[51] *Congressional Globe*, 39 Cong., 1 Sess., 3753.
[52] Bowers, *Tragic Era*, 117–18.   [53] Chicago *Tribune*, June 22, 1866.
[54] *Ibid.*, June 26, 1866.
[55] *Ibid.*, June 28, 1866. Editor Murat Halstead of the Cincinnati *Commercial* lambasted what he called the "infernal tariff" and "those damned har-
pies of Pennsylvania and New England." Murat Halstead to Rutherford

action and stick to bloody-shirt waving until after the November elections. This had the desired effect, even upon the Chicago *Tribune*, for not until after the election, when once more the Radicals took up the tariff question, did the *Tribune* suspect that it had been duped. Then it even suspected that the Radicals had no intention of carrying out their Reconstruction program. "Instead of reconstructing the South," said the *Tribune*, they "devised tariff schemes which disregard the wishes of the people and are oppressive." [56]

Another economic problem of importance to the Middle West was monopolistic transportation costs. Though concentration on the bloody shirt crowded out economic questions even in purely state elections, the antimonopoly feeling found other outlets. Following the war, the railroad and steamboat companies continued to take advantage of their favorable position by steadily increasing passenger and freight rates. In 1865 a rumor spread through Illinois of the existence of a large upper–Mississippi River railroad and steamboat combination. Two hundred and twenty leading Chicago merchants united in sending to the railroad companies a pointed questionnaire, inquiring whether they were in partnership with the elevators, transportation companies, or steamboat lines of the Chicago area. When no replies were received, the general suspicion deepened. Farmers protested through mass meetings, and commercial conventions planned new waterways and demanded legislative action. Demand for rate regulation became general. In one Illinois county the supervisors resolved to support for office only those candidates pledged to work for correction of the

---

B. Hayes, July 6, 1866, in Rutherford B. Hayes MSS., Hayes Memorial Library, Fremont, Ohio, as cited in Eugene H. Roseboom, *The Civil War Era, 1850–1873* (*The State of Ohio*, ed. Carl Wittke, Vol. IV [Columbus, 1944]), 472. See also Chicago *Tribune*, June 27, 1866, and Columbus *Crisis*, July 11, 1865.
[56] Chicago *Tribune*, February 5, 1867; Bowers, *Tragic Era*, 118.

abuse.[57] Early in 1866 other antimonopolists gathered in St. Paul for a large convention to consider the high transportation rates. The meeting was held at the suggestion of the St. Paul *Press* and had the enthusiastic backing of many other newspapers and numerous citizens. The assembled farmers and merchants voted condemnation of the monopolies, urged the patronage of independent shippers, and recommended the formation of a steamboat company to be owned by themselves.[58]

This growing antimonopoly protest, coupled with the money and tariff questions, bristled with opportunity for politicos desirous of popular issues. But few of them were looking for issues, because the bloody shirt had become the principal medium for tub-thumping. With economic issues thus hopelessly submerged, there remained no real hope for most Johnson men to win in the ensuing congressional and state elections. The major party casualty, moreover, was certain to be the Democracy. The possibility of Democratic restoration had depended upon skill in using economic issues to give the party a positive tone and submerge its war record; but by negatively following the likewise-negative Johnson, the Democracy forfeited this chance. More than that, the needless Johnson-Radical bickering over Southern Reconstruction added to the discomfiture of the already embarrassed Democracy by giving the Radicals opportunity to capitalize upon their own military victory and the copperheadism in the opposition. Johnson, in effect, had invited the enemy to rub salt in the wounds of the Democracy.

Having thus set the stage for political suicide, the Johnson-Moderate-Democratic group scheduled a final rehearsal for August, 1866. Labeled the National Union Convention, this

[57] Arthur C. Cole, *The Era of the Civil War, 1848–1870* (*Centennial History of Illinois*, Vol. III [Springfield, 1919]), 357–60.
[58] St. Paul *Press*, January 3, 4, 5, 10, 12, February 6, 8, March 23, 1866; Eugene V. Smalley, *A History of the Republican Party . . . of Minnesota* (St. Paul, 1896), 180.

was composed of Democrats and Moderate Republicans from North and South, who assembled to make final plans for the autumn elections. Many hoped that the convention would take concrete steps toward creating a new national party. Although the Copperheads were not encouraged to attend, the two most conspicuous of them put in their appearance at the Philadelphia meeting place. District Democratic conventions sent Ohio's Clement L. Vallandigham and New York's Fernando Wood. Upon discovering that he could exert no influence, Wood graciously withdrew from the conclave. But Vallandigham remained long enough to cause political jitters among the delegates and then, just before the meeting was to get underway, yielded to persuasion and retired. The convention, without organizing the dreamed-of new party, decided merely to pass resolutions endorsing the Johnson program. The delegates thereupon returned home to a political campaign that culminated in a disastrous defeat for the Democrats and the few Republicans still loyal to Johnson. The Radicals had completely outsmarted the opposition; they were now strong enough in Congress to have their way on southern Reconstruction; and they had forestalled any immediate check to their economic plans.[59]

Following the Radicals' election triumph the Democratic *Daily Milwaukee News* announced: "Wisconsin has now consented to labor for the benefit of New England; to pay New England prices for everything we wear; take what New England will give for our produce, and pay New England taxes. Well, work on . . . and help enrich the moneyed aristocracy of the East." [60] Indeed, middle-western allegiance to the Radical-dominated Republican party meant middle-western colonial subservience to eastern capitalists. Who

[59] Roseboom, *Civil War Era*, 454; Beale, *Critical Year*, 131–38; Smith, "Party Politics in Minnesota," 27; Evarts Boutell Greene, "Some Aspects of Politics in the Middle West, 1860–1872," *Proceedings of the State Historical Society of Wisconsin*, 1911 (Madison, 1912), 71.
[60] *Daily Milwaukee News*, November 10, 1866.

would step forward to rescue the region from the eastern Radicals? Perhaps the Democratic leaders would see in the situation a golden opportunity for their party's resuscitation. But it was also possible that they lacked the necessary fiber to withstand the clutching eastern brand of capitalism.

Chapter Three

Bondholders and Plow Holders 1867-1868

> *As wealth is power, so all power will infallibly draw wealth to itself by some means or other.*
> —EDMUND BURKE

EARLY IN 1867 a middle-western farmer wrote plaintively to his congressman that the money stringency was increasing and he wished Congress would do something about the problem and leave Reconstruction to a later date.[1] He was but one of the many farmers, along with many businessmen, demanding economic relief through government action. The Civil War recession had set in, and crop failures in 1866 and 1867 added to the deepening gloom.

Democrats responded to the call. One by one middle-western Democratic politicos shifted their main interest from southern Reconstruction to economic reconstruction for their own region. A spirit of economic reform entered and quickened the pulse of the party, causing some Democrats to become feverish with hope and others to be feverish with fear. The most hopeful were the remnants of the prewar Progressive Western Democracy; the most frightened were the Bourbons, who wanted no tampering with the economic *status quo*. The profession of the reformers was essentially politics, and their political strength lay mainly with the masses. The profession of the Bourbons was essentially money-making, and their political strength lay mainly with

[1] Orville Brown to Ignatius Donnelly, January 17, 1867, in Ignatius Donnelly MSS., Library of the State Historical Society of Minnesota.

their own prosperous class. The result was a struggle for party mastery which was to plague the Democracy for decades to come.

In the course of the Democratic change in emphasis from southern Reconstruction to home-front economic problems, there was considerable correspondence among reform-minded Democrats. They reported to each other on the voters' state of mind as they saw it, and they suggested tentative programs of action. One, writing to President Johnson, expressed conviction that "the masses of the people will not lay quietly and see Congress usurp the entire control of their country, through the power of the monopolies of the north and negro votes of the south." [2]

Some Democrats were willing to admit defeat on the southern issue and were anxious to turn the party emphasis entirely to economic questions. General H. C. Hobart, the Wisconsin Democracy's 1865 candidate for the governorship, asserted that the southern slaveholder had contaminated the party. He predicted that the Democrats would "always be in the minority if they sympathize with oppressors of mankind. It is because of the past connection of the Democratic party with those who held men as property, and sympathizing with traitors against the Government, that it has been beaten in every Northern state, . . . and deserves to be beaten." [3] Soon even King of Copperheads Vallandigham began to preach less on southern Reconstruction and more on questions closer to middle-western pocketbooks.[4]

Ohio's politically wise R. P. L. Baber declared that it was "useless to battle longer on a mere defensive position" and urged that the Democracy base its fight on taxation and tariff reform. His proposed strategy for the national political scene was Democratic utilization of economic issues to unite

[2] M. Martin to Andrew Johnson, October 28, 1867, in Johnson MSS.
[3] E. A. Calkins, "General Harrison Carroll Hobart," *Proceedings of the State Historical Society of Wisconsin*, 1902 (Madison, 1902), 158–59.
[4] Cincinnati *Commercial*, August 12, 1867.

the agrarians of the North and the South and thereby rescue the West from eastern dominance. He predicted that "when the passions of our people, inflamed by demagogues, have cooled," the South and West "will ultimately concentrate on tariff and taxation reforms." [5]

Some Democrats saw opportunity beckoning in state politics, for organized antimonopoly sentiment was pressing forward. In January, 1867, a nonpartisan convention of Illinois citizens demanded that the legislature regulate railroad combinations, equalize freight rates, establish a three-cent passenger fare, and require from each road an annual report of expenditures and receipts. Fuel was added to the fire when a combination of railroad managers and politicians interested in building more lines in southern Illinois blocked this and every demand for regulatory legislation.[6] In Wisconsin a Democratic legislator, echoing the sentiments of the Madison *Wisconsin Farmer* and agrarians in general, warned railroad managers against proceeding with a proposal to consolidate certain Wisconsin, Iowa, and Illinois lines.[7] But it was not a question easy to implement politically; for it cut across party lines, and leaders in both parties were blocking action. Railroad influence was powerful in both political camps, as railroad money was plentiful for political uses, railroad-stock certificates were issued to politicians, and many lawyer-politicos were retained as railroad attorneys.

In the realm of national economic policy the tariff question aroused spirited interest among middle-westerners, but it too cut across party lines. In 1866 the majority of middle-western leaders had successfully united against the eastern Republican protectionists, and during the 1867 congressional tariff debate there was the same nonpartisan unity and the

[5] Baber to Doolittle, January 11, 1867, in Doolittle MSS.
[6] Cole, *Era of Civil War*, 358.
[7] Calkins, "General Hobart," *loc. cit.*, 158; Madison *Wisconsin Farmer*, January 19, February 16, 1867.

same success. Iowa's Republican Grimes, Illinois' Republican Richard Yates, and Indiana's Democrat Hendricks led the united middle-western senatorial pack; and even eastern promises of duties on wool and foodstuffs failed to split the adamant middle-western Democrat-Republican combination. Newspapers of both parties forgot to brandish the hatchet of partisanship at each other whenever eastern protectionists started an advance.[8] The Democratic *Daily Milwaukee News* asserted, "Capital now rules the nation with despotic sway, imposes enormous taxes upon the people 'to protect itself.' Do the people of the Northwest desire such protection?"[9] Concurrently the Republican Chicago *Tribune* insisted that "taxation for one class and one section for the benefit of another, to the extent of seventy per cent of the gross consumption of the country is a crime."[10] Indeed, in the opinion of most middle-western agrarians—except the woolgrowers and some wheatgrowers—it was such a crime that no room was left for significant political disagreement. It might have served as a basis for a popular Democratic attack on the eastern Republican protectionists, but the woolgrowers' political strength in Ohio and Indiana dampened Democratic ardor in that very heart of the middle-western Democracy. The woolgrowers obtained protection in 1867, and they would frown upon politicians who talked too loudly of scaling tariffs downward.

Finally in 1867 a group of middle-western Democrats found in the currency question what seemed the key to their problem of policy sterility. Because the hard times of 1867 and the contraction of currency by the government occurred simultaneously, the public was increasingly inclined to associate the two developments. Many farmers had long been interested in a more liberal currency policy, and now even

[8] *Congressional Globe*, 39 Cong., 2 Sess., 908, 926, 1658–59; *Nation*, January 31, 1867.
[9] *Daily Milwaukee News*, January 5, 1867.
[10] Chicago *Tribune*, February 4, 1867.

some of the most conservative men of wealth admitted or
hinted that Secretary McCulloch and his Republican associates had stretched the policy of contraction beyond the
limit of decency.[11] The Chicago *Tribune* declared that
greenback withdrawal was having an injurious effect upon
business interests and causing hardship for the debtors. As
early as January, 1867, it observed, ". . . if there be one
political measure or public policy which the people of the
entire West are a solid unit in opposition thereto, it is the
scheme of currency contraction which Secretary McCulloch is forcing upon the country." [12] Chicago's pious Cyrus
McCormick, manufacturer of farm machinery and financial
godfather to the Illinois Democracy, was prepared to make
concessions to the Greenbackers to aid in driving the Radicals from control of the nation. Virginia-born McCormick
was hopeful of expanding the farm-machinery market south-
ward and had been consistently bitter against the wartime
Republican party. That, added to the fact that his attitude
had constrained him from investing in wartime government
bonds, rendered the Chicagoan willing to accept a program
taxing the United States bonds and issuing several millions
more in greenbacks.[13] On the extreme left of the soft-money
element were men of the Henry Clay Dean stripe. From the
pen of this excited Iowa Copperhead came angry attacks on
the national banks, New England capitalists, and bondholders in general. Dean demanded that the government immediately pay the national debt with greenbacks.[14]

Some business leaders, concluding that they had a bigger
stake in promotion than in their current property holdings,
leaned toward the inflationist view. Railroad promoters,

[11] Cyrus Woodman to C. C. Washburn, December 11, 1867, in Cyrus
Woodman MSS., Library of the State Historical Society of Wisconsin.
[12] Chicago *Tribune*, January 21, 1867.
[13] William T. Hutchinson, *Cyrus Hall McCormick* (New York, 1935),
II, 312–13.
[14] Henry Clay Dean, *Crimes of the Civil War, and Curse of the Funding
System* (Baltimore, 1869), no page numbers.

looking to the possibilities in the far West and the South, saw that inflation would facilitate the sale of railroad securities. Seeing eye to eye with them were many merchants and manufacturers, who envisioned a better home market through increased cash in consumer pockets and also dreamed of tapping distant markets through new railroads. In Cincinnati there was great interest in improving business connections with the South through a proposed railroad into that area. "Every intelligent citizen of Cincinnati," said the Republican Cincinnati *Commercial*, "is convinced of the great importance of the road to her interests, and to the interests of the vast section of country which will be made tributary." [15]

The Ohio Democracy was the first important group to refurbish its organization to emphasize the money question.[16] The rapidly growing popularity of the money issue was not even checked when the nervous Republican Congress passed an act in February, 1868, which temporarily stopped greenback contraction. Many did not believe that this policy would continue if the Republicans stayed in office, and many others wanted issuance of more greenbacks. Spearheading the movement in that stronghold of erstwhile Copperheads was intrepid Washington McLean. Through his position as wealthy manufacturer, Democratic boss of the county embracing Cincinnati, and owner of the Cincinnati *Daily Enquirer*, McLean was in a position to command a respectful political hearing. What is more, "Wash" McLean wanted to be heard. He had political ambitions, not for personal office-holding, but for a renewal of his pre–Civil War hobby of successfully naming candidates and influencing

---

[15] Cincinnati *Commercial*, November 21, 1865; see also issue of October 30, 1865.

[16] Two good discussions of the "Ohio Idea" or "Pendleton Plan" are Destler, "Pendleton Plan," *loc. cit.*, 171–84, and Max L. Shipley, "The Background and Legal Aspects of the Pendleton Plan," *Mississippi Valley Historical Review*, XXIV (December, 1937), 329–40.

policy in both state and national politics. His inclination was
to be a president-maker. With his sights thus leveled at the
political heights, he chose the soft-money issue as the entering wedge. and gratuitously selected George H. Pendleton
as his presidential candidate. In January, 1867, McLean attempted to induce the assembled state Democratic convention to endorse currency reform. But the delegates coldly
ignored the effrontery.[17]

The Ohio gathering, after quickly disposing of McLean's
suggestions, adopted a platform written by Vallandigham.
It dealt almost entirely with the constitutional aspects of
Reconstruction and contained but two short, vague items
on taxation and the tariff. Then the members of the Copper-
head-dominated convention nominated for the governorship one of their milder cohorts, "the Old Roman," Allen G.
Thurman—always moderate, dull, honest, and respected.
In April the more colorful "Gentleman George" Pendleton,
who had the endorsement of the Ohio Democracy and of
McLean for the 1868 presidential nomination, opened the
state campaign. He made it clear that the Ohio Democrats
had no intention of abandoning their emphasis on southern
Reconstruction in favor of the money issue. In fact, in listing the party's grievances he decried the current existence
of inflated currency.[18]

Wash McLean, meanwhile, was very busy. Upon discovering that it netted him nothing to deal directly with the
Democratic traditionalists, he used the *Enquirer* to strike out
boldly for Henry Clay Dean's extreme inflation ideas. Playing demagogue to the growing inflationist sentiment among
the masses, McLean was building up a popular following
to force Pendleton and the state organization to endorse inflation. His tactics soon awakened state leaders to action;

[17] Destler, "Pendleton Plan," *loc. cit.,* 171, 174–75; *National Cyclopaedia of American Biography* (New York, 1898–1945), I, 444.
[18] *Appletons' Annual Cyclopaedia,* VII (1867), 603; Destler, "Pendleton Plan," *loc. cit.,* 174–75.

they discovered that local Democratic conventions were endorsing Greenbackism and that Washington McLean was headed toward domination of the state party. Faced with loss of party control if they followed McLean's program or with a very weak chance of victory if they failed to advocate currency reform, state-organization leaders offered a compromise financial proposal. The particular plan upon which they concentrated was developed in its ultimate form by George H. Pendleton. It came to be called the "Pendleton Plan" or the "Ohio Idea." The scheme was very mild; it went no further in the direction of inflation than to propose a temporary restoration of the wartime circulation of greenbacks. Pendleton would substitute greenbacks both for the costly national-bank notes, which had been issued on interest-bearing government bonds, and for the costlier use of gold in retirement of government bonds. By 1881, the saving thus effected would supposedly result in a sinking fund large enough to retire the greenbacks and return the national currency to a gold basis.[19]

The plan was capable of commanding a mass following if identified with the proper candidate—and Gentleman George Pendleton, the 1864 Democratic vice-presidential nominee, seemed to fit the need. At that time he was, in the opinion of Ohio's Republican Rutherford B. Hayes, "the most distinguished and perhaps the most influential Democrat . . . actively engaged in politics in Ohio."[20] The dashing, handsome Pendleton was a prosperous lawyer with an annual income approaching ten thousand dollars. He was also an investor-promoter especially interested in the proposed railroad connecting his native Cincinnati with the South. But above all this forty-two-year-old grandnephew

[19] Destler, "Pendleton Plan," loc. cit., 175–78.
[20] Hayes, in a campaign speech at Lebanon, Ohio, on August 5, 1867, quoted in Charles R. Williams, The Life of Rutherford Birchard Hayes, Nineteenth President of the United States (Boston, 1914), I, 296.

of Edmund Randolph was a professional politician. As a youth he had been active in the Progressive Western Democracy; from 1857 to 1865, an outspoken Peace Democrat in the House of Representatives; in 1864, the Democratic vice-presidential candidate—and now he was one of the notable Vallandigham-Thurman-Pendleton triumvirate of the Ohio Democracy.[21] Regionalist and political realist, Gentleman George was an ace card in the Democratic pack.

In 1867, Pendleton's innate caution and shrewdness caused him to hesitate before succumbing to wily Wash McLean's pressure and blandishments. But McLean had selected Pendleton as his 1868 presidential candidate on a currency-reform platform, and by July he succeeded in luring the popular Ohioan into his lair. Although Pendleton did not go nearly so far off the sound-money reservation as McLean had previously demanded of the Ohio Democracy, the general outcome was a McLean victory. After all, McLean wanted chiefly to force the currency issue to the forefront and find a willing candidate. He had succeeded.[22] The other leading Ohio Democrats swung in behind Pendleton on the issue. Even the supposedly die-hard Copperhead Vallandigham decided, albeit reluctantly, to supplement his former concentration on the Reconstruction issue with doses of Greenbackism. In August he told farmer audiences, "If legal tender is good enough to pay for a bushel of corn, it is good enough to pay these bonds. . . ."[23] The state-election results showed progress for the Ohio Democracy. Although the party failed to win the governorship, it captured the legislature and consequently sent Old Roman Thurman to the United States Senate. Twelve usually Republican counties, moreover, voted with the Democracy in

[21] Roseboom, *Civil War Era*, 448–99; Destler, "Pendleton Plan," *loc. cit.*, 177–78.
[22] Destler, "Pendleton Plan," *loc. cit.*, 178.
[23] Cincinnati *Commercial*, August 12, 1867.

defeating a Republican-sponsored constitutional amendment allowing Negroes to vote in Ohio.[24] Gentleman George had cleared an important hurdle in the presidential-nomination race.

Although the Ohio success quickened the Greenback movement in other states of the Middle West, the region's party leaders in general still showed untoward reluctance to endorse the movement. Paradoxically, the most agrarian of the states—and therefore the one most needful of currency reform—embraced the least organized Democratic enthusiasm for the issue. This was due to a different balance between the wealth-getting and the vote-getting activities of the dominant Democratic leaders. While Ohio and Indiana leaders saw in the currency issue an opportunity to satisfy both their southern-expansionist and their political aims, such was not the case with most state leaders in the remainder of the Middle West. There the Democracy was less popular; and the aging party-leaders were well-heeled Bourbons, who had long since abandoned frontier-promotion economy and vote-getting Jacksonian democracy. In their thinking these Bourbons were largely anti-inflationist, antileveler, anti-agrarian.

Bourbons were very much interested in keeping Greenbackism from receiving party sponsorship. Remembering well the pioneer inflation economy with its wildcat bank currency, they shuddered at the thought of even so mild a plan as Pendleton's, for fear it would be an entering wedge to widespread currency inflation. They envisioned the dreadful specter of soft money sending all good men of property, especially themselves, to the abyss of poverty, where already dwelt so many sad-faced farmers. Better to leave the agrarians there than to lend a hand—lest *change* pull down the entire house of big profits and accumulated wealth. Beware of change! They accordingly utilized their

[24] Hubbart, *Older Middle West*, 244.

political power, which wealth and ability made considerable, to stop the "Pendleton Planners." Most Bourbons, however, shrank from seeking public office for themselves, knowing that they were too unpopular with the voters to obtain victory and being too busy as masters of capital to "waste time" campaigning. So they utilized the device of promoting stool-pigeon candidates. Better that the Republicans win, they thought, than back a popular man of the masses and a people's platform.

Wisconsin's Democratic mogul Alexander Mitchell was typical of the Bourbon operators. In 1839 two Scotsmen, Mitchell and a George Smith, had started banking in frontier Milwaukee; and after several decades of shrewd activity, including some wildcatting in the most barefaced manner, they had become fabulously wealthy. In 1853 Smith returned to Scotland, and upon his death in 1899 he left one of the most colossal fortunes in the United Kingdom. Mitchell remained in Milwaukee and soon added industrial and railroad promotion to his banking activities. He organized the Milwaukee Railroad, of which he was president until his death; and for a time he was president of the North Western Railroad.[25] Certainly Alexander Mitchell, rolling in wealth at the time when Gentleman George Pendleton was merely laying plans to roll toward wealth, would not be enthusiastic for Greenbackism. It was all right in his young days of wildcatting, when he had everything to gain and nothing to lose; but now his position was reversed. And as the most important Democrat in Wisconsin he had no intention of allowing *his* party to fall into the clutches of the money-bugs. In Milwaukee he was surrounded by a group of like-minded Bourbon Democrats, who wanted no change in the existing

[25] Gustave Pabst, Jr., "Marine Bank Celebrating 100 Years of Smith's Money," Milwaukee *Journal*, May 14, 1939; Horace White, *Money and Banking, Illustrated by American History* (Boston, 1896), 387–94; Horace White, *George Smith's Money* (an address to the American Bankers Association, Chicago, 1893 [New York, 1893]), 1–10.

economic pattern of "progress." The Milwaukee clique was so powerful in the state Democracy that Bourbons out in the state grumbled. Lawyer George Smith of Madison, in commenting on the Milwaukee cabal, complained that "the devil of it is there is nobody there or but few whose advice is disinterested or valuable." "I hope and pray," lamented Smith, "for a better condition of things." [26] Another disgruntled Wisconsin Democrat hoped that the time would come "when the Democratic Party of Wisconsin will be so strong that Milwaukee will not make any difference with us." [27]

In the 1867 Minnesota election this brand of Bourbonism was strikingly exemplified. Some local leaders wanted the Democracy to concentrate on financial reform, but the Bourbons steered the state convention into placing the emphasis upon southern Reconstruction. The only action which they took on economic problems was adopting the usual resolution against high tariffs and another asking taxation of federal bonds. On Reconstruction, however, the convention attacked the Radical Republicans for passing "enactments subversive to the liberties of the people, and . . . intended solely to secure the ascendency of the Republican Party." [28] As if to emphasize this outburst, the Bourbons called upon a visiting Copperhead editor, Wisconsin's "Brick" Pomeroy, to address the assemblage. This episode so highlighted the Reconstruction issue as to call forth an incensed polemic from the St. Paul *Press*. The *Press* believed Pomeroy to be "without exception the vilest and most malignant Copperhead in the Northwest. It was he who urged the crime that Booth committed and who dared to . . . deride the grief of the nation for its slain chief, and heap such insults upon the grave of the Martyred Lincoln as made the blood curdle with horror to read." [29]

[26] George B. Smith to H. C. Orton, January 20, 1868, in George B. Smith MSS., Library of the State Historical Society of Wisconsin.
[27] H. C. Orton to George B. Smith, January 17, 1868, *ibid.*
[28] Smith, "Party Politics in Minnesota," 33.
[29] St. Paul *Press*, July 11, 1867.

The liquor question was another issue which aroused the hopes of many Minnesota Bourbons. The Republicans had shown interest in prohibition legislation, and consequently the opposition envisioned strong German support for their Democratic party. In its platform the Democracy condemned "sumptuary laws of all kinds, as subversive of sound morality, and unwarrantable invasion of the natural rights of man." Adding more to Democratic hopes was the convention's unusual success in convincing a prominent Bourbon, Judge C. E. Flandrau, to accept the nomination for the governorship. Flandrau had been a chief justice of the Minnesota territorial supreme court and a conspicuous hero in the Indian war of 1862.[30] Even Republicans admitted that the Democrats had chosen not only a good but actually the best slate in the party's history.[31] The outcome, however, was discouraging for the Minnesota Democracy. In the absence of the currency issue normally Republican voters saw no impelling advantage in forsaking their own party. Over twice as many votes were cast as in 1865, but the proportional distribution between the parties remained about the same. For all their efforts the Democrats made but slight gains in the legislature, though they managed to defeat a Negro-suffrage amendment to the state constitution.[32]

In Illinois the Democrats possessed a better opportunity because the Republican incumbents in the state legislature were in especially ill repute. By common consent the 1867 legislature had been the most disgraceful in the state's history. The legislators had shown both dishonesty and bad manners. The senate had frequently been the scene of disorder, as members threw books and paper wads at each other and at the speaker. But the Bourbon-controlled Democracy failed to capitalize on the opportunity. The cam-

[30] Smith, "Party Politics in Minnesota," 32–33.
[31] Charles Passavant to Ignatius Donnelly, July 11, 1867, in Donnelly MSS.
[32] Harlan Page Hall, Observations . . . of Political Contests in Minnesota (St. Paul, 1904), 346; Smith, "Party Politics in Minnesota," 41.

paign was marked by factional bickering over local issues, not by a straightforward contest on important economic questions. The outcome was only a slight gain for the Democracy in candidates elected; it contained no indication of an ensuing general upswing in party popularity.[33]

The election gains of 1867 and Republican excesses nevertheless caused middle-western Democrats to be hopeful of a brighter party future.[34] A Wisconsin Democrat announced, "The Gods have made the Radical party *mad*, and its destruction is seen. By proper management we shall carry nearly all the northern states next fall." [35] Many onetime Democrats were leaving the Republican party and returning hopefully to their old camp. In December independent Democrat Cyrus Woodman, who had supported Lincoln and the Radicals, decided:

> If the Republican party is to be governed by men who are in favor of impeachment and repudiation, like Stevens and Butler, then you may count me out for good. The Republican party is in a fair way to make the name of "Copperhead" honorable. At any rate I may soon be much more willing to bear it than that of Republican. I can tell you that the people are getting tired and sick of this everlasting talk about impeachment and reconstruction. Universal Negro suffrage should not be demanded of the South. . . . Pass what laws you will the white man of the South will control and govern that country. If they cannot do it any other way they will kill off the Negroes.

But on the subject of currency, Woodman favored continuing the Radical policy of contraction.[36]

[33] Cole, *Era of Civil War*, 406; Chicago *Tribune*, March 1, 1867; Hutchinson, *McCormick*, II, 308–309. Cyrus McCormick, although then residing in New York, rendered financial assistance to the Illinois Democracy.

[34] Charles H. Coleman, *The Election of 1868* (*Columbia University Studies in History, Economics and Public Law*, No. 392 [New York, 1933]), 55.

[35] H. C. Orton to George B. Smith, January 17, 1868, in Smith MSS.

[36] Woodman to C. C. Washburn, December 11, 1867, in Woodman MSS.

The outcome of the spring elections in 1868 added still more to Democratic hopes. In April the Michigan voters rejected by a vote of 110,000 to 71,000 a proposed new constitution which provided for Negro suffrage. In local Michigan elections the Democrats gained in southern and central counties; forty towns which in 1867 had voted majorities for the Radicals now voted Democratic. In such large cities as St. Louis, Milwaukee, and Cincinnati, moreover, the Democrats made large gains. In a Chicago judicial election they swept all before them.[37]

With the approach of the 1868 national convention the purposeful Greenbackers and the die-hard Bourbons vied with each other for position. The Greenbackers had considerable cause for optimism, for they had early gained control of the party in strongly Democratic Ohio, they possessed an able presidential candidate in Pendleton, and they had a popular program and the backing of some aggressive leaders. Among the able Democrats rendering support to Pendleton was editor J. Sterling Morton of the newly admitted state of Nebraska. Although but thirty-six years old, Morton was a veteran in Democratic politics. Michigan-born, he had gone to Nebraska in 1854 when a youth of twenty-two and before being there a week had attended two political meetings and made a political speech. Through the ensuing years Morton devoted his restless energy to being an editor, booster, fruit farmer, business promoter, railroad lobbyist, and politician. He was always a Democrat, always for free trade, and always for railroad expansion. During the Civil War he was closely associated with, and made a favorable impression upon, Vallandigham, Pendleton, and other Copperheads. Now in 1868 he was again working with these perennial political thorns-in-the-flesh.[38]

---

[37] Coleman, *Election of 1868*, 66; Chicago *Republican*, April 27, 1868.
[38] James C. Olson, *J. Sterling Morton* (Lincoln, 1942), 40, 111, 118–20.

One of the services which the ambitious Pendleton hoped to receive from Morton, and one which only the illness of Morton prevented, was work for the cause among his fellow newspapermen. In April he urged Morton to visit editors in Iowa, Missouri, Wisconsin, and Michigan in an effort to "give tone to the papers and to infuse vigor into them." Morton could, Pendleton informed him, "communicate to them new ideas and new information and thus set up a chain of sympathy. . . . Your position as a leading western man, a politician, and editor and a delegate would enable you to make the trip without exciting the least suspicion that you had any other business than to recruit your health and see the country." [39]

The middle-western Bourbons, meanwhile, were slow to get into action, though they were blessed with considerable power, with more money and more newspapers than the Pendleton faction, and with powerful allies in the East. But Bourbon strength was waterlogged with confusion. Bourbons had not settled upon a presidential candidate nor defined a clear-cut, positive program. They kept telling each other over and over that they were saner in Reconstruction than the Republicans and saner on currency than the Greenbackers, but their ideas on how to demonstrate superiority were vague, if not void.

Chicago's Bourbon John M. Corse, a Civil War brigadier general and currently a railroad- and bridge-building contractor, bestirred himself a little from the political lethargy which had settled upon his clan. In January, 1868, Corse told his old friend General Henry H. Sibley of Minnesota that until recently he had thought that "the war-element" in the party was "too feeble to give any manifestations of life," but "experience has induced me to change my opinion and to believe it can be made the predominant element in

[39] George Hunt Pendleton to J. Sterling Morton, April 26, 1868, as cited *ibid.*, 149.

the party. . . . We can get sufficient representation to the
National Convention that will at least give tone and character to it if not control it." Indignantly he sputtered that the
time had come for the old War Democrats to "assert our-
selves and manifest to the country that the Democratic
party is not a Copperhead organization. . . . But, if we
remain supine and make no struggle to overthrow men like
Vallandigham and Henry Clay Dean . . . we must expect
to perish." He was convinced that the Democracy was mis-
represented by a band of "political adventurers and broken
down politicians." He neglected to include in that group
himself and the other War Democrats who had served as
officers in the Union army. In fact, he had written to many
of his fellow former officers in Illinois, Missouri, Michigan,
Indiana, New York, and Massachusetts; and their replies
demonstrated that they all desired the Democracy to be the
"exponent of the people in their integrity and devotion to
Constitutional law." Brigadier General Corse had found a
party platform—"Constitutional law." [40]

Other Bourbons demonstrated a similar lack of originality,
some expressing certainty of a Democratic victory in November and certainty that currency inflation was the worst
possible question to endorse. That done, they retreated into
meaningless verbiage. Wisconsin attorney H. C. Orton predicted victory and also bewailed the prominence in the party
of "radicals who *make haste* to start theories of finance and
internal policies that have not been sufficiently digested
and tested to be reliable, and make the principal noise about
them . . . to secure their own prominence, in advance of
the party." To him there were men in the party "just as
impractical as the members of the old abolitionist
party. . . ." He was "sorry that Pendleton had started any
theories of finance and still more regretted that there is an

[40] John Murray Corse to H. H. Sibley, January 18, 1868, in H. H.
Sibley MSS., Library of the State Historical Society of Minnesota.

effort to commit the party to them. We as a party are in no-wise responsible for the present state of things. Let the party in power suggest and commit itself to policies and theories." Then, because there existed no possibility of any proposal bringing relief, the Democracy should oppose anything that the Republicans suggested or attempted: "Our theories of government are of course all right, and are *positive*, and we may urge them with convincing power, as we shall, but I would not embarrass them by side issues of present remedial legislation for our financial embarrassments. For this reason, I would favor the nomination of some civilian and statesman, cool, calm, slow to resolve, but resolute and bold in action, like Governor Seymour." [41]

Failing to discover a program destined to satisfy both themselves and the agrarians, the Bourbons in general resorted to passing the buck to each other. But no able men stepped forward with appealing ideas or with willingness to bid for public office. A Wisconsin lawyer, Democrat George Smith, expressed apprehension over the aggressiveness of the Greenback forces and over a corresponding lethargy among his fellow Bourbons. He believed that there were enough "sound" men in the party to "control matters if they would only act together, but the trouble is that they will not act at all. Hence . . . things is left to the management of incompetent hands. So after all the real fault lies with better and not with lesser men." [42]

This general blind preoccupation with their past and their pocketbooks was too engulfing for the Bourbons to take effective action against the Greenback heresy, but outside forces might deliver them from their plight. There was one promising possibility. Their eastern Bourbon cousins, especially the August Belmont–Samuel J. Tilden clique in New York, might be successful with their drive to dominate

[41] H. C. Orton to George B. Smith, January 17, 1868, in Smith MSS.
[42] George B. Smith to H. C. Orton, January 20, 1868, *ibid.*

the national organization in the interest of Bourbonism. There was no doubting the New Yorkers' intention to prevent Pendleton's nomination.[43] They distrusted Pendleton for two reasons—his espousal of currency reform, and his interest in a West-South economic-political alliance that would isolate the East.

The New York Bourbons spared no effort in undermining Pendleton's position. They had friends working for them in the Middle West. Wisconsin's James R. Doolittle, back in the Democratic fold after a decade of Republican espousal, served as the New Yorkers' agent to gain Moderate Republican support for Horatio Seymour's candidacy. Out in the Nebraska Territory able Dr. George L. Miller served Seymour's cause. Belmont and Tilden succeeded in blocking Washington McLean's efforts to control the national committee and then dictated that New York instead of Cincinnati, would be the convention's meeting place.[44] The Cincinnati *West and South* thereupon bitterly concluded that Seymour's nomination was a foregone conclusion, for August Belmont was "master of the situation." [45]

Throughout these preconvention months the Pendleton men, on the other hand, hoped that they could keep the Bourbon strength confined to the East and the South. In his own efforts to secure the nomination, Pendleton emphasized the importance of holding the line. He told Nebraska's J. Sterling Morton that the Democrats could win "only if we agree in good faith to stand firmly together, on the doctrine which has given us strength." Pendleton observed that the New York bondholders "are zealous." Bourbons in the South were praising Pendleton as a "most ex-

[43] Perry Belmont to August Belmont, March 12, 1868, as cited in Perry Belmont, *An American Democrat* (New York, 1940), 134–35.
[44] Stewart Mitchell, *Horatio Seymour of New York* (Cambridge, 1938), 433, 460; Coleman, *Election of 1868*, p. 179; Destler, "Pendleton Plan," *loc. cit.*, 182; Omaha *Herald*, January 22, 1868.
[45] Cincinnati *West and South*, February 29, 1868.

cellent man" but one who "cannot win." They argued that
to win the Democracy "must gain two hundred thousand
Republicans," and "in order to do this we must take a war
man, perfectly sound but not subject to [the] cry of dis-
loyalty." But how ensure the middle-western solidarity
against such eastern Bourbon tactics? "This can best be
done," thought Pendleton, by "warming up" to the greenback issue, because "that takes hold on our people—that
promises relief—that affords common ground on which war
and anti-war men may stand without 'going back' on their
past actions." [46]

On July 4 came the opening of the national Democratic
convention. There was optimism in the Pendleton camp,
with many predicting a speedy nomination of the Ohioan
and an endorsement of Greenbackism. Indeed, his strength
in the delegations from the West and the South was great
enough to warrant optimism. In the West only Michigan
and Wisconsin failed to send delegates pledged to Pendleton. Michigan was pledged to Reverdy Johnson and Wisconsin to favorite-son James R. Doolittle. The position of
the Pendleton men was strong—but not strong enough for
them to avoid a contest with a strong-willed opposition.
August Belmont and Samuel J. Tilden were there, and
Horatio Seymour was chairman of the convention.[47]

In deciding upon the platform the delegates worked in
comparative harmony until they reached the money question. On the Reconstruction issue the resolution which
was adopted included a scathing denunciation of Radical
Reconstruction; declared the question of slavery and secession settled; and demanded that the southern states be restored to their rights in the Union, that amnesty be granted
former Confederates, and that franchise regulation be con-

[46] Pendleton to J. Sterling Morton, April 26, 1868, as cited in Olson,
Morton, 148–49.
[47] *Official Proceedings of the National Democratic Convention, Held
at New York, July 4–9, 1868* (Boston, 1868), 21–24, 73, 77.

fined to the states. On the tariff question the delegates blandly straddled, demanding "a tariff for revenue upon foreign imports, such as will afford incidental protection to domestic manufacturers." But on the currency question the fight lasted so long that the Cincinnati *Enquirer* believed that the Bourbons were deliberately attempting to starve out the Greenbackers with mounting hotel expenses. The plank which was finally accepted was a left-handed endorsement of the Pendleton position. It called for the payment of bonds in greenbacks only when the latter appreciated in value to an equality with gold. This emphasis upon equality with gold simply placed emphasis upon the essential conservatism of the Pendleton Plan.[48]

The Bourbons were more successful in the balloting for a presidential nominee. Although Pendleton maintained a comfortable lead throughout the early balloting, it was not sufficient to break down the Bourbon resistance. The New York delegation's thirty-three votes went first to Sanford E. Church and on the eighth ballot to Thomas A. Hendricks of Indiana. Transferring to Hendricks had the appearance of compromise. The eastern Bourbons considered the moderate Hendricks safer than Pendleton on the money question.[49]

The New Yorkers were more pleased at the rise of Hendricks' star than they would have been at merely checkmating Pendleton. The move split the middle-western Greenback front. The Ohio Pendleton supporters had no stomach for losing the mantle of middle-western leadership to Hendricks' organization from neighboring Indiana, and Ohio's delegate C. L. Vallandigham used this situation to undermine the Pendleton strength in his own delegation. At heart Vallandigham opposed placing the major Democratic emphasis on the currency question instead of on south-

[48] *Ibid.*, 58–59; Cincinnati *Daily Enquirer*, July 4, 7, 9, 10, 1868; Hubbart, *Older Middle West*, 247.
[49] *Official Proceedings . . . 1868*, 77, 111.

ern Reconstruction. He was also somewhat piqued at the
Ohio organization for having selected Allen Thurman instead of himself for the United States senatorship. Following his failure to acquire the hoped-for senatorship, Vallandigham had denounced his party's tactics of trimming
to catch Republicans votes by ignoring what he called old-
fashioned straight-out Democratic principles and Democrats. So now he reasoned that if the Ohio organization
failed to secure the nomination for Pendleton, it should
then go to someone adhering closely to the Reconstruction
issue.

This jealousy over the threatened rise of Hendricks, together with the undercurrent of dissension within Pendleton's home-state delegation, resulted in Ohio's switching its
vote to New York's Horatio Seymour. With the Pendleton phalanx thus broken at its very core, there immediately
followed a general convention shift to the silk-stocking New
Yorkers. On the twenty-second ballot Seymour became the
nominee. The convention then named for second place on
the ticket Missouri's Francis P. Blair, Jr.—perhaps the party's
most hyperthyroid critic of Radical Reconstruction. This action ensured prominence of the Reconstruction issue in the
campaign.[50]

Some people ironically estimated that the conclave's effort contained promise and promises for all those dissatisfied
with Republican rule. Humorist Petroleum V. Nasby, in a
Republican campaign book entitled *The Impendin Crisis uv
the Dimocracy*, informed the voters that in the Democracy
"every sole may find rest—in it there is sich a variety . . .
uv principle that every man, no matter wot the pekoolyer
bent of his mind . . . may find his rock upon which he
may sekoorly rest. . . . There isn't a man in the Yoonited
States who cant get out uv it what he wants. What a gorjis

[50] Coleman, *Election of 1868*, 63, 248; Cole, *Era of Civil War*, 441;
Hubbart, *Older Middle West*, 247.

seeries uv campane mottoes we ken put onto our banners!
In Noo York we shel hev 'Seemore and Gold.' In Ohio
'Blare and Greenbax.' In Kentucky 'Dimokrasy and Re-
poodiashun.' " [51]

The soft-money enthusiasts of the Middle West nevertheless felt that the net gain of their delegates at the convention added up to little more than some pleasurable outings
on Coney Island. Many felt so bitter that they threatened to bolt the ticket and form a third party. They certainly felt no better after the Seymour campaign got under
way, for very soon the New Yorker repudiated the mild
greenback plank. Even old Cyrus McCormick, a friend of
Seymour's and contributor of twelve thousand dollars to
the campaign, believed that this repudiation was a needless
aggravation of the Greenbacker discontent. But the majority of business magnates did not share the same opinion as
McCormick. Candidate Seymour operated on the theory
that the election was in the hands of businessmen. "It will
go," he informed McCormick in September, "as their judg-
ments shall dictate." [52] Certainly repudiation of the Greenback plank placed in bold relief the fact that the dominant
Bourbon strategists were essentially men of private interests
rather than of public affairs. They were first of all men of
pride and pocketbook and only incidentally men of party.

The states which the Democrats had had a chance to take
from the Republican column were mostly the soft-money
agrarian states. Had Seymour and his Bourbon friends shaken
off their prideful phobia about the Republican triumph in
the Civil War and Reconstruction and been less concerned
about their individual purses, they would have had a chance
to capture the important agrarian vote. As conducted, the
campaign caused the Democratic rank and file to sink ever

[51] David R. Locke (Petroleum V. Nasby, pseud.), *The Impendin Crisis
uv the Dimocracy* (Toledo, 1868), 3, 11, 15.
[52] Hutchinson, *McCormick*, II, 212–13; Cole, *Era of Civil War*, 441.

deeper into a morass of defeatism. There seemed no hope for the Bourbon brand of Democracy to defeat the Republican combination of a controlled Negro vote and hero-candidate General U. S. Grant. In October came election reverses in Ohio, Pennsylvania, and Iowa which were great enough to cause Cyrus McCormick to urge his friend Seymour to withdraw from the race and be replaced by Salmon P. Chase. But Seymour continued on his Bourbon way, and on election day he took his medicine. While in 1867 the party had obtained 49.5 per cent of the nation's votes, in 1868 it slipped to 46.7 per cent, not including still unreconstructed Virginia, Florida, Mississippi, and Texas. In the agrarian Middle West, Seymour's percentage was 45.[53]

Bourbonism and factionalism clipped the liberal wing of the Democracy. Even so, perhaps the masses, still living under a political system committed to the democratic process, might eventually find an oportunity to direct toward themselves more of the benefits of the rising industrial order. Perhaps they would capture one of the old parties—or in desperation resort to the formation of a third party.

[53] Hutchinson, McCormick, II, 313; Mitchell, Seymour, 468–69; Coleman, Election of 1868, 45–46, 182; McPherson, Political History, 499; Wilfred E. Binkley, American Political Parties, Their Natural History (New York, 1943), 276–77.

Chapter Four

The Democracy Reaches
Its Nadir
1869-1872

> *The Democratic party is like a man riding back-*
> *ward in a carriage. It never sees a thing until it*
> *has gone by.*
>
> —BENJAMIN F. BUTLER

WITH THE 1868 sabotage of the Pendleton Plan, the middle-western Democracy ceased to be a champion of the region's exploited masses and became instead a meaning-less collection of state and local fragments, over most of which stood watchful Bourbon sentinels. These uninspired and uninspiring Bourbons, remembering their close call in 1868, were determined that Democratic strategy would henceforth avoid sponsorship of economic reforms. Enough of schemes designed to win popular favor; enough of at-tempts to whittle down the Bourbons' enormous financial take from the existing monopolistic order! If the Democracy was going to win elections, the Bourbons sagely told each other, the victories must come through Republican excesses, driving voters in desperation into the Democratic clutches. If the party should get out of hand in such danger spots as Ohio, the Bourbons were determined this time to be well enough organized to check the infection from spreading. And, too, there were always at hand the Bourbon brethren in the East, to aid in the quarantine. There would be no truckling to leveler champions of economic unfortunates.

Confronted with this Bourbon disregard for the voters, the victory-seeking portion of the Democratic camp saw no immediate chance to win elections. Many prominent Democrats therefore retired from politics to await a better day. Some reappeared for the 1872 national contest, but others remained on the side lines for many years. In 1869, Thomas A. Hendricks, upon the expiration of his term in the United States Senate, quietly returned to his Indianapolis law practice.[1] Out in Nebraska, editor-politico George Miller announced that he was educating himself "out of all political aspiration."[2] Energetic J. Sterling Morton contemplated moving to the South and leaving Nebraska for the Republicans to worry over. He finally decided to remain but did abstain from active politics during the next decade.[3] In 1869, after a futile bid for the governorship, Gentleman George Pendleton left his soft-money crusade to lesser men and turned his energies to his new position as president of the Kentucky Central Railroad. Nine years later, by entering the state legislature, he resumed office-holding politics.[4]

Following the 1868 national campaign, however, local and state politics sputtered and flickered in the afterglow. It was a sordid kind of politics, with all its bickering over the inconsequential and its petty personality clashes, but it was not without significance in long-term Democratic fortunes. A notable result was a loosening of the Republican hold on a large number of German voters. Another and closely related result was the impetus rendered the historic trend toward urbanization of the Democracy. A recurrence of the periodic nativist outbursts supplied the political fireworks

[1] James A. Woodburn, "Thomas Andrews Hendricks," in Allen Johnson and Dumas Malone (eds.), *Dictionary of American Biography* (New York, 1928–1946), VIII, 535.

[2] George L. Miller to J. Sterling Morton, November 17, 1868, as cited in Olson, *Morton*, 152.

[3] *Ibid.*

[4] Reginald C. McGrane, "George Hunt Pendleton," in Johnson and Malone (eds.), *Dictionary of American Biography*, XIV, 420.

involved. This particular time the hair-pulling social-cleavage scrap between the "sinful" and the "sanctimonious" revolved around Demon Rum. Neither the Republican nor the Democratic hierarchy was directly responsible for this injection of puritanism into party politics, the chief instigators being vociferous social reformers among the rank-and-file Republicans. They were, more specifically, puritanical folk who were always anxious to do something dramatic and "worthwhile." For a time abolition had captivated and consumed their public interest; then the Civil War had absorbed their attention; and now they raised their battle standards for a new cause. They scented Demon Rum and went to work. They were able to bring pressure to bear for their cause partly because they possessed propaganda aids. Having been among the first to settle permanently in the region, the puritans had acquired much wealth and also controlled many newspapers, public schools, and Protestant churches.

Republican-controlled local and state governments had neglected to regulate the liquor business properly, and now the issue was being forced upon them in a politically non-professional, extremist fashion. Many Republican leaders became worried because the movement threatened to drive the large bloc of beer-loving Germans into the low-brow, traditionally antinativist Democracy. The Republicans were helpless in the face of the puritans. Blind to the broader party implications of their crusade, the inspired nativists unhesitatingly forced the Republican craft full-stern against the ever-increasing human driftwood from nonpuritan Europe. They compelled many Republican candidates to endorse their antiliquor movement, and where that failed, they offered their own candidates on separate temperance tickets.[5]

[5] Cole, *Era of Civil War,* 342–43, 421; E. L. Bogart and C. M. Thompson, *The Industrial State, 1870–1893 (Centennial History of Illinois,* Vol. IV [Springfield, 1920]), 42–43; Edgar Bruce Wesley, *Owatonna, The Social Development of a Minnesota Community* (Minneapolis, 1938), 72–73;

Jubilantly the Democrats watched the German voters bristle in response to the crusade. With glee the Democrats saw worried Republican politicos vainly attempting to turn the issue aside; they heard ambiguous assurances that any Republican candidate was, of course, "as good a Champion of Temperance as any Man can Desire." [6] Germans passed resolutions against voting for candidates pledged to liquor legislation; German, Republican leader Carl Schurz grew increasingly concerned; John V. Farwell dodged the issue in strongly German Illinois. Farwell declined a gratuitously offered Prohibition-party nomination for congressman-at-large, seeing "no practical result to follow" but the "weakening of the Republican party for the advantage and benefit of the Democratic party." [7] Here and there temperance advocates were strong enough to gain political victories: Joseph Medill was elected mayor of Chicago on an antiliquor platform; Illinois' Governor John M. Palmer and Wisconsin's Governor C. C. Washburn signed liquor-regulation measures for their respective states.

But these "triumphs" failed to worry the Democratic politicos. They reiterated their traditional stand against all "sumptuary legislation" and then smugly awaited the German voters' reaction to the laws. The drive against Demon Rum hit the Republican party squarely between the eyes. It loosened the Republican grip on the German voters to the point of causing them to vote Democratic whenever nativism captured the Republican candidates. [8]

Periodic outbursts of nativism helped further the tendency toward urbanization of the Democracy. Into the cities

---

W. W. Folwell, *A History of Minnesota* (St. Paul, 1926), III, 176–78; Herbert Wiltse, "The Temperance Movement, 1848–1871," *Papers in Illinois History*, 1937 (Springfield, 1938), 92.

[6] Bogart and Thompson, *Industrial State*, 43.

[7] John V. Farwell to editor, Chicago *Tribune*, September 16, 1870.

[8] Bogart and Thompson, *Industrial State*, 44; William L. Utley to E. W. Keyes, October 10, 1872, in E. W. Keyes MSS., Library of the State Historical Society of Wisconsin.

poured a stream of immigrants; and, coming from nonpuritan countries, they likewise poured into the antinativist Democratic party. Neighborhood Democratic leaders, of the same nationality origins as the newcomers, immediately herded them under the protective wing of the Democratic precinct clubs. As the cities grew in population and wealth, so grew the power of Democratic machines and bosses. In the middle-western cities emerged a collection of near-replicas of New York's Tammany, which became a very important factor in determining the course of the region's Democracy. So grew the threat to the emergence of a regional Democracy, a Democracy giving fair representation to farmers. Though the Middle West remained predominantly agrarian, the wealth and the voting strength of the farmers were more scattered than in closely knit city populations. Hence, each city machine could stand alone, a well-fortified island in the midst of frustrated farmers. Bourbon Democrats, by making sordid deals with corrupt ward-heeler bosses, utilized the city Democratic machines to stop champions of the farmers from gaining control of the party.

The most striking concurrent example of city-rural cleavage revolved around a political venture of eccentric Ignatius Donnelly. A decade before the Civil War, when a boy of nineteen, restless young Donnelly left Pennsylvania to settle in eastern Minnesota. He concentrated his energies on real-estate dealings until he was leveled by a devastating financial blow in the panic of 1857. Then he turned his Irish talents to law, literature, and politics—mostly politics. Immediately he emerged as a colorful public figure, with "Nininger," his farm home near St. Paul, as headquarters for his tempestuous career. As an orator Donnelly was a masterful spellbinder; as a political tactician he became a dauntless crusader. He had the ability to make even statistics entertaining to audiences. Among other activities, Donnelly attempted to prove by ciphers that Francis Bacon was the real author of Shakespeare's plays. Eventually his insistent writing and lecturing brought him notoriety in the fanciful element of the literati, and he came to be y-clept the "Sage of Nininger."

During the Civil War Donnelly was a Republican congressman; in 1866 he was re-elected after a campaign of preaching the advantages of a protective tariff. Two years later a party split in his district lost him the election. But he kept in touch with his congressional colleagues.[9] After tycoon Jay Cooke undertook the fabulous Northern Pacific Railroad project in 1869, Donnelly became his chief lobbyist. The Minnesotan, ardently interested in western railroad expansion, saw nothing wrong in getting paid for lobbying among his old congressional colleagues.[10]

The next year the Republican party in his district was split more than ever, and the organization was in the hands of the anti-Donnelly faction. The irrepressible Donnelly bid for his old seat in the House—this time as a low-tariff Democrat—and thereupon acquired the nomination. He was responding to the growing sentiment for lower rates on iron and wool. Cheaper iron meant railroad construction; cheaper wool meant more warmth in cold Minnesota. All went well in the campaign until the Bourbon-controlled city Democratic machines went into action. St. Paul and Minneapolis were in his district, and the large Irish Democratic element of St. Paul was important.

The Bourbons had no intention of delivering this controlled vote to Donnelly, an "unsafe" outsider not amenable to taking orders.[11] The Democratic St. Paul *Pioneer* ignored his candidacy. A week before the election Bourbon nervous-

[9] Hall, *Political Contests*, 160; Folwell, *History of Minnesota*, III, 160; John D. Hicks, *The Populist Revolt* (Minneapolis, 1931), 162–64; Smith, "Party Politics in Minnesota," 26.

[10] Oberholtzer, *Jay Cooke*, II, 175 n.; Josephson, *Politicos*, 106.

[11] Smith, "Party Politics in Minnesota," 68; Hall, *Political Contests*, 160–63.

ness broke its bounds; fifty-five bigwig city Democrats circulated a printed *Protest*. This document condemned the
"Proposed Prostitution of our Party by the course certain
assumed leaders had taken in attempting to foist upon us
the notorious Ignatius Donnelly." Donnelly was characterized as a "broken down, cast off, disaffected Republican,
who is trying to climb into Congress upon Democratic
shoulders, by now claiming to be a Free Trader, while his
entire political history shows him to be ultra High Tariff." [12]
The Republicans also expended extra effort to stop Donnelly. They attempted to nullify his tariff stand, adopting
for themselves a platform endorsing tariff for revenue only.
The outcome of the combined Republican and city Democratic onslaught was defeat for Donnelly. The Democracy
was again in the clutches of the city Bourbons and ward heelers.[13]

Meanwhile Democrats in the Middle West became optimistic over the outlook for the 1872 presidential election.
There was popular moral indignation at the Republican
regime. Republican President Grant was not doing well; his
party in Congress was faction-ridden. Wealthy Cyrus
Woodman thought Grant a "pretty good general and a
pretty poor President" and declared that he would "not vote
for him at the next election if a Democrat shall be nominated I
can vote for." [14] A Cincinnati *Commercial* writer observed
that "there is no more cohesion, beyond mere office holding
and public plunder, in the Republican party than there is
in a rope of sand . . . the Republicans are of one party
only in name—and each leader is the representative of a
faction in deadly hostility to some other faction. . . ." [15]

[12] Copy of the *Protest*, October 28, 1870, in Donnelly MSS.
[13] Hall, *Political Contests*, 160–61; Ignatius Donnelly to Dr. W. W.
Mayo, June 8, 1872, in Donnelly MSS.
[14] Woodman to C. C. Washburn, July 4, 1870, in Woodman MSS.
[15] Cincinnati *Commercial*, June 9, 1870, as cited in Binkley, *Political
Parties*, 294.

There was considerable middle-western indignation at Republican friendship for eastern bondholders, national banks, and the high tariff. This, declared an Ohioan, constituted a "swindle in the interest of capital." [16]

Encouraged by the situation, Democratic politicos made gestures toward fashioning a program. Where Bourbons were not in control of party machines, there was a tendency to emphasize economic issues. The 1869 state Democratic platform of Ohio emphasized taxation of government bonds, their payment in greenbacks, abolishment of the national banking system, and a tariff for revenue only. The platform asked for a "limited number of hours in government workshops" and generous land grants to actual settlers but not to "swindling railroad corporations." The Ohio delegates, nevertheless, could not resist stirring the Reconstruction cauldron; they denounced the Fifteenth Amendment, affirming suffrage to be a matter for each state to decide.[17]

In April, 1871, the Democrats in Congress cautiously moved toward digging a grave for the Reconstruction issue and cautiously hinted that the Grant administration had exceeded what the voters would stand. With their eyes on both the Copperhead element and the Bourbons, these professional-minded politicos issued an *Address of the Democrats in Congress to the People of the United States*. The "Address" dealt first with the Reconstruction issue. Offering a left-handed acceptance of the war amendments, it launched an attack upon the immediate Republican legislation for their enforcement. "Under the pretense of passing laws to enforce the Fourteenth Amendment and for other purposes," stated the declaration, "Congress has conferred

[16] A. Haines to Benjamin F. Butler, November 19, 1870, in Benjamin F. Butler MSS., Library of Congress, as cited in William B. Hesseltine, *Ulysses S. Grant, Politician* (New York, 1935), 222.

[17] Smith, "Party Politics in Minnesota," 68; Roseboom, *Civil War Era,* 469–70.

the most despotic powers upon the Executive and provided an official machinery by which the liberties of the people are menaced and sacred rights of local self-government in the states ignored, if not tyrannically overthrown."

The "Address" then dwelt on the scandalous excesses of the Grant administration in patronage and finance. The existing "pernicious system" of patronage distribution, it asserted, resulted in "enormous defalcations and widespread corruption." As for public lands, two hundred million acres which should have been "reserved for the benefit of the people" were voted away to "great corporations." The cautious "Address" failed to demand that the corporations be prosecuted for their corrupt tactics. It announced instead that existing practices caused a "handful of greedy speculators and lobbyists . . . to exercise a most dangerous and corrupting influence over state and federal legislation." No change was demanded in the currency and banking structure. The "Address" simply decried high tariff rates, high taxes, and dishonesty in tax collecting. It directed attention to the absence of "proper diligence" in collecting the "many millions of dollars" remaining due from former collectors of internal revenue.[18] Thus, Democratic congressmen laid the groundwork for a possible 1872 presidential-election platform.

The congressmen could safely have pushed on much further, inasmuch as direct action came a few weeks later from the Copperhead wing itself—action inaugurated by no other than King of Copperheads Vallandigham. In May, Vallandigham spoke out for a new Democratic approach to the nation's needs. Speaking at a county party convention in Dayton, the politically ambitious Ohioan broke with his past views and called upon the Democrats to exercise a "ra-

---

[18] *Address of the Democrats in Congress to People of the United States, Platform of Wisconsin Democracy, Speeches of James R. Doolittle* (pamphlet in Library of the State Historical Society of Wisconsin, n.d., n.p.), no page numbers.

tional toleration" toward one another on past issues. He urged acceptance of the "natural and legitimate results of the war" and asked fellow Democrats to "cordially unite upon the living issues of the day." The Democracy should go forward, contended Vallandigham, by "burying out of sight all that is of the dead past" and at the same time remaining faithful to the "vital and long established rule of strict construction."

Vallandigham's proposal called for Democratic acceptance of the three war amendments, but not upon the basis of any interpretation of them which "altered or modified the original theory and character of the Federal Government." On specific issues, he would have the party demand universal amnesty, civil-service reform, payment of the debt with "moderate Taxation," revenue reform, tariff for revenue only, taxation of wealth rather than people, speedy return to specie payments, and no grants of public lands to corporations. He also attacked President Grant's Santo Domingo venture, the corruption of Grant's regime, and the notorious Ku-Klux acts.

The county convention enthusiastically endorsed Vallandigham's "New Departure," as it came to be called, and issued a general appeal to Democrats everywhere to endorse the new movement.[19] A sizable portion of the party press and many individual Democrats immediately responded with praise. Chief Justice Salmon P. Chase wrote to Vallandigham that his action was a great service, adding, "May God bless you for it." Chase said further that "nothing can be truer than your declaration that the movement contemplated by the resolutions is the restoration of the Democratic party to its ancient platform of progress and reform. I know you too well to doubt your courage and your fidelity to your convictions."[20] Iowa's former Senator A. C.

[19] *Appletons' Annual Cyclopaedia*, XI (1871), 609–10.
[20] S. P. Chase to Clement L. Vallandigham, May 20, 1871, *ibid.*, 750.

Dodge hoped that Democratic conventions elsewhere would in like fashion deliver the party from "the odium of being revolutionary and unconstitutional." He suggested to Minnesota's former Governor H. H. Sibley that, as two old delegates to the "ill-fated Charleston Convention, whose want of union introduced sin and death, and all our woe," they "try and become members of the next convention and through wise and judicious action atone for the errors we committed in 1860." [21] As though thankful for the opportunity to shake off the unhappy past, Democratic state conventions hastened to endorse the New Departure. [22]

As the New Departure received favorable attention, so increased the prestige of Vallandigham. Since his walkout on Pendleton at the 1868 national convention, Vallandigham had not been in good standing with the strong Pendleton-Thurman wing of the Ohio Democracy. Now his New Departure was endorsed by the state convention, won for him popular support, and undermined rival Senator Thurman's pet political endeavor of attacking the war amendments. Vallandigham was making a good start toward capturing Republican John Sherman's seat in the Senate, but he did not live to learn the outcome. Two weeks after the state Democratic convention, while serving as an attorney in a sensational murder trial, Vallandigham accidentally shot himself with a pistol. Not knowing that the weapon was loaded, he pulled the trigger while showing an associate how the murdered man might have killed himself. The shot was fatal. Thus, at the age of fifty, one of the era's most colorful and tenacious political figures ended his career. [23]

Although both ideologically and officially the New Departure had led the Democracy out of a blind alley, the road ahead was extremely rough. The Republicans were well

[21] A. C. Dodge to Sibley, July 15, 1871, in Sibley MSS.
[22] Hubbart, *Older Middle West*, 250.
[23] Roseboom, *Civil War Era*, 475, 477.

aware that their triumphs under President Lincoln had won a deep hold on the populace and that the Democracy had disgraced itself with the majority. Determined to keep the public memory alive to this past, Republican leaders and newspapers sneered at Vallindigham while he was still alive, and thereafter used the same tactics on the Democratic party in general. The Cleveland *Leader*, in a manner typical of other Republican papers, questioned Vallandigham's sincerity: "Can the leopard change his spots, or the Ethiopian his skin?" [24] The Columbus *Ohio State Journal* sarcastically commented regarding Vallandigham, "It would be out of the course of nature for the Republican party not to feel some gratification that the great arch-traitor of the peace Democracy has been brought by any means to get down on his belly and humbly eat the many dirty words which have defiled his mouth . . . during the past ten years. If his repentance were sincere, and his desire to atone for his miserable past . . . could be accepted as reliable, the very angels in Heaven would rejoice over the salvation of this meanest of sinners." [25]

Factionalism within the Democracy contributed to nullification of the New Departure. Sputtering continued between War Democrats and Peace Democrats, between Bourbons and Greenbackers. Some insistently fixed their attention on Reconstruction, explosively attacking President Grant's enforcement of the Ku-Klux acts and loudly demanding universal amnesty. Some Vallandigham haters were angry over the Ohioan's coup. Bourbon James R. Doolittle steered the New Departure through the Wisconsin state convention but could not resist exhibiting distaste for Vallandigham. He declared to the delegates that the substance of the new movement had already been proclaimed in the Democratic congressmen's *Address*, and that al-

---

[24] Cleveland *Leader*, May 20, 1871, as cited *ibid.*, 476.
[25] Columbus *Ohio State Journal*, as cited *ibid.*, 475–76.

though it was "new to Vallandigham," it certainly was not to the Democratic congressmen.[26]

While the Democrats continued to flounder in a condition of disunity, the many anti-Grant voters became discouraged. Voters were prone to distrust the probable course of Democratic policy. Some voters feared that the party would follow the soft-money Ohioans; others feared that the party would not do so. The voters in general approved the New Departure, but the feeling increased that it would not be adhered to if the Democracy actually gained control of the national government. Conservative Cyrus Woodman watched the Democracy in the hope of finding a means to rid the country of Grantism, but by September, 1871, he concluded that the Democrats "generally act like cursed fools." The public, he observed, still feared that if the Democratic party should gain power, the war amendments "would be abrogated if possible, the rights of the Negro be ignored and the public debt be repudiated." [27] A bitterly anti-Grant editor in Iowa lamented: "If the democracy could muster up courage enough to go into the next presidential contest on the live questions of the day . . . there might be a chance for success. But we have little hope of seeing so much sense in the democratic party. The everlasting negro question must be fought over again and again." [28]

The New Departure helped bring together the erstwhile Peace and War Democratic elements, but to many voters it was a union of more sentimental than practical value. This superficiality was revealed in a continued party split on such basic economic questions as monopoly, currency, national

[26] *Address of Democrats . . . , Speeches of James R. Doolittle;* Hesseltine, *Grant,* 258–59.

[27] Woodman to E. W. Farley, September 22, 1871, in Woodman MSS.

[28] Clinton (Iowa) *Age,* November 17, 1871, as cited in Frederick E. Haynes, *Third Party Movements Since the Civil War, with Special Reference to Iowa: A Study in Social Politics* (Iowa City, 1916), 22.

banks, and government bonds. In Ohio and Indiana, the Democracy championed the people, but elsewhere the Bourbons disregarded public demands. In Wisconsin a state politician told Bourbon James R. Doolittle, "You are represented as being the favorite candidate of the monied monopolies and corporations," and one who, if elected governor, "will be even more subservient to their views and interests" than the Republican incumbent. "I know there is a deeper and wider feeling on this subject than you are aware of. The anti-monopolist mob is stronger . . . than the vote of the monopolists, and if the issue is made it will" beat the Republican governor. "Cannot the Democratic candidate," he asked, "be as much of a peoples' man as the Republican?" But Doolittle and other Bourbons paid no heed to such pleading.[29]

On the money question, the non-Bourbon Ohio Democracy set an example of moderation, but its suggestions were brushed aside by middle-western Bourbons. The 1871 Ohio platform declared "that while we reject repudiation, we equally reject the proposition to pay bondholders more than the contract demands." It declared "that if bondholders have rights, so have the taxpayers, and we insist upon justice being done to both; that the creditor . . . be paid in the same currency he loaned to the government." If the creditor "loaned greenbacks, he should be paid in greenbacks," but not so if the "contract otherwise provides." The true mode of returning to specie payments, moreover, "is to make customs duties payable in legal tender currency, whether paper money or gold." [30]

The ensuing Ohio campaign failed to bring victory to the Democracy.[31] The party, however, acquired enough votes to demonstrate that despite inadequate funds and

[29] J. A. Noonan to Doolittle, September 25, 1871, in Doolittle MSS.
[30] *Appletons' Annual Cyclopaedia*, XI (1871), 611; Roseboom, *Civil War Era*, 476.
[31] Roseboom, *Civil War Era*, 478.

Governor Rutherford B. Hayes' popularity, it had offered a program which the Bourbons, if they really wanted to capture additional votes, might use as a basis for compromise.

Many Democrats, in looking toward the 1872 presidential election, revealed a willingness to kowtow to the eastern wing of the party. Iowa's former Senator A. C. Dodge thought Thomas A. Hendricks a "worthy, able and excellent man." He also thought that in "Iowa and Illinois, and . . . throughout the Northwest, there is a strong feeling in favor of" the moderately Greenback Indianian. Dodge, however, expressed doubt that he would run as well in "Pennsylvania and some other Eastern states" as would General Winfield Scott Hancock. Why not, therefore, "move heaven and earth to nominate" this military man. It did not seem in the nature of most middle-western Democratic leaders to put up a fight for candidates who would aid their region. They persistently met the Republicans on Republican grounds. Pennsylvania "has never failed to give preference to military men"; therefore, beat General Grant with General Hancock in that state and forget about one's own region.[32]

Other Democrats became so discouraged that they advocated consigning the party to the bone yard. A year before the presidential elections an Iowa Democratic editor suggested that it would be folly to use the old party name in the 1872 contest. He would have the Democracy "disband" and its members support one of the Republican factions.[33] In January, 1872, a Wisconsin Democratic paper suggested that they "abandon the name Democrat, and form a new party." [34]

While around and around went this Democratic swivel-

[32] A. C. Dodge to Sibley, July 17, 1871, in Sibley MSS.
[33] Burlington (Iowa) *Hawk-Eye*, November 2, 1871, as cited in Haynes, *Third Party Movements*, 23.
[34] Madison (Wis.) *Democrat*, January 4, 1872.

chair politics, the Liberal Republicans stepped forward to grasp the anti-Grant scepter. This Republican group embraced professional politicans jealous of the clique surrounding Grant, and a large coterie of reformers. In general the Liberal Republican movement was a protest against high protective tariffs, such foreign adventures as Grant's Santo Domingo affair, the existing Reconstruction policy, and, above all, the despicable party spoils system then in operation. These were items which the Democrats could heartily endorse. They left the initiative to the Liberal Republicans, with the expectation of a combined onslaught on President Grant's re-election bid.

Delegates representing the Liberal Republicans enthusiastically convened in Cincinnati to design a platform and designate a slate for the national campaign. Petty politics immediately took command and dampened the high moral spirit which had accompanied the movement. The result, especially for the Democrats, was disappointing. Low-tariff Democrats witnessed the tariff reformers' demands whittled down to an innocuous resolution which "remanded to the people in their congressional districts" the tariff question. The resolution was devised largely to placate protectionist Horace Greeley and his New York *Tribune*. Then, to cap the climax, wirepulling politicians stampeded the convention into nominating the eccentric, aging Greeley for the presidency.[35] It was, as Governor Rutherford B. Hayes observed, "a queer result." "Free traders nominate their bitterest and most formidable foe. A party whose strength is mainly in the German element which is clamorous against temperance fanaticism nominates the author of that fanaticism. Democrats are required to support a man who said he would go for Grant in preference to any Democrat!"[36] It was indeed "a queer result." It would be even

---

[35] Josephson, *Politicos*, 153–54, 159; Hesseltine, *Grant*, 271–73; Binkley, *Political Parties*, 297–98.
[36] Rutherford B. Hayes, *Diary and Letters of Rutherford Birchard Hayes*, ed. Charles R. Williams (Columbus, 1924), V, 204.

queerer if the Democrats added their endorsement. Certainly it would not be easy for them to swallow as a candidate the man who, back in 1860, had remarked: "I never said all Democrats were saloonkeepers. What I said was that all saloonkeepers were Democrats."

The Democratic leaders were chagrined at this turn of events, but having allowed the initiative to fall to the Liberal Republicans, they could see no alternative to Greeley to beat Grant. Some Democrats talked themselves into believing that he was a pretty good choice. Bourbon James R. Doolittle's "first feeling was that of blank astonishment, the next a broad grin of laughter, the third a serious question." After all, he asked, "Is not this the man to break up the Republican party and to beat Grant? If we run a separate ticket, will not the election go to the House of Representatives almost to a certainty, where Grant with his carpetbaggers will be sure to be elected?" On the tariff, Doolittle initially thought that the Liberal Republican "resolution looked like a dodge." He finally decided that "really the House of Representatives has jurisdiction on the question of revenue, and the dodge after all of saying the East and West differ and will discuss it in the Congressional districts is as frank as the common expression of judicious Tariff, or Revenue tariff with discriminations." [37] Doolittle conveniently overlooked Greeley's having said, "If I had my way, if I were king of this country, I would put a duty of $100 a ton on pig iron and a proportionate duty on everything else in this country." [38]

Politically, the situation was not promising for the Democratic party, but the Bourbons exhibited no marked disappointment. After all, the immediate future was protected against a political onslaught from the lower economic strata of society. The Bourbons thus were free to enjoy the

[37] Doolittle to George B. Smith, May 7, 1872; and *id.* to *id.*, May 17, 1872, in Smith MSS.
[38] Binkley, *Political Parties*, 298; Josephson, *Politicos*, 162.

sprightly, harmless game of anti-Republican politics. First
Democratic leaders, then state conventions, and finally the
national convention at Baltimore, meeting in July, went on
record for Greeley.[39] A minute proportion of Democratic
leaders refused to co-operate. These so-called "Straights"
held a convention at Louisville, with the financial aid of
Grant Republicans, who saw in the movement a chance to
divert Democratic votes from Greeley.[40] Charles O'Connor,
despite his insistence that he would not accept the honor,
was designated as the presidential candidate. He continued
to refuse the nomination, and consequently the Straights
conducted no campaign.[41]

In the Greeley campaign the Democratic and Liberal
Republican managers presented fusion tickets for the various elective offices. Where the Democrats were traditionally
popular, they secured top places. They were able, for example, to obtain such a plum as the nomination of Thomas
A. Hendricks to the Indiana governorship. In many other
areas, however, the Liberal Republicans obtained the choice
nominations.[42]

Everywhere the fusion effort was marked by considerable bickering, jealousy, and suspicion. The greatest dissension was in Illinois, where Democrat Cyrus McCormick
stepped out of his retirement from active politics and insisted upon dominating the state campaign. He was piqued
over having been ignored by the fusion organization which
Democrat Melville W. Fuller and Republican Governor
John M. Palmer had established. Upstart Fuller, thought
tycoon McCormick, needed a political spanking, and the

[39] Saterlee Clark to Doolittle, May 10, 1872, as cited in Horicon (Wis.)
Reporter, May 12, 1905; George B. Smith to *id.*, May 13, 1872, in Doolittle MSS.; Herman J. Deutsch, "Political Forces in Wisconsin, 1871–
1881" (unpublished doctoral dissertation, University of Wisconsin,
1926), 23; Hubbart, *Older Middle West*, 252; Hutchinson, *McCormick*,
II, 316–17.

[40] J. H. Howe to Keyes, August 23, 1872, in Keyes MSS.

[41] Hesseltine, *Grant*, 284.

[42] Mayo to Ignatius Donnelly, July 18, 1872; and J. L. MacDonald to
id., July 30, 1872, in Donnelly MSS.

best way to administer it was to withhold the funds which he had promised for the Greeley campaign. McCormick had offered ten thousand dollars to the national organization, and he saw to it that the committee sent no money to Illinois until his control of the state campaign was assured.[43] Realizing the necessity of the McCormick financial backing, Fuller finally withdrew, declaring that if his presence on the committee interfered with McCormick's liberality, "it is little to sacrifice me and let him shell vigorously." When a man of McCormick's wealth, added Fuller, "seeks political notoriety or preferment, he should be willing to pay liberally. . . . Consider my head in the basket as soon as the proper number of ducats can be coined out of the political life stream expected thereupon to leave my veins— 'the blood of the martyrs is the seed of the Church.' " [44] Palmer also resigned, and soon McCormick moved the headquarters from Springfield to Chicago. This, according to the Springfield *Daily Illinois State Journal*, was "to get it out of the control of Springfield Liberals and nearer to the dollars and dimes of McCormick." [45]

In the actual campaign in the Middle West the public response to Greeley was discouraging for the managers. Antitemperance Germans were frigid; so also was the more important mass of farmers. Many farmers considered the Greeley candidacy a farce. They looked upon Greeley as an amateurish urban theorist in agricultural matters.[46] In Wisconsin a Grant worker reported, "Things never looked better. . . . The only Greeley Republicans to be found are in the cities and villages." [47] And on election day the middlewestern citizens, as in most corners of the North and several

[43] Hutchinson, *McCormick,* II, 317–24.
[44] Melville Fuller to ———— (unknown, but probably J. M. Palmer), as cited *ibid.,* 321 n.
[45] Springfield *Daily Illinois State Journal,* September 9, 1872, as cited *ibid.,* II, 324 n.
[46] Hesseltine, *Grant,* 287; Charles E. Payne, *Josiah Bushnell Grinnell* (Iowa City, 1938), 271.
[47] E. L. Browne to Keyes, August 19, 1872, in Keyes MSS.

in the South, turned in a majority vote for Grant. The President, winning in practically the same northern counties as had Lincoln in 1860, was re-elected with 56 per cent of the popular vote and a score of 286 to 62 in the electoral college.[48]

With this fiasco the Democracy reached its nadir. The public was disgusted. Cyrus Woodman, even though dreading Grant as president for another four years, declared that "Democrats are away up Salt River," and that is "just what they deserve." He believed that "New hands must be in at its resurrection, and make a solid platform of principles."[49] Nobody seemed inclined to extend sympathy to the Democrats. Bourbon George B. Smith could elicit no kind word for his party, even from his old friend Republican Matt Carpenter. When Democrat Smith confessed to being "now fully satisfied that Greeley was not a strong candidate," the prominent Wisconsin Republican sent a curt reply: "Democrats no longer have any foresight; it is gratifying to see that *one* of them is recovering his *hind* sight."[50]

There was some compensation for the Democracy in the few election victories—like Thomas A. Hendricks' successful bid for the Indiana governorship—and, more important, in the furtherance of the New Departure spirit. A large number of Democrats and Republicans had demonstrated willingness to bury enough of their Civil War bitterness to work together in a common endeavor. Proof was thus at hand that to a Democracy which would offer something worthy, many Republican voters would lend an ear. Alas and alack, the idea-killing, vote-killing Bourbons were braced to hold the party from moving the next step forward, from the New Departure to a New Progressivism.

[48] Binkley, *Political Parties*, 300.
[49] Woodman to Farley, November 10, 1872, in Woodman MSS.
[50] George B. Smith to Matt Carpenter, November 7, 1872; and Carpenter to George B. Smith, November, 1872, in Smith MSS.

Chapter Five

Cowcatcher Campaigning
1873-1874

He who has money has in his pocket those who have none.

—LEO N. TOLSTOI

DURING 1873 and 1874 the Bourbon guardians of the middle-western Democracy had an altogether disconcerting experience with the masses. A large number of voters, especially farmers, were kicking over the old party fences and building their own. They were placing emphasis on men and measures instead of, as customarily, on blind fealty to party. The economic plight of the farmers was transcendentally acute; and because there was not a flicker of evidence that either the Democratic or the Republican leadership would act in their behalf, the farmers determined to act for themselves. Many nonfarmers were likewise willing to turn their backs on both the old parties, as they had done in the Liberal Republican spasm of 1872. Murat Halstead, prominent editor of the Cincinnati *Commercial*, repeatedly encouraged the trend. "We are weary of old parties," he declared, "and we think the country weary of them." [1] The result was an emergence of effective third parties in most states of the Middle West.

Inherently the upheaval was a peoples' regional protest against the politico-business partnership, which was keeping the little man from having a voice and opportunity in the existing order. Regional in scope and spirit, the move-

[1] Hubbart, *Older Middle West,* 254.

ment nevertheless varied in its specific goals. In Ohio and Indiana it aimed primarily at achieving national greenback legislation. Elsewhere in the area the insurgents sought state legislation to curb railroad and warehouse monopolies.

All during the post-Civil War years the greenback question had plagued the Bourbon Democrats. Ohio Greenbackers were especially bothersome to the Bourbons. Ever since Wash McLean and Gentleman George Pendleton had educated them on the money question, many unhappy Ohio voters had concentrated on currency reform as their chief economic need. They had been successful in utilizing the Ohio Democracy as their political outlet, but by 1873 the Democratic leadership was turning its back on Greenbackism. Senator Allen Thurman, the leading Ohio Democrat, was responsible for this shift of party policy to the Bourbon hard-money position. Thurman had been bitten by the presidential bug! He reasoned that espousal of soft money would incur the wrath of eastern Bourbons and hence kill his chances to obtain the nomination.

Many Ohio Democrats were in no mood to remain in a party which bent its policies to Thurman's wishes. Times were hard in 1873; this was no time for Greenbackers to forsake their favorite panacea. Thereupon a group of insurgents in a traditionally Democratic county organized a People's party. Its popularity spread rapidly. The new party's state convention in July listened with approval when Democratic General Thomas Ewing declared that the Democratic party had "outlived its usefullness." Finally Senator Thurman went into action, trembling lest Democratic voters escape his corral. Concessions were in order, so he persuaded his uncle, old Democratic war-horse William Allen, to run for the governorship on the People's party platform, whereupon the new party united forces with the Democracy.

It soon became apparent that the People's party had been

a little hasty in making common cause with the Thurman cabal, for candidate William Allen "forgot" to mention the money question in his campaign.[2] The leonine-voiced and craggy-headed Thurman thought it discreet to say a few words of encouragement to the Greenbackers. Although endorsing an early return to specie-paying currency, Thurman made it clear that the move should not be made "before it can be reasonably effected." [3] He left the voters to guess what he considered a reasonable time for resumption of specie payments. Because the Republicans offered no such room for speculation, the People's party was victorious in the October election. During the Senate discussion of the currency question in 1874 Thurman made some mildly anti-inflationist remarks. Ohio voters responded with acrimonious protests. The Democratic Cincinnati *Enquirer* vehemently turned upon him and asked its readers to remember that Thurman had been elected as a currency expansionist.[4]

Elsewhere in the Middle West the greenback issue failed to receive the prominence accorded it in Ohio. There were a few signs of interest. In Indiana many voters were discouraged over Democratic leader Joseph E. MacDonald's failure to espouse Greenbackism; there was a small flurry of revolt among the rank and file. In the autumn of 1873 a few local meetings were held, at which old party ties were severed. There was enough of a Greenback tinge within the Indiana Democracy, however, to prevent a widespread revolt. Thomas A. Hendricks was known to be sympathetic with soft-money ideas, and "Tall Sycamore of the Wabash" Daniel Voorhees was outspokenly in favor of Greenbackism. Some Indiana Republicans, notably Oliver P. Morton,

[2] Reginald C. McGrane, "Ohio and the Greenback Movement," *Mississippi Valley Historical Review*, XI (December, 1924), 527–28; O. O. Stealey, *Twenty Years in the Press Gallery* (New York, 1906), 441–43.

[3] Cincinnati *Enquirer*, October 9, 1873.

[4] *Congressional Record*, 43 Cong., 1 Sess., 2593–98; McGrane, "Ohio and the Greenback Movement," *loc. cit.*, 528–29.

also leaned in the soft-money direction. In the following spring, however, a state convention of Independents assembled. The delegates wrote a Greenback platform and nominated candidates. The Indiana Democracy met the challenge of the new Independent party by evincing interest in Greenbackism and inducing two Independent nominees to forsake the party and accept places on the Democratic ticket. Another Independent convention filled the vacancies, but in the election the rising tide of Greenbackism was communicated chiefly through the Democracy. Though the Independents secured minor victories, the general result was a sweeping Democratic triumph.[5] Voters in the other middle-western states were slower to show spirited interest in the soft-money issue—1873 platforms of the Democratic and new parties indicated a preference for a return to specie payments.

The next year, however, the Greenback feeling quickened, though only in Illinois was there any marked action. There the Independent Reform party, outvoting the protests of a vigorous and sizable minority, inscribed Greenbackism in its platform. Illinois Democrats straddled the issue, happily realizing that the election result turned on the more prominent antimonopoly issue.[6] Thus it was only in Ohio and Indiana, and to a slight degree in Illinois, that the movement showed tangible signs of mustering a large following.

Simultaneously with the greenback question the Granger antimonopoly crusade advanced. The scene of this upsurge was the commercialized agricultural area at the core of the Middle West—an area dependent upon off-the-farm mar-

[5] Solon J. Buck, *The Granger Movement* (Cambridge, 1913), 93–94; Hubbart, *Older Middle West*, 256.

[6] Chicago *Tribune*, July 30, August 12, 1874; Bogart and Thompson, *Industrial State*, 102–105; *Appletons' Annual Cyclopaedia*, XIV (1874), 404.

FOUR BOURBONS

Above, left: WILLIAM F. VILAS (courtesy of the State Historical Society of Wisconsin); *right:* CYRUS H. McCORMICK (courtesy of Chicago Historical Society).

Below, left: JAMES J. HILL (courtesy of Minnesota Historical Society); *right:* J. STERLING MORTON (courtesy of Nebraska State Historical Society).

kets. Farming in this region was wholly dependent upon railroads, warehouses, and factory-made machinery and hence was very vulnerable to monopolistic control of these instruments of production and marketing. True, all the middle-western states included some surplus-producing agriculture; but it was most extensive and most widely vulnerable to monopoly in Iowa, Wisconsin, Minnesota, and Illinois. Together these states constituted a distinct area—the Granger Northwest.

In comparison with neighboring Ohio, Indiana, and Michigan, the Granger Northwest had not only a larger proportion of commercialized farmers but also more specialization in costly-to-ship grain. It embraced fewer large cities affording nearby markets and was farther from the eastern markets and ports. And, compared with the neighboring states to the west, the Granger area was at a different stage in agricultural development. The Granger Northwest already had railroads into most of the farming areas. Although the rail lines and the Mississippi River were inconveniently far away for some farmers, they were nevertheless close enough for use and thus to cause the farmers to think considerably about freight rates.[7] Such areas as Nebraska and the Dakotas were still concentrating on acquiring transportation—an essential instrument of marketing. Not until more railroads arrived to make commercialized agricultural activity widespread would there emerge in the plains area a mass protest against monopoly. In 1873, Nebraska's J. Sterling Morton was telling the farmers to leave the service of railroads to be governed by the law of supply and demand: "Are they not subject to the laws of competition? If the roads of the West pay exceedingly well, will not more

[7] Horace S. Merrill, "An Early History of the Black River Falls Region" (unpublished master's thesis, University of Wisconsin, 1933), 69–70; Black River Falls (Wis.) *Banner-Journal*, January 2, 1869, and March 16, 1927.

railroads be constructed . . . in a contest for our carrying trade?" [8] Henry Lotham urged Nebraskans to concentrate attention upon securing railroad connections with the rich gold and silver mountain areas to the west.[9]

The antimonopoly protest or Granger movement was more purposeful, more angry, than the Ohio People's party. The incensed farmers saw clearly, and experienced directly, the effects of monopoly. They saw just as clearly a way to remedy their plight. The Granger plan, in its political aspect, sought state regulation of railroads and warehouses— if necessary, to the point of fixing maximum rates. The idea was not new; in the sixties it had actually been tried in Illinois. And in 1871, on the eve of the Granger upsurge, Minnesota had enacted a rate-regulation measure.[10]

In 1873 the farmers, completely fed up with the failure of both Republicans and Democrats to champion their cause, went into politics themselves. They found the Grange organization a convenient medium for their political action. The Grange, founded in 1867 as a farmers' lodge called the "Patrons of Husbandry," now became a dynamic political vehicle. Granger orators inflamed public opinion; Granger journals poured out antimonopoly vitriol; Granger leaders organized state political parties. Antimonopoly, Reform, and Independent parties sprang into being. On Independence Day, 1873, Granger conventions throughout the area of protest endorsed a "Farmers' Declaration of Independence." This document set forth the farmers' grievances and forth-

[8] J. Sterling Morton, *A Speech Delivered at Nebraska State Fair at Lincoln,* September 2, 1873 (Nebraska State Board of Agriculture publication, in Library of the State Historical Society of Wisconsin), no page numbers.

[9] Henry Lotham, *Address at State Fair of Nebraska at Lincoln, September, 1872* (Nebraska State Board of Agriculture publication, in Library of the State Historical Society of Wisconsin), no page numbers.

[10] Fred A. Shannon, *The Farmer's Last Frontier, Agriculture, 1860–1879* (*Economic History of the United States,* Vol. V [New York, 1945]), 310–11.

rightly announced their determination to obtain relief.[11]

In the Granger political movement much effort was expended in educating the public on the low state of the old parties and the evils of unquestioned loyalty to party. Concerning politicians' utterances, the Chicago *Industrial Age* declared: "*Words* are cheap, and professions often hollow. It is *Acts* that we need. . . ." This newly established farm organ lambasted the "sleek and well-fed partisan" editors, office-seekers, and corporate officials in positions of local or state influence. None of these likes "to have his . . . personal comfort interfered with by a lot of rusty farmers. . . . It is because of this blind spirit of party fealty, more than . . . any other one cause, that the monopolists have the country by the throat." [12]

The traditional parties received a blistering going-over. The widely circulated Chicago *Prairie Farmer* was much pleased when farmers' conventions condemned both parties as being "tools of grabbers and monopolists." [13] Special attention was given to the Democracy, to forestall voters from registering their disgust with the party of the "ins" simply by switching to the party of the "outs." The *Industrial Age* attacked the Democrats for having voted with Republicans for monopolist-favoring legislation: "Almost without exception . . . the Democratic members voted for and urged the adoption of the most injurious monopoly measures." More than that, proclaimed this journal, "in some of the Western States . . . the Democratic party is, par excellence, the monopoly party of those States. . . . There is no blinking it, both of the old parties are owned, controlled and run by the moneyed corporations." [14] In Minnesota an Antimonopoly editor, a friend of Ignatius Donnelly, ob-

---

[11] Buck, *Granger Movement*, 86–87.
[12] Chicago *Industrial Age*, August 20, 1873.
[13] Chicago *Prairie Farmer*, June 21, September 13, 1873.
[14] Chicago *Industrial Age*, August 20, 1873.

served that it was a patent fact that "certain Democrats who boasted of their origin and principles voted in the interests of the railroads." [15]

The Bourbon Democrats were at long last caught in a position where it would be expedient to perform less as Bourbon dictators and more as Democratic politicians. Now they confronted the "people," and the people were in no mood for condescension or blandishment. Unless the Bourbon managers acted quickly, the new movement might permanently replace the already wobbly Democracy. Unless they did something to blunt the edge of the Granger scythe, Antimonopoly legislation might destroy the source of ill-gained Bourbon wealth. To meet this double threat against them as Bourbons and as Democrats, they decided to fake friendship for the Granger cause and to unite with the Grangers to defeat the Republicans. Then they could use whatever means they had at their command to sabotage the Antimonopoly program.

Like-minded Bourbons held strong positions in the Democratic organizations of all the Granger states, but the application of like-mindedness varied in intensity and effectiveness. In Iowa, where the Democracy was especially weak, the Bourbon effort was correspondingly feeble. In the Iowa election of 1873 the Democracy quickly bid for Granger friendship by giving the movement its blessing and unreserved support, hoping the result would be a Republican defeat in 1873 and a Democratic victory in the next election. As Bourbons the Democrats had nothing to lose, for railroad regulation was certain to come in any case. Republican Governor Cyrus C. Carpenter was a known enemy of the railroads, and many Republican legislators were now prepared to vote for regulation. So from the standpoint of Bourbon pocketbooks it made no difference which party won.

[15] M'Carthy to Ignatius Donnelly, March 24, 1874, in Donnelly MSS.

In June the Bourbons helped the Grangers organize for political action; in August John P. Irish, chairman of the Democratic state committee and editor of the Iowa City *State Press*, delivered a friendly address before the Anti-monopolist state convention. He said that Democratic leaders would gladly co-operate in the new party, and he even declared the Democracy dead. The Democratic state committee resolved not to hold a Democratic convention and issued an address urging Democrats to support the Anti-monopoly ticket. But because from no source were forthcoming enough funds to conduct an adequate campaign, and because some Grange members remained within the Republican party, the Democratic strategy did not result in a general Republican rout. Republican Governor Carpenter, a member of the Grange, was re-elected; the Antimonopoly party obtained enough seats in the legislature to wield considerable influence. The following March Governor Carpenter signed a carefully drawn act to regulate railroad rates, but Iowa continued to be the Gibraltar of Republicanism.[16]

In Wisconsin the Bourbons fell heir to a choice political opportunity.[17] The Republicans' liquor-regulation Graham act, passed in 1872, had greatly incensed the sizable German population. The Germans were in a mood to vote for the traditionally antinativist Democracy in the 1873 election. The Grangers, aware of the Democratic hold on the large German bloc, were willing to unite forces with the Democracy. The Bourbon Democrats were even more anxious to join forces with the Grangers, for they saw a chance to advance their Democracy and protect their

[16] Chicago *Tribune*, September 2, 1873; Buck, *Granger Movement*, 90–91; Haynes, *Third Party Movements*, 70; Hubbart, *Older Middle West*, 254–55; W. A. Anderson, "The Granger Movement in the Middle West with Special Reference to Iowa," *Iowa Journal of History and Politics*, XXII (January, 1924), 42.

[17] Deutsch, "Political Forces," 100–16, contains excellent material on the Granger movement in Wisconsin, which this author has used extensively as a guide to source material.

monopolistic interests. Paradoxically, they envisaged a
Granger victory as a railroad-monopolist victory. Republican Governor Cadwallader C. Washburn was seeking re-
election, and wealthy manufacturer Washburn was incensed over the high railroad rates. This influential and
politically experienced governor seemed to the Bourbons a
much greater danger to the railroads than any conceivable
Granger amateur candidate.

The Wisconsin Bourbons were ably led in their battle to
unseat the Republican officeholders. Center of the Bourbon
organization was the Milwaukee wing of the party, and the
kingpin was Alexander Mitchell. He was a banker–railroad
magnate and a member of Congress. His chief agent was
George H. Paul, editor of the *Daily Milwaukee News*. And
out in the hinterland was cohort Gabe Bouch, who looked
with contempt upon the Granger movement and farmers
in general. To him it seemed that the "reform movement
is based upon small potato men." As for farm voters, "They
take a newspaper, believe in and swear by it, and the bigger the cockbull story, the more likely" they are to believe
it. He further observed, unwittingly making reference to
his own type of political activity, that farmers have a "perfect abhorrence of being controlled, and yet are always controlled"—and "by the biggest rascals and the least talent of
the country. They are the capital stock in trade of the barna-
cles around every court house. To this must be added the
influence of ignorant itinerant ministers." [18]

By fall the Mitchell-Paul-Bouch triumvirate had fashioned
a corresponding organization of the disaffected. This was
a Democratic–Liberal Republican–Granger combination,
grouped under the party name of Liberal Reform. A state
convention was held, an antimonopoly platform written by

---

[18] Gabriel (Gabe) Bouch to George H. Paul, September 13, 1873; and
id. to *id.*, August 22, 1873, in George H. Paul MSS., Library of the State
Historical Society of Wisconsin.

editor Paul was adopted, and nominations for the state offices were divided among the different groups. The gubernatorial nomination went to Granger William R. Taylor.[19] As president of the State Agricultural Society, he was a logical Granger candidate; being a rank amateur in political manuevering, he was acceptable to the scheming Bourbons. As a campaigner, farmer Taylor would have an advantage over manufacturer Washburn; as a governor, he would be more subject to Bourbon-monopolist control than the shrewder Washburn.

The Liberal Reform offering was indeed a hard one to beat, and the Republican leaders realized it. Some Republicans remained optimistic,[20] but not the state Republican chairman, "Boss" E. W. Keyes. He circulated among his state workers a warning that they were faced with a tough battle, correctly pointing out that there was "no disguising the fact that our opponents have worked up . . . a plausible programme and ticket. They profess to represent the people, to be opposed to the monopolies, and to be in favor of reform generally; while the facts are, that the old Bourbon Democrats are the main spirit of the effort—that their convention was run and controlled in the interests of railroads and that the candidates, . . . notwithstanding the pledges in their platform are wholly under the influence of these corporations." [21]

On election day, able and admirable Governor Washburn wrote to his friend Cyrus Woodman that the "combined powers of darkness, Whiskey, Beer, Railroads, and a sprin-

[19] Paul to Dr. O. W. Wight, September 21, 1873, *ibid.;* Milwaukee *Sentinel*, September 3, 1873; Madison (Wis.) *Democrat*, September 3, 1873; Solon J. Buck, *The Agrarian Crusade* (*Chronicles of America*, Vol. VL [New Haven, 1921]), 38.

[20] Charles Seymour to Keyes, August 29, 1873; George W. Allen to *id.*, October 14, 1873; A. C. Dodge to *id.*, October 17, 1873; Frank Leland to *id.*, October 30, 1873; and H. S. Socket to *id.*, October 31, 1873, in Keyes MSS.

[21] Keyes to political workers, October 7, 1873, *ibid.*

kling of Grangers, have been on my trail and are confident of my defeat." [22]

Election day did bring victory to the Liberal Reform party—the governorship for Taylor, control of the Assembly so that Gabe Bouch could become speaker, and but one member short of control of the Senate. The Bourbons were so pleased with themselves that they could not resist hinting how it was done. Alexander Mitchell said that the outcome was no surprise to the "few who knew the machinery at work and understood the quiet under-current of public feeling." Bourbon George Smith crowed to a prominent Republican friend over having beaten "you fellows awfully." "*We* did it," he said; "but who is *We?* . . . Why the Democrats, Grangers, Reformers, Liberal Republicans, aided a little by other influences . . . not necessary now to mention." [23] Those looking at election statistics for the cause could conclude that the Liberal Reform strategy had had the effect of neutralizing the farm vote into indifference. Farmers could see no real difference between the prospects under antimonopoly Washburn and those under supposedly antimonopoly Taylor. Many Grange voters had thus remained at home on election day and left the antiprohibition element to vote the "party of puritanism" out of office.[24]

When the Liberal Reform victors took office, the Bourbon Democrats were on hand to see that the antimonopolists did not get out of hand. Gabe Bouch did become speaker of the House, and George Paul became the close adviser of Governor Taylor. Editor Paul's first assignment was writing the Governor's inaugural address. Taylor humbly told his scribe that he felt "impelled to suggest" that he include

[22] C. C. Washburn to Woodman, November 4, 1873, in Woodman MSS.
[23] Alexander Mitchell to Ignatius Donnelly, November 8, 1873, in Donnelly MSS., as cited in Deutsch, "Political Forces," 109.
[24] Milwaukee *Sentinel*, November 7, 1873; Deutsch, "Political Forces," 110.

a recommendation for a board of railroad commissioners. Taylor entertained the notion that "the people seem to demand" such action. He did think it permissible, however, to include a "saving clause," by saying that "in the states where tried it has not been eminently successful." [25] Paul happily conformed, and the administration's antimonopoly program emerged as an extremely mild one. [26]

The Republicans, relying upon their majority of one in the Senate, were determined to embarrass and split the hodgepodge Liberal Reform group. They permitted repeal of the antiliquor Graham act and outreformed the administration on the monopoly question. Much to the chagrin of Alexander Mitchell and his hirelings, the Republicans introduced a drastic railroad-regulatory measure—the Potter bill. Much to the surprise of the Republicans and the railroad interests, public pressure was great enough to overcome the Bourbon whip and ensure final passage of the proposal. [27]

The Republicans now possessed an antimonopoly record, and soon they were able to demonstrate that the Bourbon Democrats added a monopolist tinge to the Liberal Reform party. [28] The Republicans needed but to draw the attention of the voters to the activities of Bourbon George H. Paul, who was using his *Daily Milwaukee News* to urge repeal of the Potter Law. [29] Republican Charles Seymour publicly declared that "the veil that covers the carcass of Bourbon Democracy is too thin to deceive honest and intelligent men." [30] Nor did the antimonopoly farmers forget. In 1878,

[25] W. R. Taylor to Paul, November 26, 1873; and *id.* to *id.*, December 7, 1873, in Paul MSS.
[26] Deutsch, "Political Forces," 115.
[27] Utley to Keyes, November 16, 1873; and J. M. Brockitt to *id.*, November 18, 1873, in Keyes MSS.
[28] J. H. Waggoner to *id.*, June 12, 1874, *ibid.*
[29] Tom Reid to *id.*, November 9, 1874; C. L. Colby to *id.*, November 12, 1874; and S. S. Merrill to *id.*, December 4, 1874, *ibid.*
[30] Madison *Wisconsin State Journal*, October 2, 1874.

J. A. Noonan, farm-paper editor, reported that the Reform party had "fooled and cheated the Grangers so badly I fear for the worst next fall." Indeed, the Bourbon-controlled Wisconsin Democracy had thrown a boomerang that came back with discomforting speed. They lost as Bourbons; they lost as Democrats! [31]

In neighboring Minnesota the Democracy, after considerable bickering, reluctantly moved toward endorsement of the Antimonopoly ticket and platform. Throughout the weeks of negotiating for a Democratic–Liberal Republican–Antimonopoly joint effort the state organizers experienced considerable sullenness in the Democratic camp.[32] A Rochester editor reported that "the little Democratic clique that hangs on to the Court House ring here is fierce against the farmers movement, worse than the Republicans." [33] At one point in the maneuvering it was widely suggested that all the parties and factions endorse for governor the Republicans' reform candidate, C. K. Davis. In a separate convention the Antimonopolists could then concentrate on naming candidates for the other positions who would not be subject to the Republican "ring" which was determined to control Davis.[34] But many Democrats opposed that move, one editor claiming that it was asking a little too much of Democrats to vote for a Republican nominee. "I never have been in so tight a place before," he added.[35] St. Paul Bourbons were not enthusiastic over supporting Davis for governor [36] because he would be out of their control if he attempted railroad regulation. Bourbon W. P. Clough, St. Paul railroad

[31] Noonan to Ignatius Donnelly, April 26, 1875, in Donnelly MSS.

[32] E. J. Hodgson to *id.*, July 18, 1873; and M. F. Barnes to *id.*, May 19, 1874, *ibid.*

[33] H. H. Young to *id.*, August 18, 1873, *ibid.*

[34] Mayo to *id.*, July 17, 1873; *id.* to *id.*, July 21, 1873; and Daniel Pickit to *id.*, August 7, 1873, *ibid.*

[35] J. H. McKenny to *id.*, July 24, 1873, *ibid.*

[36] H. M. Burchard to *id.*, August 8, 1873; and Frank Mead to *id.*, August 14, 1873, *ibid.*

attorney, sought to discredit Davis as an antimonopolist, claiming that there was no real ground for considering him antimonopolist in sentiment. Clough added that "Mr. Davis is nothing but what the *St. Paul ring* has made him." [37]

Finally an Antimonopoly convention nominated an entirely separate ticket, and a Democratic–Liberal Republican combination held a separate convention to record its endorsement. Republican Davis was elected, although his party's usual majority was drastically reduced. Two of the fusion candidates were elected to state offices, and the Republican majority in the legislature was sharply cut. In the Senate the Republicans had but a one-vote margin over the combined opposition faction. For the farmers, the result was speedy passage of a railroad-regulatory act.[38]

The Minnesota Democrats, because of their lack of enthusiasm during the campaign, had not raised their standing with the mass of farm voters. Their subsequent actions in the legislature were even less commendable. Many Democratic legislators were tools of the monopolists, and they were bent upon blocking the ambitious Antimonopolist Ignatius Donnelly. Newly elected to the state senate, Donnelly had the backing of the Antimonopolists and Liberal Republican legislators, and all he needed was the Democratic bloc to ensure him a United States senatorship. But a combination of blind party loyalty and monopolist proclivities kept the Democrats from supporting the uncontrollable Donnelly.[39] A St. Paul Democrat expressed his "Democratic

[37] W. P. Clough to *id.*, July 29, 1873, *ibid.*

[38] St. Paul *Press*, July 17, 1873; St. Paul *Pioneer*, July 17, September 25, 1873; Folwell, *History of Minnesota*, III, 49.

[39] Ignatius Donnelly to H. W. Lambertson, March 25, 1874; Lambertson to Ignatius Donnelly, March 26, 1874; MacDonald to *id.*, March 26, 1874; L. E. Fisher to *id.*, March 30, 1874; *id.* to *id.*, April 2, 1874; Ignatius Donnelly to Fisher, April 1, 1874; Henry Hayes to Ignatius Donnelly, May 15, 1874; MacDonald to *id.*, May 23, 1874; J. H. Wiswell to *id.*, June 2, 1874; and W. R. Colton to *id.*, June 20, 1874, in Donnelly MSS.

disgust and nausea at the idea of being dosed with Anti-
Monopoly germifus to dissolve the Copperhead mucus in
the system. . . ."

The Democrats were clearly out to bury the Antimonopoly party before it got out of hand and absorbed the
Democracy. Donnelly was informed by a Democrat that
"the Democratic party *won't dissolve*, it will fuse. It will
almaganate [*sic*]. It will even yield principles and dilute its
Bourbonism to the weakest, wish-washy slop. But it must
have the old name—however foolish it may be to insist on
a misnomer. . . . Moreover, the *leaders* do not propose to
abdicate and be shelved by new recruits with strange banners and prejudices! We are masters of the situation and you
can win no victories without us." [40] If the Democrats had
good reason to dislike Donnelly, they showed no inclination to offer a better candidate. They simply made clear their
preference for having a Republican as United States senator
rather than Antimonopolist Donnelly. After months of
bickering a Republican was selected. The Democratic Bourbons continued to sit on the party lid.[41]

In Illinois industrialist Cyrus McCormick was the guid-
ing spirit of the Democratic policy in dealing with the
Grangers. As chairman and financial godfather of the state
Democratic central committee he had great influence in the
state. As a manufacturer of farm implements he had an acute
interest in the Granger movement. For a long time McCormick had watched the Illinois antimonopoly movement gain
momentum.[42] During the late sixties laws were passed in Illinois to restrain the elevators and the railroads; in 1870 the
new state constitution included a specific mandate for regulatory legislation. In 1871 this was implemented with a supposedly effective board of railroad and warehouse com-

---

[40] J. W. McClung to *id.*, May 22, 1874; and *id.* to *id.*, May 27, 1874, *ibid.*
[41] O. H. Page to *id.*, February 16, 1875, *ibid.*; Hall, *Political Contests*,
143–52.   [42] Hutchinson, *McCormick*, II, 334.

missioners. But the railroad interests managed to safeguard their monopolistic position in the face of each successive attack. Their most recent victory had been to obtain from the state supreme court a decision declaring the 1871 law unconstitutional.

That was too much for the Grangers. They were determined to effect a political house cleaning of the state government. Immediately after the Illinois supreme court announced its decision, an incensed Antimonopoly convention registered a vehement protest. In a few weeks another impressive gathering frightened the legislature into passing an improved regulatory measure. The Grangers quickly followed up their initial victories by going directly into politics. In the spring elections they easily defeated Chief Justice Charles Brush Lawrence, the judge most instrumental in killing the 1871 law. Onward the movement swept, reaching a very spirited pitch with the July 4 meetings which proclaimed the farmers' "Declaration of Independence." There was no Illinois election for state offices in the fall of 1873, but the Antimonopolists entered candidates in over half the county contests and won in most of them.[43]

During 1873 it was plain to Cyrus McCormick and everyone else that the Grangers were in no mood nor need for outside leadership. "If," declared the Chicago *Prairie Farmer*, "those that see the necessity of this great movement being made political in order to accomplish the overthrow of the monopolies . . . should make the mistake of attempting to attach it to the Democratic party, they will soon discover that they cannot accomplish their undertaking." This Granger organ thought that both parties were tools of the monopolists. Anyhow, declared the *Prairie Farmer*, it would be bad politics to place the movement under the Democratic banner, for Republican members of

[43] Buck, *Agrarian Crusade*, 32–34; Buck, *Granger Movement*, 85–89; Bogart and Thompson, *Industrial State*, 97.

the antimonopoly "Clubs and Granges will not, as a general thing, support the Democratic party, and the Republican party will thus be enabled to continue to rule the country in the interest of the great monopolies." [44]

Most Democratic politicos, state and local leaders alike, were worried—but not mogul McCormick. Like so many manufacturers, he was happy to witness the railroad monopolists' getting their beards singed. He disliked high railroad rates, for reasons comparable to those for his distaste of high tariffs on foreign goods. He wanted a free flow of goods wherever it would promote his own business and his dream of prosperity for the Middle West and his native South. Low freight rates would mean for him cheaper steel for his farm machinery, cheaper delivery costs to farm purchasers of his products, more farm purchasing power, and less cost in shipping his machines to the ports for entering the foreign market.

In its broader aspect McCormick's antirailroad attitude involved his dreams for a dynamic economic regionalism in the Middle West and the South. It was a regional spirit aimed at circumventing the economic lordship of the easterners. He would free the South and the Middle West from their colonial subservience to the East. He would link those regions and Europe into an economic chain that would, in turn, free them from vassalage to eastern-controlled railroads, capital, markets, and raw materials.

This practical dreamer believed that Europe offered a larger market for middle-western surpluses than did the East and that New Orleans and Mobile were better ports for middle-western purposes than were New York and Philadelphia. If enough capital was forthcoming, the Mississippi River could be developed into a freight route. In 1867, while visiting abroad, McCormick outlined his plan to many English businessmen and became convinced that they were

[44] Chicago *Prairie Farmer,* June 21, September 13, 1873.

willing to invest capital in the project to build a transportation system linking the Middle West, the Gulf States, and Europe.[45]

As a middle-western economic regionalist, McCormick was thus in accord with the Granger attack on the East-West partnership of railroad extortionists. He did not, however, relish the nonpolitical aspects of the movement—the Granger-owned farm-machinery factories. But he saw no harm in the Grangers' antimonopolist fight against the railroads. In fact, he could use his political power to keep the drive aimed at the railroads and away from his own McCormick Reaper Company. Perhaps, as the *Prairie Farmer* suggested in September, 1873, McCormick's company backed the bitterly antirailroad *Industrial Age*.[46] In any case, that farm journal voiced a middle-western regionalism akin to McCormick's. It expressed belief that there was no good reason why "Iowa, Wisconsin, and Illinois should not make all the clothes they need, as well as their boots and shoes. . . . The Northwest abounds in iron and coal, and has the skilled labor to make almost any implement or article made from iron. Why not do it and save the heavy freights from the East?" [47]

When it came time to prepare for the 1874 elections, McCormick decided that it was also time to push his Democratic organization into co-operative action with the Antimonopolists. Bourbon state leaders were opposed. They wanted to ignore the Antimonopolists and even divorce the Democracy from the Liberal Republicans. They wanted a "Democracy pure and simple." McCormick wanted it otherwise —and McCormick was used to having his way. Addressing his Democratic state central committee in July, McCormick announced his willingness to support railroad regulation,

[45] Hutchinson, *McCormick*, II, 590–98.
[46] Buck, *Granger Movement*, 323.
[47] Chicago *Industrial Age*, December 6, 1873.

lower tariffs, and a more liberal currency policy. He felt that the "agricultural community has unquestioned and grievous wrongs to complain of, and the Democracy should stand pledged to their redress, without however violating a single vested right or resorting to the extreme legislation which has proved so embarrassing to other States." On currency, his attitude was consistent with his past views on the subject, reflecting distaste for eastern bondholders and recognition that the money stringency hindered the sale of his own farm implements. He would have "no immediate resumption of specie payments, and no sudden, reckless inflation." [48]

In August the state Democratic convention bowed to McCormick's program on monopoly and the tariff, but on the money question it leaned further than McCormick in the direction of hard money. The platform called for a resumption of specie payments as soon as practicable. The Antimonopolists, meeting as a separate Independent Reform party, had already adopted a similar program; but they advocated inflation by the use of greenbacks. In selecting candidates the Democrats endorsed the Independents' nominee for state superintendent of schools but made a separate choice for state treasurer. The election outcome was victory for the fusion candidate for superintendent and victory for the Republican candidate for treasurer. In the congressional elections Democrats and Independents captured several seats from the Republicans. The Republicans lost their majority in the state legislature to the Independents.[49]

These two years of political insurgency had placed a heavy strain on the Bourbon Democracy of the Middle West. The Bourbons had seen their control of the party, and the very party itself, shaken and exposed. But they were still on the

[48] Chicago *Tribune*, July 30, 1874; Hutchinson, *McCormick*, II, 335–36.
[49] Chicago *Tribune*, July 30, August 12, 1874; Bogart and Thompson, *Industrial State*, 102–105; *Appletons' Annual Cyclopaedia*, XIV (1874), 404.

party lid, trying to smother every regional effort of the people. Only in Illinois, where regional-minded Cyrus Mc-Cormick held the reins, did the Democracy show signs of harmonizing with voter interests. McCormick's regional economic philosophy and his limited action pointed the way to a more prosperous Middle West; but his own high-price practices in the farm-implement business reduced his appeal to the masses. The area needed leaders whose profession was regional politics. But no such leaders had emerged during these two years of opportunity. In Ohio Senator Thurman and his subservient state machine had turned to eastern kowtowing. Some Indiana Democratic leaders were cautiously straddling the fence. The Iowa Democracy was spiritless. In Wisconsin the party was revealed as a cheap monopolistic tool for hoodwinking the voters. The Minnesota Democracy consisted of Bourbon-dominated, cantankerous diehards. Almost everywhere the cold grasp of selfish Bourbonism controlled the Democratic pulse.

Chapter Six

The Spirited Evasion of 1876

*All political questions, all matters of right, are
at bottom only questions of might.*
—August Bebel

THE PRESIDENTIAL election of 1876 approached;
Grantism and the panic of 1873 made the voters impatient
with the Republicans; the Democrats judged the time aus-
picious to capture the presidency. Could the real voice of
the Middle West be heard in this Democratic bid? Not with
the Bourbons in the Democratic driver's seat. In preceding
national elections the Bourbons had found it convenient to
forget the people of the Middle West, heeding instead the
voices in the caves of Wall Street. They had made no plausible gesture toward the middle-western masses living in
colonial subservience to the East. The Bourbons were themselves making money out of the eastern brand of capitalism
—a brand which contained nothing but crumbs for the mass
of such little men as the middle-western farmers. And the
Middle West was predominantly a region of farmers. Nor
was the rising number of urban wage earners given a hearing
in Democratic policy. Laborers were organizing and asking
the political leaders to secure for them better working conditions and shorter hours of labor, farmers were crying for
help, but the Bourbon Democracy paid no heed.

Within the Democracy the cult of Bourbonism had a
self-perpetuating quality. When challenged from without,
the Bourbons had joined forces with the opposition to sabotage the movement. Bourbon self-perpetuation was further
ensured by absorption of discontented leaders. Riding the

wave of expanding big business, Bourbonism possessed an attractiveness for successful politicians. As professional politicians proved their ability, the doors of business opportunity swung open to them. Gentleman George Pendleton found his position as railroad president a convenient substitute for anti-Bourbon politics.[1] Eastern Bourbons also were a great help in perpetuating the middle-western branch of the clan. When a professional politician such as Ohio's Allen Thurman became famous enough to entertain hope for the presidency, he suddenly realized the impossibility of obtaining the nomination without the combined support of eastern and middle-western Bourbons. As for actual election to the presidency, Thurman and others doubtless subscribed to the theory enunciated by Bourbon Horatio Seymour at the time of his 1868 campaign for that office. Seymour operated on the "theory . . . that this election is in the hands of business men. It will go as their judgement shall dictate." [2]

The Bourbon sect also ensured its permanence by absorbing young men of promise. Even neophytes with humanitarian, progressive inclinations gradually came under the spell. There was, for example, Wisconsin's Colonel William F. Vilas, son of a well-to-do and prominent Democrat. One August evening in 1873 this young Civil War veteran and lawyer sat writing in his diary. He had just returned to his hotel room after paying a nocturnal visit to a Lake Superior ore dock. Musingly he recorded that "all around are the ore trains . . . discharging their rich contents into the vessels lying by. They seem to work all night. These rich men are hard taskmasters and the men who get 20 shillings for 12 hours are toiling, toiling night and day to fill their pockets. So it goes. . . ." Two days later he visited an Indian settlement and recorded in his diary how the red men "suffer greatly from hunger and cold and are subjected to great

[1] McGrane, "Pendleton," *loc. cit.*, 420.
[2] Hutchinson, *McCormick*, II, 312.

privations while the Agents uniformly rob them." [3] Upon returning to his home community, where he was known as a "people's lawyer" and a friend of the exploited, Vilas launched into active work in behalf of the Liberal Reform movement. Early in 1874 Governor Taylor offered this thirty-three-year-old lawyer the honored position of chief justice of the state supreme court. But young Vilas refused the post. He had bigger opportunities coming, his father told him.[4] In the dollar sense his father was correct, for young Vilas was soon a prosperous and influential railroad attorney, lumber magnate, and Bourbon Democrat. For Democratic leaders, young and old alike, there seemed no escaping the lure of Bourbonism.

Bourbonism also operated effectively against social-minded reformers who managed to attain influence. Thomas A. Hendricks was the most prominent of that group still in active politics. But Hendricks was very much alone in the party leadership and hence easily overlooked by the Bourbons when it came to selecting a presidential candidate. The middle-western Bourbons winked at each other and then pompously declared how sad it was that eastern Bourbons would not accept this soft-money Indianian. Farther down in the party the Bourbons employed various devices to keep reformers like Ignatius Donnelly from crashing into the party's inner circle. They brushed Donnelly aside as a rank outsider, unfit to be included in the Democratic sect or even to receive Democratic support to beat the Republicans.

To be an independent Democratic leader in the face of the Bourbons was difficult and discouraging. Few had the tenac-

[3] "Journal of Lake Superior Trip, August 13 to 27, 1873," in William F. Vilas MSS., Library of the State Historical Society of Wisconsin.

[4] Burr W. Jones, "Colonel Vilas and the Law School," *Memorial Services of William Freeman Vilas, October 20, 1908* (Madison, 1908), 17–18; Madison *Wisconsin State Journal*, November 10, 1873; Madison *Democrat*, November 10, 1873; Milwaukee *Sentinel*, January 10, 1874; Clara L. Hayes, "William Penn Lyon," *Wisconsin Magazine of History*, IX (March, 1926), 260.

ity to play the part, but now and then some individualist would emerge and remain. Such a man was William R. Morrison of Illinois. After years of effort to regain the political popularity which he had lost during the Civil War, Morrison finally fought his way back. And he did it by winning the deep respect of the voters. In the 1872 campaign the droll and sincere Morrison started emphasizing to Illinois citizens the evils of the high protective tariff. The panic of 1873 helped him, for after reminding voters that the Republicans had claimed that postwar prosperity was attributable to the Republican high tariff, he drove home the logical point that the same party and the same tariff policy were, therefore, responsible for the current depression. His reward in 1872 and again in 1874 was election to a seat in Congress which was normally occupied by a Republican.[5]

Morrison had chosen the hard way. Instead of relying on an emotional appeal or upon winning simply through Republican default, he had patiently educated his constituents on a fundamental economic problem. Throughout the Middle West there were voters ready to listen to speeches on basic economic issues. The Republicans knew this, and they knew that they were vulnerable. Wealthy Cyrus Woodman advised his Republican friend E. B. Washburne of Illinois that if he expected to catch farmers' votes he had better steer clear of advocating a high-protective-tariff policy. "The 'poor farmer' would like to have the tariff reduced," said Woodman, "so that he can get his iron and his coat and even a silk dress for his wife at a price he can afford to pay." [6] But only Morrison stepped forward to make real capital of that fact.

The Bourbons not only possessed firm control of the

[5] Franklin D. Scott, "The Political Career of William R. Morrison," *Transactions of the Illinois State Historical Society*, 1926 (Springfield, 1926), 137–42; Franklin D. Scott, "William Ralls Morrison," in Johnson and Malone (eds.), *Dictionary of American Biography*, XIII, 232.

[6] Woodman to E. B. Washburne, July 16, 1875, in Woodman MSS.

Democracy but also had good prospects of defeating the Republicans in the 1876 election. The widespread disgust with Grantism and the hardships following the panic of 1873 had faded the Republican halo. Thus, with self-assurance the Bourbons dared to ignore such fundamental economic issues as the tariff. They turned instead to capitalizing on other Republican weaknesses. Bourbons saw many Republican voters put on rose-colored glasses to look at the Democracy —voters who saw nothing basically different from what they were accustomed to seeing in the Republican party, except that the Democratic banner and faces were not directly connected with Grantism and the panic of 1873. These voters, with minds free from the constantly haunting specter of personal economic hardship, tended to concentrate their wrath on the moral degradation of the Republican stewardship. They demanded better administration of the existing economic policies. Upon this group the Bourbons pinned their main hope.

It would not be as easy to capture the support of the economically more needy voters. These less fortunate citizens fixed worried and embittered stares on governmental policies which sanctioned greedy exploitation of the little man and the fruits of the God-given natural resources that seemed within the reach of all but actually were not. These people were for more than better administration; they were for better policies to be administered. The Bourbons reasoned that by accenting better administration they could divert public attention from Bourbon neglect of better policies. Republican negligence was also driving some voters into the Bourbon lair.

The largest single group of victims of unrestrained big-business exploitation outside the South were the middle-western farmers. They had grown up in an environment of habit and creed which taught that the road to security and prosperity was studded with obstacles which only hard work, and not panaceas, could remove. Most of them had traveled a little way toward security and had no desire to risk untried cure-alls which might destroy their hard-won grubstakes of home-owned farms and equipment. But they were having a hard time hanging on. Farmers had borrowed money to get their starts at interest rates which, at the time of their borrowing, seemingly could be carried—for wheat had sold for as much as $1.25 per bushel, and other farm products had brought a comparable return. Now, however, the farmers were compelled to carry the burden of high interest rates, together with high railroad charges and high machinery costs, at a time when wheat brought about half its former return. They wanted, as a result, to be assured by intelligent leaders that currency reform and tariff reform would help them. Or if there was a better plan for relief, they wanted it put into effect. They were not expecting something for nothing, but they were expecting something that would give them a fair chance to plant and reap and prosper in this land of plenty.[7]

The leaders of the once-honored political parties offered nothing but shopworn platitudes about the blessings wrought by God and the industrial revolution. In desperation the most daring—and usually these were the ones with the least to lose—turned to pinning hopes on, and making demands for, currency reform. In Ohio and Indiana respected Democratic leaders like Pendleton had told the people in 1868 that currency reform would help. As a result, in those states the devotion to Greenbackism permeated more deeply than elsewhere into the rank and file of conservative farmers. Finally, the hard times following the panic of 1873 caused the already smouldering greenback question to flare with liveliness throughout the entire Middle West.

The middle-western Bourbon Democrats, in preparing for the 1876 election, were constantly reminded of the dread

[7] Shannon, *Farmer's Last Frontier*, 291–309.

threat of Greenbackism. It was sweeping in from the hinterland and throwing a shadow over the ostentatious mahogany furniture of Bourbon business offices. In 1873 and 1874 it had wrung concessions from the Democracy in Ohio and Indiana and had permeated the Independent Reform party of Illinois. It had even received a half-nod of approval from pious Cyrus McCormick.[8] Some Republican leaders, no less, were showing an inclination to endorse soft money. Indiana's Republican Senator Oliver P. Morton, remembered sorrowfully by the Bourbons as an effective Copperhead-baiter, was flirting with the soft-money idea.[9] And Morton's was a big name with a big following.

The Bourbons continued to sit tight, guarding with determination their bags of gold, which automatically increased in value as deflation sent prices on goods rocketing downward. They hoped to defeat the Republicans without bending to the "currency craze"; but in any case they would not bend, win or lose. Their policy on money followed that which President Grant had set for the Republicans early in 1874. A politically jittery Congress had passed a measure fixing the number of greenbacks that could be issued. The bill closed the door to excessive inflation; but because it authorized some issuance of greenbacks, the hard-money reactionaries were incensed. President Grant, remembering the 1868 soft-money storm as having contained more wind than lightning, calmly vetoed the bill. The Bourbons rejoiced! [10]

Then came the congressional elections of 1874, which brought a tidal-wave victory for the Democracy. Not since 1860, fourteen years before, had the Democrats controlled any branch of the national government. In 1874 they not only overthrew the Republican two-thirds majority in the House but captured control of that body. They elected 169

[8] Hutchinson, *McCormick*, II, 334.
[9] Hubbart, *Older Middle West*, 256.   [10] Hesseltine, *Grant*, 333–35.

representatives to the Republicans' 109.[11] The Bourbon Democrats were gleeful. It appeared that they could win the presidency without committing their party to Greenbackism. They continued to hold the line in favor of hard money, as did the Grant Republicans.

In the 1875 Lame Duck Session of Congress the badly defeated Republicans, having finally decided to follow Grant's hard-money policy, passed the Resumption Act. This provided for the gradual accumulation of a gold reserve which would be large enough to resume specie payments by January 1, 1879. The soft-money element responded with fury; the reactionary Republicans and Bourbon Democrats were elated.[12]

During 1875 and the early part of 1876 the Bourbons experienced some political headaches in the Middle West. The tidal wave of 1874 was receding, and the trouble was chiefly that the Bourbons were standing pat on the money question. Their role in the third-party upsurge of 1873 and 1874 had disgusted many farm voters, and now the Bourbon refusal to endorse soft money caused the Republican voters to see no reason to forsake their traditional party. In the state election held in Minnesota Ignatius Donnelly strove fruitlessly to inject a greenback pledge into the Democratic platform.[13] The Democratic bid thus remained as weak as ever. As one Minnesotan informed Donnelly, "A great many think there was a great blunder at the Democratic convention in their platform. The way it is now there is no issue between the Republican party and Democratic on the financial. If your measure had been adopted on that question," he added, "there would not have been the least doubt in my mind but it would carry the State. But people think as long as there is no issue on the most vital part of the financial question it makes but

[11] Binkley, *Political Parties*, 302.   [12] Josephson, *Politicos*, 195, 260.
[13] Page to Ignatius Donnelly, February 16, 1875; J. E. Doughty to *id.*, June 3, 1875; Young to *id.*, June 28, 1875; and A. Barto to *id.*, August 11, 1875, in Donnelly MSS.; Hall, *Political Contests*, 143–52.

little difference which side wins." He thought that the Democrats "ought to have adopted the Ohio platform." The result was the usual Republican victory.[14]

Neighboring Wisconsin also held a state election, one with the currency issue carefully buried. The politicians in the Bourbon-controlled Liberal Reform party bickered instead over whether the citizens should re-elect Granger Governor William R. Taylor. Many farmers did not like Taylor because he had failed to enforce the antimonopoly Potter law; the Bourbon Democrats did not like him because he had signed the bill in the first place. Finally the Democrats, not wishing to admit openly their previous error of sponsoring Taylor, decided to renominate him. The confused voters delivered the governorship and control of the state legislature to the Republicans and elected to the other state offices the Liberal Reform candidates.[15]

The 1875 Ohio governorship contest was the election most closely watched by the politicians. Both the Democrats and the Republicans aimed at keeping the voters confused on the money question, and observers wondered how the voters would react to the confusion. Former Governor Rutherford B. Hayes was the Republican nominee. He had managed to steer clear of close contact with the Grant regime and was friendly with the hard-money group. Governor William Allen was the Democratic nominee. His party traditionally leaned in the soft-money direction, but Allen and his friends adroitly decided that it would be wise to be very circumspect on that issue. If they played their cards with finesse, Gov-

---

[14] S. G. Cummings to Ignatius Donnelly, July 25, 1875, in Donnelly MSS.

[15] S. A. Pease to Paul, September 3, 1875, in Paul MSS.; Noonan to Ignatius Donnelly, April 13, 1875, in Donnelly MSS.; E. E. Bryant to Lucius Fairchild, August 19, 1875, in Fairchild MSS.; J. T. Carr to Wendall Anderson, February 14, 1876, in Wendall Anderson MSS., Library of the State Historical Society of Wisconsin; Keyes to Jeremiah M. Rusk, in Jeremiah M. Rusk MSS., Library of the State Historical Society of Wisconsin; Ralph Gordon Plumb, *Badger Politics, 1836–1930* (Manitowoc, Wis., 1930), 68.

ernor Allen or his nephew, Senator Thurman, might secure the nomination for the presidency. So the Ohio Democratic managers wrote a vague money statement in their platform and endeavored to exhibit all shades of opinion during the campaign.

The Ohio Republicans did likewise, in accordance with their own inclination and the advice of National Chairman John Binny.[16] Early in September, Chairman Binny told the Ohio Republican leaders that it would be "unwise to make the currency a prominent part of the canvass, as it would divide and weaken the Republican ranks." He thought it "better to keep this an open question on which Democrats and Republicans are divided in opinion."[17]

The Ohio voters could easily conclude that Hayes favored hard money, but the issue was played down so much that they tended to make their decision on other factors. In fact, some soft-money men campaigned for Hayes, and some hard-money speakers campaigned for Allen. Only the German voters were given a forthright lecture on money. Carl Schurz paid them a visit and preached on the evils of inflation. He doubtless obtained many votes for Hayes. A local religious question, involving a measure to make religious instruction available to inmates of public institutions, was another factor in determining the outcome. The personalities and reputations of the candidates, both of whom were figures of long-standing prominence with loyal followers, also contributed to the final decision.[18]

Hayes emerged the victor, although by a narrow margin. The Ohio Republicans had shown that the Democratic tidal wave of 1874 was subsiding, even in a state where the Democracy was traditionally strong. The Republican victories in Minnesota and Wisconsin and in the eastern states of Penn-

[16] Hubbart, *Older Middle West*, 255–56.
[17] John Binny to Keyes, September, 1875, in Keyes MSS.
[18] McGrane, "Ohio and the Greenback Movement," *loc. cit.*, 529–30; Hubbart, *Older Middle West*, 255–56.

sylvania and Massachusetts added emphasis to the trend. The Democracy needed to do something more than simply ride the tide of discontent; it needed to offer the people something positive.

Early in 1876, as the time drew near for the Democracy to settle upon a national policy and a national ticket, middle-western pressure for currency reform pressed insistently upon the Bourbons. Even in Wisconsin, where the soft-money program was never as strong as in many parts of the Middle West and where it had been condemned in the 1873 Liberal Reform platform, there was now a different feeling. Many farmers were bitterly opposed to the Resumption Act, and many were demanding greenback inflation. Local politicians sent insistent warnings to the vexed Bourbon policy makers to unstop their ears to the clamor. One local Wisconsin Democratic leader wrote to Bourbon George B. Smith, "You have no idea of the strength of the money Element with the masses. . . . It seems nine-tenths of the farmers and the masses of the people think that this is the vital question and will vote for no one in favor of resumption." [19] Another reported, "While 'soft money' notions have made little or no gains with the newspapers and party leaders in the larger towns and cities, . . . with the common people, farmers especially, there has been a wonderful change going on in the last six months in that direction." He expressed belief that a soft-money policy would carry Wisconsin.[20]

Local party workers in Wisconsin pointedly informed the policy-making Bourbons that they had better not waste time in taking a stand for currency reform. State Democratic Chairman Wendall Anderson received word from a loyal Democrat that "without *some* policy on this question there is not much use in doing very extensive work in the way of

[19] P. Orton to G. B. Smith, June 17, 1876, in Smith MSS.
[20] D. C. Fulton to Anderson, March 18, 1876, in Anderson MSS.

drawing party lines." [21] Another insisted that the Democracy "must have a real issue or something, or else fight the rebellion over again as the staple of the campaign. We cannot agree with the Republican party on the money question, the tariff in the main, and hope to win." [22]

The soft-money element was very impatient. Greenback parties sprang up, and plans were made for a national convention. The national Democratic chairman, General Thomas Ewing of Ohio, attempted to buy time by requesting Greenback party leaders to postpone their convention until the day after the Democrats met and then endorse the Democratic slates. An Illinois Greenback leader, D. H. Pinney, optimistically reported the proposed fusion to Ignatius Donnelly. Pinney believed that a union of Democratic and Greenback forces could carry Illinois and Indiana and very likely Ohio and "other doubtful states." [23]

While Pinney built castles in the air, other Greenback party leaders remained dubious of the Bourbon Democrats' willingness to co-operate. The reformers had been fooled too many times in the past. In May they held a national Greenback or Independent convention at Indianapolis and nominated New York's eccentric Peter Cooper for the presidency. They could not hope to win against the well-organized traditional parties, but they were angry. They were somewhat hasty in their action, for in nominating the sixty-five-year-old Cooper they did the rank and file an injustice. The great mass of reform-hungry voters would certainly refuse to support the eccentric Cooper; however distracted they might be, they would surely be too cautious to vote for such an oddity. The nomination was more outlandish than the 1872 nomination of Greeley and was carried out by a group more visionary than the Liberal Republicans.

[21] T. S. Heller to *id.*, February 24, 1876, *ibid.*
[22] Fulton to *id.*, March 18, 1876, *ibid.*
[23] D. H. Pinney to Ignatius Donnelly, April 14, 1876, in Donnelly MSS.

The voters wanted something "safer" than the Greenback party and Peter Cooper. A soft-money friend of Ignatius Donnelly was "convinced that Peter Cooper would not get as many votes in Minnesota . . . as would elect him school trustee." [24] The discontented "plain people" were thus thrown upon the mercy of wily moguls of the Republican and Democratic parties.

The Bourbon Democrats, by their Fabian tactics, had won the first and most crucial round. The most spirited agitators of the soft-money element had sidetracked themselves into the new Greenback party, and it was a party too weak to force the Democracy into even a compromise stand on the issue. So the Bourbons went blithely ahead with a "safer" issue. Their approach was to augment the usual state-rights froth with a demand for administrative reform to replace the wasteful and corrupt practices of the Grant regime. True, the agrarian middle-westerners had not been excitedly interested in the question because the monopoly and money issues absorbed their attention, but their sense of decency would cause many farmers to vote for administrative reform if that were the theme of the campaign.

The Bourbons not only possessed an issue—they had a candidate. This was New York's multimillionaire governor, Samuel J. Tilden. The cold, austere Tilden had accumulated one of the nation's biggest fortunes and the title, the Great Forecloser. His vast wealth came largely from his astute corporation-law activities, in connection with which he had served such unscrupulous manipulators as Jay Gould, Jim Fisk, and William Tweed. Shortly after the Civil War historian James Parton wrote a *Manual for the Instruction of "Rings," Railroad and Political*, which was designed to expose Tilden's highhanded tactics in financial manipulation. Tilden had demonstrated adeptness at stock-market rigging, and now he turned to acquiring a corner on this book. It

[24] J. Manning to *id.*, July 2, 1876, *ibid.*

proved to be simply a matter of obtaining from a corrupt New York court an order confiscating the entire edition of the book. The only error was that at least one copy escaped the officials and turned up later to plague Tilden.

The Great Forecloser had shown uncanny ability in politics. Although his favorite companions were men of letters and he liked good books and fine wines, Tilden did not overlook political conversations with unsavory "Boss" Tweed of Tammany and the politicos in cloakrooms and caucus meetings. Eventually, however, Tilden and some of his wealthy New York friends decided that friendship with Tweed and Tammany paid poor dividends. The Tweed ring, through outlandishly high city taxes, was picking the pockets of its "respectable" benefactors. So in 1871 Tilden stepped forward to become instrumental in the crusade that soon smashed the Tweed ring. In 1874, after resigning as state Democratic chairman, Tilden rode the Democratic tidal wave and his own reform wave into the governorship. There he continued with his new-found reforming zeal, and within a year the odious state canal ring crumbled before his onslaught. He had become the Democratic patron saint of administrative reform. The Great Forecloser had become the Great Reformer.[25]

Tilden's record as a ring-buster brought him considerable well-earned notoriety, and the broad intellectual and historical framework with which he surrounded his actions added to his stature as a national leader. He called upon the Democracy to revitalize itself and lead the people back to the days when the principles of Jeffersonian democracy were taken seriously. Upon resigning from the state chairmanship, Tilden told his fellow Democrats that "what the country now needs is a revival of Jeffersonian democracy, with the principles of government and rules of administration, and . . . the high standards of official morality which

[25] Binkley, *Political Parties*, 281, 303–304; Josephson, *Politicos*, 150–53.

were established by the political revolution of 1800." Tilden, the administrative reformer and state-rights advocate, compared the situation preceding Jefferson's first administration with the contemporary Reconstruction period. To Tilden, "the demoralization of war—a spirit of gambling adventure, engendered by false systems of public finance; a grasping centralization, absorbing all functions from the local authorities; and assuming to control the industries of individuals by largesses to favored classes from the public Treasury of money wrung from the body of the people by taxation— were then, as now, characteristic of the period."

Turning to the Federalists and their leader, Tilden declared, "The party that swayed the government . . . was dominated . . . by the ideas of its master spirit, Alexander Hamilton. Himself personally pure, he nevertheless believed that our people must be governed, if not by force, at least by appeals to the selfish interests of classes, in all forms of corrupt influence."

Then the gifted Tilden pointed to the solution of this evil: "As a means to the reaction of 1800, Jefferson organized the Democratic Party. He set up anew the broken foundations of governmental power. He stayed the advancing centralization. He restored the rights of the States and of the localities. He repressed the meddling of Government in the concerns of private business. . . . He refused to appoint relatives to office. He declined all presents. He refrained while in the public service from all enterprises to increase his private fortune. . . . The reformatory work of Mr. Jefferson in 1800 must now be repeated." [26]

The Bourbons saw no need to look farther for a presidential candidate. Tilden was a proven vote getter, had a reputation for administrative reform, was unreservedly for hard money, and had money of his own to conduct the cam-

[26] Bowers, *Tragic Era*, 487.

paign. The middle-western Bourbons, now that they had ridden out the greenback storm, were prepared to nominate their New York brother-Bourbon. The party machinery was well in hand. At the end of May the Des Moines *Weekly Iowa State Register* reported on the Iowa state convention in a manner which might well have caused the Bourbons to blush but also to wink at each other with pleasure. The *Register* observed that the "greenback men had control of the Convention, but the wily leaders of the party had control of them." [27] Tilden's corporation connections were also a help in spreading the gospel among delegates scheduled to attend the national convention. Perry Smith, vice-president of the Northwest Railroad, wrote in a friendly manner to delegate George B. Smith of Wisconsin. The New York *Times* and the Milwaukee *Sentinel* printed Republican assertions that the "public spirited" Perry Smith canvassed all the leading Democratic delegates in behalf of Tilden.[28]

Back in February a Wisconsin Tilden supporter had informed state chairman Wendall Anderson that "it will be hard work to secure his nomination," and had expressed doubt that it could be done.[29] Much had transpired in the Democracy since then and when the national convention met on June 27. Although enough middle-western regional-minded politicos slipped into the conclave to give Thomas A. Hendricks 140½ votes on the first ballot, the Bourbon influence netted Samuel J. Tilden 404½ votes. The second ballot gave eleventh-hour reformer Tilden the necessary two-thirds majority for the nomination. Soft-money Hendricks was granted the vice-presidential accolade. The platform was primarily an invocation to the creed of administrative reform and a harkening to the people's desire for

[27] Des Moines *Weekly Iowa State Register*, May 26, 1876, as cited in Haynes, *Third Party Movements*, 154.
[28] P. H. Smith to George B. Smith, June 11, 1876, in Smith MSS.
[29] Carl Schmidt to Anderson, February 2, 1876, in Anderson MSS.

"honest men from another party." Ten planks began with "Reform is necessary . . . ," but none emphasized the liberal demands of middle-western agrarians. The platform asked for repeal of the Resumption Act, but the stated reason was that the measure constituted a hindrance to accomplishing specie payment.[30]

The Bourbons had outsmarted the people, but as usual they were left without much wind in their sails. The Republicans nominated Ohio's Governor Rutherford B. Hayes, who had a mild record of civil-service reform and was in no way tainted with Grantism. That left the campaign with no vital issue. The only question awaiting the voters' decision was which candidate and party would administer the government the more honestly and efficiently.[31] The Republicans' nomination of Hayes removed their party from the purely defensive role of having to defend the sordid Grant administration and placed upon the Democracy the unhappy task of convincing many normally Republican voters to switch their party allegiance from quasi-reformer Hayes to eleventh-hour reformer Tilden—from a party carrying the putridity of Grantism to one with the lingering aroma of copperheadism.

The campaign was superficial but spirited. The Democrats saw their best chance to win since the days of Stephen A. Douglas, so old-timers came out of retirement to croak or roar at political audiences and were joined by young recruits fired with new faith in the party's future. While Tilden sat in his library writing campaign handouts, the Democratic campaign committee, with wealthy ironmaster Abram Hewitt at the head, skillfully gathered and spent huge sums in directing the Democratic "revival meeting."

[30] Allan Nevins, *Abram S. Hewitt* (New York, 1935), 308; Bowers, *Tragic Era*, 483–84; Alexander C. Flick, *Samuel Jones Tilden, A Study in Political Sagacity* (New York, 1939), 286–91.

[31] James G. Blaine, *Twenty Years of Congress* (Norwich, Conn., 1884–1886), II, 578–79; Josephson, *Politicos*, 221.

There were many rallies, considerable oratory, and an out-
pouring of newspaper broadsides.[32]

The Democrats at first attempted to concentate their guns
on the evils of Grantism and the reform record of Tilden
and to put life into the skeleton issue of state rights. The
Republicans countered the attacks with eulogies on Hayes's
reforming proclivities, Tilden's questionable Civil War and
reform record, and the Democracy's Copperhead reputation. Tilden's supposed failure to report a considerable portion of his income for taxation in 1863 furnished the Republicans with a good talking point. In Illinois the Democrats
were embarrassed when the state Republican committee discovered a stray copy of the suppressed Parton book expos-
ing Tilden's financial machinations and turned out ten
thousand reprints.[33]

The Republicans, especially in the Middle West, turned
their heaviest fire on the opposition's Civil War record.
Tilden was scored for not having supported the Lincoln
administration in its method of conducting the war, and
a dark picture was painted of the evils that would transpire
if the Democracy gained control of the nation and allowed
the South to fall into the hands of southern rebels.[34] Candidate Hayes wrote to James G. Blaine, "Our strong ground
is the dread of a solid South, rebel rule. . . . I hope you
will make these topics prominent in your speeches. It leads
people away from 'hard times,' which is our deadliest foe."
Masterful Republican orators like James G. Blaine, Roscoe
Conkling, Oliver P. Morton, and Robert Ingersoll outdid
themselves in kindling the flames of hatred and of terror for
the dread consequences of rebel rule. Renowned orator
Robert Ingersoll reminded the voters that "every man that

[32] Henry W. Clendenin, *Autobiography of Henry W. Clendenin*
(Springfield, 1926), 117; Nevins, *Hewitt*, 316; Hubbart, *Older Middle
West*, 257; Bogart and Thompson, *Industrial State*, 115–16; Hutchinson,
McCormick, II, 341–44.
[33] Binkley, *Political Parties*, 304.   [34] Josephson, *Politicos*, 207–209.

tried to destroy this nation was a Democrat. . . . The man that assassinated Abraham Lincoln was a Democrat. . . . Soldiers, every scar you have on your heroic bodies was given you by a Democrat." [35]

The Democratic campaigners rose to the bait with such enthusiasm that it appeared that they, too, were anxious for a chance to divert the voters' attention from economic frustrations. They seated Civil War veterans in conspicuous places on speakers' platforms, while the speakers themselves held forth in heated defense of the Democracy's loyalty to the Union. Young Colonel William F. Vilas, a gifted orator, fervently expounded on the war record of Democrat John M. Corse, relating to a Wisconsin audience the famous story of how Colonel Corse held Allatoona Pass until his command "was shattered and himself shot to pieces." He told about Corse's then signaling to General Sherman that "one cheek was shot away, one eye gone, but he could hold the pass against all the southern armies and the combined forces of Hell." That same brave warrior, Vilas continued, now headed the movement for a convention of soldiers to meet in Indianapolis to endorse the Tilden ticket. [36]

Such Democratic efforts as Vilas' might save some votes but could not be expected to *make* votes. For there simply was no impelling reason for normally Republican voters to switch to Tilden. [37] The Democrats promised no noticeable degree of tariff reform, currency reform, or anything that would relieve the hard times. The voters listened to Democratic claims of being the more honest, efficient and loyal; the voters heard their own Republican orators pronounce the same claims in just as convincing a manner. Republican C. C. Washburn, distinguished Civil War general and re-

[35] *Ibid.*, 223–25.
[36] La Crosse (Wis.) *Morning Liberal Democrat*, October 21, 1876; Stanley F. Horn, *The Army of Tennessee: A Military History* (New York, 1941), 376.
[37] C. H. Roberts to Ignatius Donnelly, July 21, 1876, in Donnelly MSS.

spected former governor of Wisconsin, grunted disdain-
fully at Vilas' oratorical effort. Washburn remarked that
"any soldier voting for Tilden is either ignorant or has a
sore head." [38] Many voters were certain to agree. Many
would also certainly agree with the sentiments which Washburn expressed to his old friend Cyrus Woodman. "I sup-
pose," he wrote Woodman, "that you support Tilden because of his great personal integrity conceived in such a
marked manner by cheating the government out of the
taxes he owed, as well as for his skill in stealing railroads, the
Galena and Chicago Union Railroad being a conspicuous
example. I don't know of a man on God's earth that I think
is a bigger God d——d cuss than Tilden." [39]

When the voting finally came, Hayes carried all but one
middle-western state. Indiana, home state of vice-presidential
candidate Hendricks, was in the Democratic column. It was
still a question, however, which candidate had a majority
in the national electoral count. The decision hinged on the
outcome of the ensuing dispute over who was entitled to
the votes of South Carolina, Louisiana, and Florida. The
contest was so heated that many feared it would culminate
in an armed clash. But the fears were ill-founded, because
the mass of people grew weary of the lengthy partisan scrap
over such a trivial matter. In the agrarian Middle West the
voters were much more concerned over the continued hard
times than over this personality and patronage contest.
When the decision finally ended in Hayes's favor, all except
the middle-western farmers could claim some measure of
victory: the Republicans had defeated the Bourbon Democrats, and both had defeated the farmers. For the agrarian
Middle West the spirited evasion of 1876 was merely a diversionary eastern road show, which might well have borrowed the title, *Much Ado About Nothing*.

[38] La Crosse *Morning Liberal Democrat*, October 21, 1876.
[39] C. C. Washburn to Woodman, September 22, 1876, in Woodman
MSS.

Chapter Seven

Travail and Triumph for Laissez Faire 1877-1880

> *We farmers and mechanics have been political slaves in all countries because we are political fools.*
>
> —JOHN TAYLOR OF CAROLINE

IN 1877 the nation was still floundering in the devastating quicksand of economic depression. Farmers and wage laborers were suffering the most, while monopolists and investors managed to reap a harvest of profits at their expense. In the masses' struggle toward security and progress, either the Fates or ingenuity usually brought them some measure of relief and occasionally the illusion of prosperity. This time the wait for the Fates was proving very long and very burdensome. The farmers had been sinking ever more toward penury, and there seemed no end to the downward spin. Money was at a high premium and going steadily higher, creating an especially trying situation for many debtors and those needing to borrow. Farmers were having to pay higher interest rates and satisfy debts in dollars worth far more than at the time when they were borrowed. From the Civil War to 1877 the value of the dollar, measured in terms of commodities, had gradually risen to a point almost two and one half times the 1865 level, and there was no predictable break in the devastating trend. Also in a desperate economic plight was a host of nonagricultural wage earners. Between 1873 and 1877 wages had dropped 60 per cent, and unemployment had reached the three-million mark. The laborers were, like the farmers, in a mood for direct action.[1]

Associate Justice Samuel F. Miller, then probably the most able member of the Supreme Court, sought an explanation for the low economic state to which the national life had sunk. While most other intellectuals were theorists preaching the blessings of freedom for individual enterprise, in keeping with the doctrines of *laissez faire* and frontier individualism, Justice Miller was examining what lay about him. Writing in 1878, he revealed a particular distaste for powerful and parasitical business leaders. He avowed having "met but few things of a character affecting the public good of the whole that have shaken my faith in human nature as much as the united, vigorous, and selfish effort of capitalists,—the class of men who as a distinct class are but recently known in this country—I mean those who live solely by interest and dividends."

The indignant justice believed that this class was brought into being during the Civil War. He said that prior to the war the financial leaders were small in number and "had no interest separate from the balance of the community, because they could lend their money safely and at high rates of interest." The transition from economic parochialism to the new centralization, Justice Miller thought, came partly through the wartime increase in the quantity of currency. The fortunate holders of this surplus liquid wealth were aided by the government and private entrepreneurs. One place to invest the money and reap a profit in interest came with "the creation of a national funded debt, exempt from taxation." This type of "resource for investment was

[1] Samuel Gompers, *Seventy Years of Life and Labor* (New York, 1925), I, 139–40; A. M. Arnett, *The Populist Movement in Georgia* (*Columbia University Studies in History, Economics and Public Law,* No. 104 [New York, 1922]), 69.

quadrupled by the bonds issued by the States, by municipal corporations, and by railroad companies." One consequence, continued Justice Miller, "has been the gradual formation of a new kind of wealth in this country, the income of which is the coupons of interest and stock dividends." Accompanying this new wealth was the emergence "of a class whose only interest or stake in the country is the ownership of these bonds and stocks. They engage in no commerce, no trade, no manufacturing, no agriculture, they produce nothing." [2]

While scholars analyzed the deplorable state of affairs, the desperate masses moved into action. In July, 1877, railroad workers staged a widespread strike, which began in West Virginia and rapidly spread westward. The intervention of militia restored order, and the workers returned empty-handed to their jobs—but not in a spirit of final resignation. They turned with interest to watch, and later to join, the farmers' battle against the lords of big business. The farmers were vigorously pressuring their congressmen to act quickly on the money question. Early in 1877, Congressman James A. Garfield, hard-money Ohio Republican, recorded in his journal: "January 7. The financial craze has let down upon America a fog denser than London's through which I see no signs of an early sun but many signs of an eclipse of national honor. I am fighting against the majority of my own party and state and I grow weary of the contest. If it were one of logic, reason, sense, I could enjoy it, but it is a fight of interest against honor, of brute force of votes against knowledge." [3]

Seventy per cent of the nation's population were farmers, and when aroused to a high pitch of anger they were certain to make a dent in the armor of office-holding politicians. In 1877 the majority of congressmen from the

[2] Cited in Felix Frankfurter, "Justice Holmes Defines the Constitution," *Atlantic Monthly*, CLXII (October, 1938), 486.
[3] Smith, *Garfield*, II, 662.

agrarian areas were more frightened by the popular clamor than by eastern lords of the counting rooms. The farm voters had their angry countenances fixed on Congress, and the congressmen knew it. They knew that the farmers were bent upon acquiring a more liberal currency program.

The Democratic majority in the House had adopted a policy of hamstringing and embarrassing the Republicans. A part of their tactics was the passing of popular legislation which President Hayes would certainly veto, thereby acquiring public enmity. Representative Richard Bland, Democrat from the border state of Missouri, stepped forward with the initial challenge to eastern Bourbon Democrats and eastern Republican spoilsmen. Early in November, 1877, "Silver Dick" Bland introduced in the House an inflationary measure. Instead of the usual soft-money formula of calling for additional greenbacks, Bland's bill provided for the "free and unlimited coinage of silver" on the basis of 412½ grains per silver dollar. Because silver was now being produced in enormous quantities in the far West, silver men and soft-money advocates united on this proposal to turn the output into a flood of silver currency. The bill also provided for repeal of the 1875 Resumption Act. The hard-money leaders of both parties were unable to check the onslaught, and the measure passed in the House by a huge majority.[4] James A. Garfield, Republican whip in the House, observed that in voting against the bill he was alone among the Ohio delegation.[5]

The hard-money element was furious. Financiers had been operating on the assumption that the road to recovery which would not harm them was the one leading to currency based on gold. As devotees of individualism and laissez-faire finance, they reasoned that human beings should not be allowed to interfere with the law of nature which imbued gold with the right to determine the supply of cur-

⁴ Josephson, *Politicos*, 262.   ⁵ Smith, *Garfield*, II, 662–63.

rency. The Resumption Act was designed to return the national currency to the protective wing of the yellow metal—which was held sacred in proportion to the amount of gold to which one had ready access.

Old Bourbon Democrat August Belmont, a wealthy banker closely connected with the European Rothschild financiers, was greatly upset over the heretical inflationist developments in Congress. He warned that "capitalists and banks on both sides of the Atlantic will not buy a bond at par in gold" if a ninety-cent silver dollar was to be legal tender for paying off the bond when it reached maturity.[6] Belmont might have added that the extremists among the soft-money people were now attacking the financiers with the same type of weapon that he and his friends had long been using on the less fortunate. The soft-money element had been paying taxes to maintain a gold value on bonds previously purchased with cheap Civil War greenbacks. The lordly Belmont might also have added that the extremists in the soft-money movement were as crass as the hard-money advocates. The creditor class had been enriching itself and impoverishing the debtors through its government-supported policy, permitting the value of dollars to increase; now some debtors apparently would lead the government to the opposite extreme, cutting the value of the dollar below the level at which the debts were originally incurred.

When it became clear not only that the proposed measure would pass but also that both branches of Congress would override a presidential veto, hard-money men frantically fashioned a substitute measure. Wily Senator William B. Allison, Republican from Iowa, produced a bill which avoided the "unlimited coinage" feature. It provided for a "limited" silver coinage of from two million to not over four million dollars per month. The new measure, the Bland-

[6] Josephson, *Politicos*, 262.

Allison bill, proved a welcome escape for the many legislators who at heart were not extreme inflationists. It was passed early in 1878, over President Hayes's veto. The Treasury found it possible to continue accumulating a gold reserve in preparation for the resumption of specie payments. The hard-money advocates were thus still at the helm, heading the craft of state for the "sound" gold-standard harbor.[7]

The soft-money congressmen also made a drive to guard against the Treasury's retiring any more of the $346,000,000 in greenbacks which was still in circulation. The Resumption Act of 1875 was ambiguous on what to do with the greenbacks after the Treasury accumulated the necessary amount of gold to ensure specie payments. The soft-money leaders succeeded, in the Bland-Allison Act of 1878, in putting an immediate stop to further greenback cancellation and ensuring continued circulation of those notes, with the stipulation that all notes coming into the Treasury "shall be reissued and paid out again and kept in circulation." [8] The Treasury was thereby required, if it was to maintain specie payments, to be prepared to redeem in gold $346,-000,000 in greenbacks.

In the face of the mounting public restlessness the new currency laws constituted a very weak sop. They would not supply jobs for the unemployed laborers or decent wages for the scores who had angrily participated in the great railroad strike of 1877. They would not satisfy the desperate straw-grasping inflationists, who looked upon their program as a cure-all. They would not alleviate the condition of the unnumbered rank and file who were trying to be patient and hopeful. Nor could they impress favorably the sincere, scholarly students of public affairs. From many corners, an insistent protest thus continued against the existing political and economic overlordship.

[7] *Ibid.*, 263.
[8] Alexander D. Noyes, *Thirty Years of American Finance* (New York, 1898), 49–50.

Soft-money men, thoroughly suspicious of both the Republicans and the Democrats, carefully scrutinized the congressional legislation for flaws and formulated plans for independent political action. Joseph Goar, an amateurish but shrewd currency reformer, forwarded his analysis to fellow Minnesotan Ignatius Donnelly. Attacking both the Democrats and the bankers, Goar said that the "Democrats claim . . . too much importance for their action in Congress in getting the destruction of greenbacks stopped. . . . All this was necessary for the National Banks, for how could they have maintained specie payments with every importer of goods presenting their [sic] paper and calling for coin?" He believed that it would require all the gold and silver and the greenbacks to keep them in a healthy condition of resumption.

On the matter of resumption, Goar failed to foresee any advantage accruing to the people from repeal of the Resumption Act. In fact, he believed that the bankers' opposition to repeal was a mere pretense, for through currency contraction they had already reaped the harvest of their manipulations. Without the Resumption Act, the bankers would again be able to play the devastating game of expansion and contraction. "It was not specie resumption the money power wanted—it was contraction." There lay the money moguls' great gains—"gobbling up the valuable property of all who are unable to help themselves, after the large amount of money on which they intended to operate with had been withdrawn from circulation." [9] Illinois' Democratic congressman William R. Morrison was likewise unenthusiastic over repeal of the Resumption Act as a cure for the sins in high finance. Morrison, in a speech before the House, declared that repeal would increase fivefold the power of the monopolistic banking interests.[10]

[9] Joseph Goar to Ignatius Donnelly, July 15, 1878, in Donnelly MSS.
[10] Scott, "Political Career of William R. Morrison," loc. cit., 142, 146–47.

Every champion of change seemed to have his own pet solution. Minnesota's Goar, sensing the real key to the solution, advocated overhauling the national banking structure.[11] Some leaders concentrated on repeal of the Resumption Act, while others would have gone much further by using the inflationary device of greatly augmenting the amount of paper and silver currency. Cyrus McCormick, always the internationalist, preferred the trade dollar and an international conference to settle the entire matter. He had no faith in panaceas, believing, "The present financial crisis . . . is due to improvidence, extravagance, overtrading, and excesses, and recovery can only come from economy, industry and frugality. . . ." [12] Some leaders, notably William R. Morrison, saw the protective tariff as the most poisonous cause of the nation's economic coma, for it slowed the healthful flow of trade.

There was much difference of opinion regarding the best political means to bring about recovery. Many were loath to break with the old parties, but at the same time an increasing number of farmers and laborers organized into independent parties. As early as February 22, 1878, deputies from twenty-eight states gathered in Toledo and organized a National Greenback-Labor party. The delegates represented all the dissenting groups in the nation, from utopian socialists to woman-suffrage advocates, with farm and labor leaders by far the most numerous. Previously the wage earners had demonstrated but slight enthusiasm for direct political action, and their interest in pushing greenback legislation was very recent. During the depressed seventies the issue gradually became a little more popular among the workers, as more of them felt that currency inflation would bring a rise in prices and hence industrial prosperity. In 1876 they contributed very few of the scant hundred thou-

[11] Goar to Ignatius Donnelly, July 15, 1878, in Donnelly MSS.
[12] Hutchinson, *McCormick*, II, 354.

sand votes polled by Greenback candidate Peter Cooper, but with the failure of the 1877 railroad strike the incensed wage earners turned in large numbers to the "greenback craze." [13]

At the Toledo gathering, although the emphasis was on the specific demand for greenback inflation, there was evidenced some very sober and enlightened thinking about the traditional concepts of American political and economic life. Having experienced the futility of getting results with the old approaches and recognizing the childishness of panaceas in the face of the existing big business–political colossus, certain enlightened spirits were feeling their way toward something new. They saw a new centralization and a more complex order enveloping their old way of life. They saw that little men could not slay this Goliath with the old individualistic weapons of frontier days. They began to doubt the validity of placing their accustomed emphasis on traditional frontiersman-Jeffersonian precepts of individualism, localism, and *laissez faire*. The economic and political diseases were national in scope; reformers saw the need for a national cure. The national government would be turned into a servant of the people, channeling to them the credit now controlled by bankers and extending to the masses a fairer share of the fruits of productive enterprise. The Greenback leader giving most spirited and effective voice to this approach was sincere General James B. Weaver. Asking the people to think in terms of national action, Weaver said that the new party should strike at the nationwide monopolies, the "privileged classes of creditors." He would remove the burdensome resumption policy, take money control from the bankers, and establish a "rigid regulation of interstate commerce and transportation." [14]

[13] Selig Perlman, *A History of Trade Unionism in the United States* (New York, 1922), 58, 60.
[14] Haynes, *Third Party Movements*, 92–93; Josephson, *Politicos*, 259, 264–65.

Emphasizing the national and unique character of the movement was the unprecedented phenomenon of having a large national political convention mid-term between presidential campaigns. In the purely tactical aspect, the Greenback party's first target was the 1878 election of congressmen. This threw the Republican and Democratic machines off balance, for their party organizations were not patterned to emphasize congressional-district units. The most able party managers were state chairmen, state central committeemen, or national committeemen. The greatest amount of effort and money was usually concentrated on state and national campaigns. In presidential election years congressional candidates rode the coattails of the national campaigns. In the off years there usually were adjustments to the exciting governorship contests—if state elections were held.

In the absence of a presidential or governorship race, congressional candidates had to struggle against public apathy through desultory and isolated district organizations. Only the most colorful congressional candidate could whip up marked public interest in a campaign which had at stake neither a governorship nor the presidency. It often happened in an off-year election that nonorganization candidates slipped into Congress. This often worked to the advantage of the party of the "outs," for it escaped confronting the normally superior national-campaign drive of the party of the "ins." This factor likewise would work to the advantage of the newly created Greenback party. The future looked dark for the old parties—with the Greenbackers aiming with frenzied intent at the congressional elections, with public interest in their cause growing, and with the opposition caught off balance in off-year elections.

In meeting this heretical Greenback cause and heretical Greenback tactical approach, the Bourbon Democrats were caught high and dry, isolated in their state central committees and the national committee while district conventions took over. Most of the Bourbons were relieved to be by-passed, for thereby they escaped the inevitable defeat await-ing them if they attempted to control matters in the dis-trict Democratic conventions. The Bourbon state and na-tional leaders discreetly remained at home or went fishing. The silence of Wisconsin's William F. Vilas and his known friendship with certain prominent Republicans gave cre-dence to a subsequent rumor that he was going to join the Republican party.[15]

Only here and there did a Bourbon attempt to stem the flood. In Iowa, where the Democrats were very few and far between anyhow, state chairman John P. Irish and a few other Bourbons were very outspoken in their opposi-tion to soft money. But they could not keep the plague out of the party. In September the Democrats replaced their chosen candidates with Greenbackers in four Iowa con-gressional districts, and in two districts they had already fused with the Greenback party.[16] In Ohio, meanwhile, Sen-ator Allen Thurman managed to accumulate some more enemies by taking an emphatic stand for hard money. But he could not induce his party to follow in his wake.[17] In general, the 1878 campaign was for Bourbons everywhere pretty much as one of them described it to his state chair-man in October: "Of all campaigns since my entry into po-litical life this is decidedly the worst mixed; we are drifting where and in what direction, God only knows." [18]

As for the Greenback party leaders of the various con-gressional districts, they faced the tactical problem of what to do with the soft-money Democrats. Each district or-

[15] A. M. Thomson (then of Chicago *Tribune*) to William F. Vilas, November, 1879, in Vilas MSS.; Milwaukee *Sentinel*, May 12, 13, 1880.
[16] Frederick E. Haynes, *James Baird Weaver* (Iowa City, 1919), 102; Haynes, *Third Party Movements*, 154.
[17] *Appletons' Annual Cyclopaedia*, XVIII (1878), 669; McGrane, "Greenback Movement," *loc. cit.*, 537-38.
[18] Joseph Rankin to Anderson, October 6, 1878, in Anderson MSS.

ganization decided independently, and the outcome was subject very much to the numerical strength and reputation of the Democrats in each district. In certain areas Greenback-Democratic fusion slates appeared; in some of these the Greenbackers endorsed the Democratic offering, and in others the reverse transpired. Where the Democrats were weak or in ill repute with the soft-money element, Greenbackers did not hesitate to voice their disgust for the Democracy. Iowa's James B. Weaver, successful congressional candidate running on an exclusively Greenback ticket, was one of the most outspoken critics of the Democracy. He later related in a congressional speech his reasons for disliking the party. This ex-Republican declared that in 1868 he had become converted to the Pendleton Plan and had consequently intended to join the Democracy. But about the time that he became converted, the party dropped the program, thereby removing the only possible reason he could have for becoming a Democrat. The Democracy, Weaver further declared, "in its whole history has simply camped every four years exactly where the Republican party camped four years before." He attacked it for having failed to "adhere strictly to the principles it has enunciated before the public." On that score he thought the Republican record much better, because it at least was "open and bold in its piracy." [19]

A striking case of Greenbacker distaste for Democrats occurred in the Minnesota district where Ignatius Donnelly was again trying to recapture his old seat in Congress. Donnelly, the only important leader of the antimonopoly Granger movement still in active politics, was now a Greenback party leader. Realizing the difficulty of election without the backing of the large bloc of St. Paul Irish Democrats, the Sage of Nininger urged his Greenback compatriots to unite with the Democracy under one banner.

[19] Haynes, *Weaver*, 186–88.

But his friends found it most difficult to forget their past experiences with the Bourbon-dominated machines of St. Paul and Minneapolis.[20] We "will be betrayed by the Democrats," said one.[21] Another mused that the Democrats would surely be glad to "make any concessions, . . . but instead of being swallowed, [they] always in the end prove to be the swallowers." The Greenbackers, he declared, would become nothing more than "flesh and meat to Democratic skeletons." [22] Joseph Goar, in a letter to Donnelly, dwelt upon the Republican angle. "It is," said he, "the aim of both" the Republican and Democratic parties "to ignore us and keep up the old hate; and as long as we favor any coalition with the Democratic party, that long the Republican leaders will hold the party together and defeat us." He reported that upon talking with soft-money Republicans in districts where the Greenback and Democratic parties had formed coalitions, the Republicans had switched back to their own party, knowing that the Democrats would "claim all as a Democratic victory." [23]

The outcome was a separate Greenback party nomination for Donnelly, with a subsequent Democratic party endorsement. The Republican candidate was a wealthy miller and long-time political bigwig, W. D. Washburne.[24] The campaign developed into one of the bitterest political contests in the state's history. Currency became a minor issue as the contestants worked themselves into a white heat over the manner in which farmers were treated by Washburne's grain buyers and millers. The Donnelly forces contended that the buyers corruptly manipulated the brass kettle used for grading wheat [25] and charged that Washburne

[20] R. Thornton to Ignatius Donnelly, July 30, 1878; N. C. Martin to *id.*, August 8, 1878; and E. A. Cramsie to *id.*, August 27, 1878, in Donnelly MSS.
[21] Fred Hawley to *id.*, August 31, 1878, *ibid.*
[22] Doughty to *id.*, June 29, 1878, *ibid.*
[23] Goar to *id.*, July 15, 1878, *ibid.*
[24] Folwell, *History of Minnesota*, III, 117.
[25] Hall, *Political Contests*, 225-27.

headed a wheat ring [26] "which is endeavoring to keep down the price." They pointed out that wheat was eleven cents higher outside the area of the ring operations.[27] The farmers were much impressed by the Greenbacker efforts in this so-called "Brass Kettle Campaign," [28] but the city folk failed to get excited. Nor did the Bourbon Democrats exert any effort to deliver the St. Paul Irish vote to Donnelly. "I am fearful that those damned old Bourbon Democrats will not come up to the mark," said a rural Democratic adherent of Donnelly's.[29] Washburne won the city vote, and Donnelly the rural vote, the slight difference between the two sliding the wealthy miller into first place.[30]

Similar contests raged throughout the nation, as laborers and farmers pulled the beards of old party leaders. In the final count the Republican party received a drubbing for its failures as the party of the "ins." Both parties of the "outs" could boast of triumphs. The Democrats captured control of the Senate, and in the House their majority became overwhelming. The Greenback party, narrowly missing its goal of a balance of power in the House, captured fourteen seats. The total Greenback vote was 1,060,000, as compared with the less than 100,000 of two years previous.[31]

With the 1880 presidential election only two years off, the outlook for the Republican spokesmen and the Bourbon Democrats lacked its usual auspiciousness. The Republican party appeared slated for defeat, and the Bourbons faced a stiff fight if they attempted to recapture their party from the people. The Fates, operating through time and nature's

[26] T. M. Newson to Ignatius Donnelly, October 15, 1878; and H. G. Rising to *id.*, October 26, 1878, in Donnelly MSS.

[27] Robert Miller to *id.*, September 14, 1878, *ibid.*

[28] T. G. Mealey to *id.*, October 20, 1878, *ibid.*

[29] Mealey to *id.*, August 28, 1878, *ibid.*

[30] Folwell, *History of Minnesota*, III, 118; Hall, *Political Contests*, 229–30.

[31] Josephson, *Politicos*, 265.

gifts to laissez-faire capitalism, came to the rescue of both these wobbly political guardians of the system. Secretary of the Treasury John Sherman, with stubborn devotion to the sacredness of the gold-standard theory, triumphed in his drive to accumulate the necessary amount of specie to place the nation's currency on the gold standard by the specified January 1, 1879. The victory for hard money had come at a devastating cost to the masses; but when it came, there came also a restoration of financiers' confidence in the future. Money began to flow more freely, as investors optimistically opened their moneybags to optimistic seekers of credit who had the urge to launch again upon the cyclical road of expansion. The flow of money brought higher prices —to the joy of employers, wage earners, and farmers.

A few months after the nation wearily took the last dreary step toward resumption of specie payment, it received a sudden and propelling boost from the least-expected source. The farmers received from the golden goddess of nature and from *laissez faire* the double miracle of a bumper crop and high prices. In 1879 the harvest of grain was bounteous, and at the same time crop failures in Europe brought a high-price foreign demand for wheat.[32] In 1879, American farmers harvested over twenty-eight million more bushels of wheat than they had in 1878, and during the same period the price jumped from $0.78 to $1.11 per bushel.

Interest in politics languished as American frontier optimism again captured the farmers, laborers, speculators, and business promoters. Few could get excited over political issues while land values boomed, the epochal westward march of homeseekers continued, railroad construction revived, and trade flourished on every hand. The Greenback party rapidly shriveled, as party gatherings attracted but a fourth of the usual comers. With insufficient funds, no patronage, and no newspaper support, the Greenback party

[32] *Ibid.*, 266.

was in a poor position to follow through with its initial drive against laissez-faire capitalism and localized government. In the other parties most of the currency-reform element quickly dropped the issue and jumped upon the optimism band wagon or turned to less spectacular reform crusades.

During 1879 and 1880 the Democratic party in the Middle West, as elsewhere, rapidly reverted to Bourbon domination.[33] The re-instated Bourbons resorted to their old practices of nominating and financing stooge candidates, being themselves satisfied with dictating "safe" party policies and entertaining the hope that someday they might find juicy public offices through a "sure thing" election. Certainly there was no immediate possibility of Democratic victories in the normally Republican states of the Middle West. Regarding public policies, the two major parties were in a remarkable condition of equilibrium. Never had they been so obviously in such close agreement. The leaders seemed too relieved and exhausted after their mutual escape from the Greenback craze to turn with much spirit to attack each other in their usual warfare.

The situation in the Bourbon Democracy of Wisconsin exemplified the general tenor of Democratic apathy. In 1879 the Wisconsin Democrats nominated Milwaukee's railroad-banking king, Alexander Mitchell, for the governorship. He refused the honor. The convention then turned to railroad attorney William F. Vilas. He, too, refused. Back in 1875, when Democratic hopes were higher, Vilas had fruitlessly sought the nomination on the Democratic-Reform ticket.[34] His brother subsequently wrote to him from Chicago, "Of course you could hope for nothing from the convention—only demagogues and whelps get anything. I wish you would come here where you have a field

---

[33] John P. Irish to George F. Parker, November 8, 1879, in "Letters Written by John P. Irish to George F. Parker," *Iowa Journal of History and Politics*, XXXI (July, 1933), 423.

[34] Milwaukee *Sentinel*, September 9, 10, 1879.

for great success and let the damned politics alone. Away with the two-cent grangers." [35] In 1879 Vilas was still interested in politics, but he reported that there were reasons "plenty as blackberries" why he did not want the gubernatorial nomination. Although four years older than when he made the 1875 bid, he now considered himself, at the age of thirty-eight, too young for the position. Nor did he consider it possible to abandon his law practice without great sacrifice—nor think that there was "any juncture of affairs as renders duty to the public superior in its exigency." [36]

The Wisconsin Democrats finally found a gubernatorial candidate in Milwaukee's James G. Jenkins. As a close friend of Republican United States senator Matt H. Carpenter and as a lawyer for the Northwest Railroad, candidate Jenkins well represented the current Democratic temper—or lack of temper.[37] His campaign effort was described in a state Republican paper, the Janesville *Gazette*, as having "reached a high political plane." This journal further reported, "He virtually ignores the old Democratic party, and in some respects preaches more Republicanism than Democracy. His aim is to stand between the two parties, and condemn that which he sees is wrong in either, and counsels [*sic*] a better feeling between the parties, and between the North and the South." The paper also observed that Jenkins "ignored the issue of the day, did not wave the flag nor make the eagle scream, did not charge the Republicans with fraud nor attack their public men, did not refer to the recent elections, denounced the political murders in the South, advised moderation in politics, complimented [Republican] Governor Smith." [38] A dispatch to the Re-

[35] Dr. Charles H. Vilas to William F. Vilas, October 7, 1875, in Vilas MSS.
[36] Madison *Democrat*, June 22, 1879.   [37] Plumb, *Badger Politics*, 74.
[38] James G. Jenkins, "Scrapbook of James G. Jenkins," Library of the State Historical Society of Wisconsin, 11.

publican Milwaukee *Sentinel* included slightly more evidence of anti-Republicanism in the Jenkins speeches, for the candidate was reported as pointing out the danger of concentrated government, decrying Republican-fostered sectionalism, and claiming the Democracy as the only true national party.[39] Following this noble effort, the Republicans carried the election.

This Wisconsin campaign was in tenor very much a preview of the ensuing national presidential campaign, except that nationally *both* major parties entertained high hopes of victories through offering nothing. Indeed, the national strength of the Democracy had been steadily growing and seemed about to reach a remarkable balance with the Republicans. Since 1877 all the southern states had been back in the political arena, under conditions which made possible a Solid South of 138 electoral votes for the Democracy. In the North, particularly in the Northeast, Democratic city machines afforded the party a chance to carry important industrial areas. If the Democrats could capture two or three of the large northern states, victory would be theirs. Already the Democracy had an overwhelming majority in the House of Representatives, and now the party leaders were out to ride the trend into complete control of the national government.

In selecting candidates, both parties demonstrated a decided preference for mediocrity. The Democrats, after Samuel J. Tilden's withdrawal from the scene on grounds of ill health, finally settled on a military man, General Winfield Scott Hancock of Pennsylvania. Hancock's lack of experience in public office rendered it impossible for anyone to determine his political capacity or lack of it; but as he was a hero of Gettysburg, his nomination would subdue Republican bloody-shirt hyperbole. For the vice-presidency

[39] Clipping from Milwaukee *News,* October 20, 1879, in "Jenkins Scrapbook," 11.

the Democrats chose William H. English, governor of doubtful Indiana.

The Republicans also settled upon a military man for the presidential nomination—Brigadier General James A. Garfield. His military rank and reputation were less than Hancock's, but his experience as the conservative minority leader in the House of Representatives gave him some standing as a politician. What is more, Garfield had been born in a log cabin and when a boy had taken a vacation trip on a canalboat. Political orators could thus relate his rise from log cabin and canal life to national fame. The Republicans' vice-presidential offering was New York's Chester A. Arthur, handy man of "Boss" Roscoe Conkling.

The platforms of both parties were as innocuous as the candidates; and in the subsequent campaign over economic questions the currency issue was buried, and only the tariff threatened to divert the emphasis away from the personalities of the candidates. The tariff threat soon proved abortive. The Democratic platform declared a "tariff for revenue only," but when the Republican campaigners sought to make an issue of it, "Hancock the Superb" proved equal to the challenge. He asserted that "the manufacturing or industrial interests of the country . . . [would] have as much protection" under the Democracy as under Republican generalship. He also declared that the tariff was a "local question." This brought widespread ridicule upon his head, but actually the issue was more local than either Hancock or his detractors realized. Oratory on party records was also less in evidence than dramatic verbiage on the qualities of the "log cabin boy" and the military triumphs of Hancock the Superb. The party records were simply too feeble to stand up before the onslaughts from each side. The Hayes Republican administration had produced nothing; the Democratic Congress had offered nothing but partisan sniping at the Republicans.[40]

The election effort was essentially one of patronage seeking and of buying protection for big business. Money flowed freely and in a manner reflecting the low moral state of the national political life. Both parties obtained huge sums from "interested" business barons. Some moguls began the practice of giving money to both sides. In Minnesota a prominent railroad president later said that he had contributed twenty-five thousand dollars to each of the Republican and Democratic campaigns.[41] The Republicans, with a proven record of safety on the tariff question, managed to obtain the greatest financial aid. This factor aided not a little in the final Republican triumph in doubtful Indiana, New York, and Ohio. Garfield won by a very narrow margin: in the total vote of over nine million, his edge over Hancock was about nine thousand. Local elections also resulted in the Republicans' recapturing, with narrow margins, both branches of Congress.

While the Republicans and the Bourbon Democrats bid for place and patronage, the voice of the people was heard only through the almost-drowned-out Greenback party. The Greenbackers nominated James B. Weaver for the presidency and presented an enlightened program. The platform proposed an eight-hour day for labor, a graduated income tax, national regulation of railroads and all other interstate commerce, and both paper and silver inflation. Public apathy and Republican-Democratic noise caused the Greenback effort to receive but a slight hearing. Weaver received little more than three hundred thousand votes, less than a third of his party's 1878 total.[42]

---

[40] Josephson, *Politicos*, 287–99; Flick, *Tilden*, 459–66; Smith, *Garfield*, II, 970–1043.

[41] Hall, *Political Contests*, 360.

[42] Smith, *Garfield*, II, 1018–43; Josephson, *Politicos*, 289–90, 299–301.

For the common people everywhere, the years of acute depression and apparent recovery had culminated in political travesty. Neither the Republican spoilsmen nor the Democratic Bourbons had contributed a single basic legislative act to ameliorate or strike at the roots of the nation's economic ills. There was nothing to check the business cycle from again throwing the masses back into hardship. The people, too, had failed to measure up to a true appreciation of the reforms necessary. Economic optimism and relative political apathy resulted in their forsaking the start made by the Greenback party. Business moguls were likewise swept into a state of optimism and felt no urge to sacrifice personal effort in public life, but they possessed the convenience of being able to hire professionals to guard the political front against impostors. The simple use of a checkbook ensured the friendship of political policy makers— both Republican and Democratic. The masses, on the other hand, had no powerful agency working for them, and hence they went unrepresented when themselves too bored or too busy to remain on the political battle front. The masses needed able leadership, political-economic education, convictions, and the moral fiber to fight consistently for their rights.

Chapter Eight

Bourbons Stumble into Power 1880-1884

> *Only the rich can get justice; only the poor cannot escape it.*
>
> —HENRY DEMAREST LLOYD

A DECADE and a half had transpired since Appomattox, and the Republican and Democratic political armies of occupation were still camped on agrarian middle-western soil —still helping industrialist-financier victors of the Civil War to plunder the region's earnings and resources. Republican spoilsmen did the political managing; Bourbon Democrats winked approval. Both groups received a cut of the melon. These political armies, or parties, were largely bands of mercenaries and friendly middle-western vassals attached to eastern lords of wealth. During that decade and a half, time, fate, machines, and men had wrought changes which brought in their wake storms of economic depression and public protest. But the system of exploitation persisted. Industrialization was leaping westward, and with the cyclical spurt of the early eighties it moved with new rapidity into the eastern fringe of the agrarian Middle West. Michigan was absorbed into the industrial orbit without its frontier agricultural system ever becoming widely refined into a highly commercialized endeavor. In the chief agricultural areas of Michigan the farms had averaged but ten acres in size [1] and had thus escaped great dependence on the capital,

---

[1] Harriet M. Dilla, *Politics of Michigan, 1865–1878* (*Columbia University Studies in History, Economics and Public Law*, No. 118 [New York, 1912]), 236.

machinery, and railroads controlled by extortionists. The westward industrial expansion had been eating into Ohio and Indiana—a long-time core of agrarian protest. During the eighties the old agrarian spirit of protest rapidly declined in Ohio and Indiana, as the new industrialism afforded the farmers flourishing nearby markets. Nearby factories purchased the farmers' wool, and nearby wage earners bought the farmers' foodstuffs. Thus did eastern industrialism gradually absorb much of Michigan, Ohio, and Indiana. Economically and politically the farmers of those states were less colonials of the East and more the advanced guard of expanding industrialism. No longer were they strictly a part of the agrarian Middle West.

Farther westward, in Illinois, Wisconsin, Minnesota, Iowa, and Nebraska, industrial cities grew rapidly in the midst of the vast agrarian expanse. Such centers as Chicago, Milwaukee, Minneapolis, St. Paul, and Omaha flourished but continued to remain colonial islands of eastern business interests. Farm land was too rich and too plentiful to be used merely to supply a handful of cities in the region, and thus agriculture continued its dependence on distant markets. Numerically this area remained a region of farmers; economically it remained a region of commercialized agriculture geared to distant markets. Nor did the agrarian Middle West shrink in size as industrialism enveloped its eastern fringe; it was expanding westward into Nebraska and later the Dakotas and onward. The Middle West also gradually became more united with the agrarians of the recently chaotic border states and somewhat more friendly with those of the South. Indeed, industrialization had still not turned the Middle West away from its predominantly agrarian status. Although the capitalists rapidly continued to acquire ownership of some farms and mortgages on others, the farmers continued to work the land, vote, and entertain hopes of a better day.

There also was evidenced a change in the Democratic party. The national Democracy, based chiefly on the Solid South and on eastern city machines, was now a strong vote-getting organization. Though the Republicans held a majority in the Middle West, a Democratic victory in a presidential campaign would net the middle-western adjunct of the party a welcome patronage windfall. Recent off-year congressional elections had been kind to the Democracy, moreover, and it was thus not fantastic to hope that the party could soon capture the state governments and the presidential electoral vote.

With hope welling up, the middle-western Bourbon leadership began to expand its energies. The Bourbons, especially the younger element, felt that it was time to bestir themselves from merely sitting on the party lid as guards against radical agrarians. They began to vie for favor with the eastern Bourbons, in preparation for the day when their eastern cousins would have patronage and campaign funds to dispense. The Bourbons were also pleased to discover an increased number of business barons shelling money into Democratic coffers. Some of these were merchants, bankers, and railroad moguls who disliked Republican tariffs. Others were simply expedient men, who, seeing the probability of Democratic victory, decided that it would be discreet to prove their friendship for the party of Jefferson. Some eagerly gave money to both parties.

This new aggressiveness among the Bourbon Democrats was most marked in the new and younger Bourbons. The older generation, including such men as Cyrus McCormick, James R. Doolittle, Henry H. Sibley, and Alexander Mitchell, were rapidly retiring to the side lines to become sage elder statesmen. Cyrus McCormick, for example, no longer possessed the health necessary to carry on with active politics. After 1880 he concentrated his public activities on further development of the Presbyterian Theological Seminary, a Chicago project which had long been a recipient of his interest and finances.[2] Intrepid leaders of the onetime Progressive-Copperhead group, such as Allen Thurman, George H. Pendleton, Daniel Voorhees, and Thomas A. Hendricks, were still on the hustings; but they were operating in states now outside the agrarian Middle West. No longer were they concentrating on specifically agrarian problems. Thurman was an outspoken hard-money advocate. Pendleton, in the United States Senate after the 1878 election, was showing especial interest in administrative reform through civil-service legislation.[3] Even old Daniel Voorhees was no longer a strictly agrarian champion. Now a United States senator, this Tall Sycamore of the Wabash was eventually to forsake his old soft-money hobby. He frankly explained his switch on grounds of not wishing to cut off his old Indiana Democratic friends from the Bourbon patronage.[4] No, the leadership of the Democracy was not the same as of old.

In single file, able and ambitious new Bourbons cautiously moved forward in the political arena throughout the early eighties. Some slipped into the public spotlight, and others remained in the shadows to manipulate the intensity and direction of the light. Chicago's Melville W. Fuller, overcoming his old enmity for Cyrus McCormick, moved forward in the Illinois Democracy. Soon Nebraska's J. Sterling Morton caught the political fever and resumed the politico role which he had forsaken back in 1868. Business tycoons, like railroad magnate James J. Hill of St. Paul, invited themselves into party councils of war and often took over the directorship. Demagogic city-machine politicos, like Carter H. Harrison of Chicago and Albert A. Ames of Minneapolis,

[2] Hutchinson, *McCormick*, II, 335.

[3] Stealey, *Press Gallery*, 383–84, 444; Allan Nevins, *Grover Cleveland, A Study in Courage* (New York, 1934), 177.

[4] Champ Clark, *My Quarter Century of American Politics* (New York, 1920), I, 322.

made their appearance.[5] And here and there in the Democracy or at its outskirts were some lonely, non-Bourbon champions of the people—such as conscientious William R. Morrison and erratic Ignatius Donnelly.

Ready at hand, in the tariff question, was an economic-political issue which appealed to the program-seeking Bourbons. An attack on Republican protectionism fitted well into the shopworn Democratic tradition of endorsing the theory of *laissez faire* and the credo of individualism. With single-track purposefulness, Congressman William R. Morrison had already made good use of the low-tariff cry in catching Illinois votes. Now others, particularly William F. Vilas and J. Sterling Morton, stepped forward to add Bourbon influence to the crusade. It was a strange meeting of minds—Morrison, the droll and sincere friend of prairie folk, and the elegant Bourbon associates of corporate interests. Yet both seemed to look upon tariff reform as the gateway through which hard-working people could pass into a virtual economic heaven. Morrison was interested in it for the masses and as a political issue that brought him votes. Bourbons were not necessarily averse to recognizing those same factors, but above all else they had their eyes trained on what free trade would mean to the capitalistic system and their own niches in it. The Bourbons were primarily guardians and benefactors of a system, not humanitarian servants of the people. Their system was *laissez faire,* dressed up in the provocative garb of American frontier individualism. They believed, or at least they proclaimed, that individual enterprise would automatically take care of all worthy workers in field and factory.

Supporting the Bourbons was a large coterie of intellectual spirits, past and present, who served to add an aura of high-

[5] Olson, *Morton,* 252; Hutchinson, *McCormick,* II, 338, 356; Harold Zink, *City Bosses in the United States, A Study of Twenty Municipal Bosses* (Durham, 1930), 338.

mindedness to whatever mercenary purposes might be ascribed to the Bourbons. Adam Smith had emphasized the glorious benefits of *laissez faire*, and subsequently other intellectuals had brushed his theory almost clean of its original recognition that some governmental safeguards would help the people. Many post–Civil War intellectuals were proclaiming that individualism, without governmental limitations, was the true path to prosperity. On every hand men of intellect wrote and preached the blessings of individualism and the evils of the protective tariff, which they felt was a crutch used by those unwilling to rely on their own talent and effort. Among the apostles of individual enterprise were Professor William Graham Sumner of Yale University, Professor Arthur Latham Perry of Williams College, and famed statistician David A. Wells.[6] These and others of eminence served the Bourbons not only through writing books but also as counselors, orators, and organizers. They co-operated with the Bourbons in the flourishing Free Trade League and wrote free-trade platforms for their political friends.

Professor Perry was of particular help to J. Sterling Morton, journeying twice to Nebraska to deliver speeches on the sins of governmental tampering and the unconstitutionality of the protective tariff. Morton had first imported him in 1874 and had listened with appreciation to his state fair address on "Foes of the Farmers." The good professor, in speaking to an audience of sad-faced farmers, whose crops had been stricken by drought and grasshoppers, saw nothing incongruous in listing as the chief foes of the farmers paper money, the protective tariff, regulatory legislation, and debt.[7]

[6] John Herman Randall, Jr., *The Making of the Modern Mind* (Boston, 1940), 637; Merle Curti, *The Growth of American Thought* (New York, 1943), 635–56; Vernon L. Parrington, *Main Currents in American Thought* (New York, 1927–1930), III, 102–103, 268–70, 274; David A. Wells to William F. Vilas, December 5, 1887, in Vilas MSS.; Scott, "Political Career of William R. Morrison," *loc. cit.*, 164.

[7] Olson, *Morton*, 202–203.

Tariff reform, aside from its exciting theoretical implications, was a particularly fortunate political-economic medium for Bourbons to espouse. It had the dual advantage of appearing to be a boon both to the lowly voters and to Bourbon bank accounts. Bourbons thus escaped their normal role of defending or advocating policies which were too obviously devices of exploitation. Now the Bourbons could talk in terms of principle—of how the consumer was being victimized by protectionists and of the historic anti-protectionist stand of their party. At the same time, because many Bourbons were involved in enterprises not dependent on tariff protection, they could preach reform without entailing self-sacrifice. Many Bourbons connected with railroads looked upon free trade or lower tariffs as a stimulus to their carrying business to and from ocean ports. They also desired cheaper steel and iron for rails and equipment, and a lower-tariff program would facilitate lower prices. Many large-scale merchants, like Chicago's Franklin McVeagh, with their businesses geared to a quick turnover of goods at attractively low prices, found protective tariffs a hindrance. Some manufacturers even favored a limited degree of tariff reform, hoping that they could maneuver a reduction of rates on the raw materials which they imported without interfering with the protection of the finished products which they produced. A few well-established industrialists, like Cyrus McCormick, entertained the hope of fostering a greater foreign market for their products through abandonment of the protectionist system.

Concentrating political fire on the protectionists was a convenient vehicle for by-passing many unsavory economic practices involving the tariff reformers themselves and at the same time affording a plausible consistency to their position. Bourbons, by expounding on their devotion to individualism, could attack tariff protection as government interference and on the same grounds lambaste governmental regulation of railroads, natural resources, and moneylenders.

Only when it became convenient to their own personal economic interests did the Bourbons make political fodder of the exploitation of human beings and of nature's gifts of raw materials. It was a long time before Bourbons raised a voice against the nonindividualistic practice of providing governmental help to special interests through gifts to railroad promoters. The Bourbons endorsed governmental interference when it involved a gift to themselves but not when it involved any form of protection for the people or for industries in which none of their own money was at stake.

Not until the railroad companies in which they were personally interested had managed to obtain land grants and other forms of subsidies did the Bourbons turn upon promoters who sought government favors to facilitate the construction of competing lines. In the late seventies some Bourbon politicians found it politically safe—and convenient —to attack unrestrained governmental aid to railroad promoters. Some, like Senator Allen Thurman, were doubtless sincere in their indignation at the existing policy, but in no case did the Bourbons champion the public interest if it involved personal sacrifice of their own economic interest. Senator Thurman set the pattern for the new Democratic attack on the subsidy system by introducing a measure designed to force the reluctant Pacific railroads to repay the enormous government loans made for their construction. After several years of obstructionism the bill finally passed.[8]

While the Bourbons concentrated on individualism and *laissez faire* in general and on tariff reform in particular, they winked at the rapid growth of industrial centralization and "private government." It worried them not at all that railroad monopoly was injurious to individual enterprise in

[8] Ignatius Donnelly to Samuel Kilpatrick, September 25, 1880, in Donnelly MSS.; Josephson, *Politicos*, 268–71.

certain other fields of endeavor, nor did they cringe when
such combinations as Standard Oil interfered with *laissez
faire*. Politically, the Bourbons realized that such monopolists as Jay Gould and Collis P. Huntington sometimes pushed
Democrats into political office, and the traditional state-
rights stand of the Democrats was a convenient political device for keeping regulation schemes out of the national
government. Financially, many Bourbons entertained no
thought of interfering with the monopolies, for many
Bourbons were corporate attorneys and security holders.[9]

The Bourbons ignored the anticentralization protests
which had recently emanated from General James B.
Weaver and his Greenbackers. Nor did the Bourbons heed
the warnings of Henry Demarest Lloyd, who was decrying
the monopolistic device of railroad-rate discriminations.
In 1881, in the *Atlantic Monthly*, Lloyd wrote that the
power of money and industry had outgrown the forces of
our government. He urged action, stating that "our treatment of the 'railroad problem' will show the quality and
calibre of our political sense. . . . It may indicate whether
the American democracy, like all the democratic experi-
ments which have preceded it, is to become extinct because the people had not wit enough or virtue enough to
make the common good supreme." [10]

The middle-western Bourbon politicos most strikingly
expounding economic individualism were Nebraska's J.
Sterling Morton and Wisconsin's William F. Vilas. Both
were intelligent and wealthy; both were involved in the
railroad monopolies and Democratic politics; both were
tariff reformers. Morton was an enthusiastic, uncompromising advocate of free trade; Vilas was more given to com-

---

[9] Josephson, *Politicos*, 345; Olson, *Morton*, 219–25.
[10] Henry Demarest Lloyd, "The Story of a Great Monopoly," *Atlantic Monthly*, XLVII (March, 1881), 318.

promise and political expediency in his crusade for tariff reform.

In the early eighties Morton discovered that newspaper articles did not suffice to maintain the program for economic life in Nebraska cherished by him and by his railroad sponsor; for Nebraska had now reached the railroad-agrarian stage which had prevailed in the Granger Northwest a decade before. In Nebraska the Republican party and the almost defunct Democracy were traditional accomplices of the railroads. In 1880 the energetic Morton came out of the political retirement which he had imposed upon himself following the 1868 election and revitalized the state Democratic organization into a medium for "educating" the public. Too many railroad-regulation bills were being introduced into the Nebraska legislature! Morton also saw a possibility of a presidential victory for Hancock and doubtless wanted to be in on the expected patronage barbecue. At the state convention Morton obtained the chairmanship of the Nebraska Democracy and wrote a platform attacking protective tariffs and endorsing sound currency.

His task in the ensuing campaign was not easy. He not only was forced to pay almost all the campaign expenses out of his own pocket, but also was constantly plagued with the chore of recruiting candidates to replace those who withdrew. One congressional candidate, Dr. R. R. Livingston, thought his services as head of the surgical department of the Union Pacific Railroad were too important to neglect for campaigning. "I know I ought to stick," he wrote, "but my obligation to the Co. . . . is such that I cannot. . . ." [11] Chairman Morton also let himself in for a lambasting from the enemy. When he came out in opposition to the further issuance of bond subsidies to railroads, the Nebraska City *Press* observed that it was like "Satan Rebuking Sin." [12]

[11] Olson, *Morton,* 252–60.
[12] Nebraska City *Press,* September 9, 1880, as cited *ibid.,* 258.

The Omaha *Bee* recalled Morton's earlier advocacy of issuing county bonds to subsidize railroad construction. The paper wondered "who is responsible for Mr. J. Sterling Morton's sudden conversion." [13] Perhaps this criticism came because Morton was interested in the railroads already in operation.

Voters could not be expected to forget Morton's long service as a paid public-relations servant of the railroads; for years he had been supplying newspapers all over the Middle West with prorailroad propaganda and making speeches in the same vein.[14] Back in 1874 he had informed readers that regulatory "Statute spawning" was an evil "equal to the grasshopper, weevil, chinchbug, and dry weather." He had pointed out that in Wisconsin, where the regulatory Potter law existed, "communism, of the legislative sort, is the most pronounced and athletic." Consequently, "No capital seeking investment looks over into Wisconsin. . . ." [15] The 1880 election outcome was a terrific drubbing for the Nebraska Democracy.

Two years later Morton exhibited still more energy in the state election. The antimonopolists were becoming very much of a nuisance. They had forced passage of a regulatory act, and now they were making a direct political bid through separate antimonopoly parties and using almost forgotten local Democratic organizations as steppingstones. Morton, along with Dr. George L. Miller, who had helped promote New York's Horatio Seymour for the presidential nomination in 1868, kept a tight lid on the state organization. Most of the delegates arrived at the state convention either on railroad passes or on greatly reduced fares, and they quickly nominated Morton for the governorship. He had already imported—at his own expense and with a railroad pass—Professor Perry of Williams College to aid in

[13] Omaha *Bee*, September 28, 1880, as cited *ibid.*
[14] Olson, *Morton*, 189-96.   [15] Chicago *Times*, November 27, 1874.

spreading the doctrine of free trade. Together Morton and Perry wrote the Democratic platform, based on the blessings of individualism and honest government spending. It attacked tariff legislation and liquor legislation as interferences with individualism and included no reference to railroads.

The ensuing campaign was marked by Morton's attacks on protective tariffs and railroad subsidies. He lambasted the Republican party for being a tool of the railroads, and at the same time he refused to admit the need of railroad-regulatory legislation. The outcome was the usual overwhelming election defeat for the state ticket. Local Democratic candidates had better luck, for twenty-three Democrats, along with a number of Antimonopolists, were elected to the state legislature. Combined, they could defeat the Republican choice in the ensuing United States senatorship contest. Morton entertained hopes of obtaining the post, but despite friendly communications from railroad interests, his ambition was not brought to fruition.[16] S. H. H. Clark, operating superintendent of the Union Pacific, informed an Omaha friend of Morton's that his railroad preferred Morton for the senatorship. Morton's friend reported that Clark was fully convinced "that the next administration would probably be Democratic and therefore a Democratic senator would be able to help them more than a Republican of equal ability (provided they had such to elect which he admitted they had not)." The only catch was that apparently "quite early in the campaign before present results were dreamed of he gave [governorship-aspirant] Jo Millard encouragement of assistance which perhaps he may feel bound to carry out." [17]

[16] Virginia Bowen Jones, "The Influence of the Railroads on Nebraska State Politics" (unpublished master's thesis, University of Nebraska, 1927), 13; Olson, *Morton*, 266–75.

[17] E. B. Chandler to J. Sterling Morton, December 15, 1882, as cited in Olson, *Morton*, 276.

As it finally turned out in the legislature, the senatorship went to Republican General Charles Manderson after considerable balloting, during which lobbyists circulated among the legislators; the Democrats scattered their votes. The legislators had decided that a Republican was more suitable than Morton.[18] They appreciated Morton's having originated Arbor Day but wished he would confine his public life to making speeches at tree-planting ceremonials.

Morton then turned, with crusader-like zeal, to advance the cause of free trade. He took an active and enthusiastic part in the Free Trade League and spent much time in Iowa converting Democrats to the cause. Early in 1884 he went to Washington as lobbyist for the Chicago, Burlington, and Quincy Railroad and there devoted his spare time to free-trade espousal. He picked Delaware's Senator Thomas F. Bayard as his presidential candidate because of Bayard's free-trade position. Senator Bayard called tariff protection "legislative communism."

Upon the nomination of Grover Cleveland, disgruntled Morton returned to Nebraska and bid again for the governorship. He campaigned under the auspices of one of those strange fusion tickets of Democrats and Antimonopolists. In the previous election the combined vote of those elements had been greater than the Republican total, and thus stimulus was given to the fusion idea. Morton's free-trade espousal had raised him in the estimation of some Antimonopolists. Although he continued frankly to oppose railroad-regulatory legislation, Antimonopolist political leaders accepted Morton and the Democracy as the only way to beat the Republicans. After an extremely vituperative campaign, Morton again lost to the Republicans. Many rank-and-file Antimonopolists had refused to vote for lobbyist Morton.[19]

[18] *Ibid.*, 276–81.   [19] *Ibid.*, 282–314.

The other especially conspicuous middle-western Bourbon, Wisconsin's William F. Vilas, preached and practiced individualism in a manner more smug than that of his Nebraska counterpart. He was more the lid-sitter, less the crusader! In oratory Vilas was flowery; Morton, impulsively direct. Although Vilas was more given to compromise than Morton, there was no mistaking his position. He would compromise with his wealthy friends who differed on the tariff question, but on no score would he sacrifice his position to compromise with the masses.

When Vilas was a young man just getting started as a lawyer, he had noticed the plight of the masses and had written in his diary that "man's inhumanity to man has made countless millions mourn." [20] Now, as a well-to-do railroad attorney, he saw less of the people and more of miraculous financial feats of individuals and the corporate system. At the 1881 Minnesota State Fair, he told an audience of farmers about his great hopes for the future. "Who forbids," said Vilas, "that electricity shall become a farm servant, and leave the noble horse for the enjoyment of the highway and the track." Regarding the farmer's current economic plight, lawyer-politico Vilas declared, "Demagogues love to thrum our eardrums with their clamor of the wrongs of agriculturist sufferers, and stir a spirit of unrest." He admitted that "corporate powers and corporate values have advanced with a more rapid step than the invention of our statesmen and law-makers," but his only suggestion for effecting a cure was patience. The corporation managers, argued Vilas, "dare not" make the railroad an enemy of the farmer. Moreover, Vilas would have disgruntled farmers pause and "reflect that a single invention—the steel rail—has reduced the freight tariff forty per centum." He thus would have everybody "trust somewhat to time and

[20] "Journal of Lake Superior Trip, August 13 to 27, 1873," in Vilas MSS.

FOUR ANTI-BOURBONS

Above, left: JOHN PETER ALTGELD (courtesy of Chicago Historical Society); *right:* WILLIAM JENNINGS BRYAN (courtesy of Nebraska Historical Society).
Below, left: HORACE BOIES (courtesy of Iowa State Department of History and Archives); *right:* IGNATIUS DONNELLY (courtesy of Minnesota Historical Society).

genius to relieve the inconveniences, and continue to enjoy its blessings with composure." [21]

Vilas put great trust in Providence, and divine aid did seem to net him handsome rewards in profits and influence. Providence helped a great deal in his lumbering operations, prompting him to explain in *Harper's* the working of the divine plan: "That no reproduction of the valuable pine takes place, a worthless species only springing up in its stead, seems a pregnant testimony that the purpose of this great provision was for temporary uses, more durable mineral material being substituted in after-developed prosperity. . . . Immense as is the annual consumption, many years will be required to exhaust the generous supply of nature." [22]

Vilas the politician would have the Democracy, as an agent of Providence, guard against interference with individual enterprise. Let business put its own house in order! Let the public confine its reforming activity to the public business of choosing governmental officials who were honest, efficient, and possessed of no heretical notions about government interference in private business.

What then would be the Democracy's political issues? Vilas was weary of the southern question, and in 1879 he announced through the Madison *Democrat* that the southern states "are states in the union, and if they cannot maintain their internal peace and law, let them suffer." [23] Administrative reform, on the other hand, had interested him since the heyday of Samuel J. Tilden. Vilas would throw dishonest and boorish rascals out of political offices. "Too often," said Vilas in 1875, "the unprincipled adventurer

[21] William F. Vilas, *Selected Addresses and Orations of William F. Vilas* (Madison, 1912), 114, 127–31.
[22] William F. Vilas, "The State of Wisconsin," *Harper's Magazine,* LXXXII (April, 1891), 688.
[23] Madison *Democrat,* June 22, 1879.

has secured possession of our seats of statesmanship, and un-bred upstarts have been upheaved from the social depths to become our rulers." He warned against voting for such persons, observing that "the minds of the People have become poisoned by these sudden and marvelous accessions to place, and accumulations of unearned wealth." [24]

In the eighties Vilas, like so many other patrons of the individualism precept, gave increased attention to tariff reform, along with his interest in administrative reform. He declared, "The Augean stables must be cleaned of long accumulated corruption, our public trusts set utterly above the reach of political beasts of prey, our trade made free of taxes which rob the general people, our commerce to ride the waves of every sea. . . ." [25]

Politician Vilas maneuvered shrewdly and cautiously within the Democratic hierarchy. His eloquent oratory brought him public attention far beyond the confines of Wisconsin. Thirty years afterward Mark Twain recalled Vilas' famous 1879 Chicago banquet toast to General Grant. "I can vividly see him," said Mark Twain, "as he stood upon a table, with his lips closing upon the last word of his magnificent speech, and his happy eyes looking out in contentment over a sea of applauding soldiers glimpsed through a frantic storm of waving napkins. . . ." [26] Vilas served with competence as temporary chairman of the 1880 national Democratic convention and thus won the favorable attention of many delegates and news reporters. [27] Soon many persons were suggesting him for the 1884 vice-presidential nomination, or for a cabinet post if the Democrats won. [28] In 1883 John O'Day, attorney for the St. Louis

[24] Vilas, *Selected Addresses,* 24.   [25] *Ibid.,* 147–48.

[26] Samuel L. Clemens to Mrs. William F. Vilas, October 13, 1909, in Vilas MSS. and also in Vilas, *Selected Addresses,* 83.

[27] *Official Proceedings of the National Democratic Convention, held in Cincinnati, June 22ᵈ, 23ᵈ, 24ᵗʰ, 1880* (Dayton, 1882), 7; Alexander M. Thomson, *A Political History of Wisconsin* (Milwaukee, 1902), 258.

[28] Moses M. Strong to William F. Vilas, September 20, 1882; W. E.

and San Francisco Railroad and also chairman of the Missouri state Democratic committee, was one of the many favoring Vilas for the vice-presidency. "I will see," he informed his fellow railroad attorney Vilas, "that the matter is kept before the public in . . . states traversed by our line of railroad. . . ." [29]

Vilas himself showed special interest in the eastern Bourbon friends whom he had made back in the 1876 convention that nominated Tilden. One that he did not overlook was New York's Daniel Manning, Bourbon bigwig lieutenant of Samuel J. Tilden.[30] In Wisconsin politics Vilas kept in the background, turning aside the suggestion that he accept the 1884 nomination for the governorship. His avowed reason, and one which some of his associates agreed was valid, was that as a railroad attorney he would have no chance of winning the election. Also, as J. Sterling Morton had discovered in Nebraska, railroad companies with which he was not connected were loath to support the attorney of a rival concern.[31] Wisconsin Bourbons believed that Vilas could be elected with the support of the St. Paul Railroad added to that of his own Northwest Railroad; but a friend of Vilas', after putting out a feeler, reported, "From what I have learned since I saw you I fear the St. Paul people will not give you . . . hearty support." [32] Vilas decided to continue his program of concentrating on the cultivation of New York Bourbons.

The active interest in tariff reform shown by Morton, Vilas, and many others was precipitated by more than mere intellectual theorizing and special-interests pressure. The

Todd to *id.*, November 25, 1882; G. A. Dickey to *id.*, May 30, 1883; and J. J. Stark (of La Cygne, Kansas) to *id.*, June 26, 1883, in Vilas MSS.

[29] John O'Day to *id.*, September 18, 1883; and *id.* to *id.*, September 24, 1883, *ibid.*

[30] Chicago *Chronicle*, July 8, 1895.

[31] George W. Bird to William F. Vilas, August 11, 1884, in Vilas MSS.; Cedarburg (Wis.) *News*, as cited in Madison *Democrat*, August 14, 1884.

[32] A. K. Delaney to William F. Vilas, August 25, 1884, in Vilas MSS.

tariff question was brought to a head by the hard times which settled upon the country in 1882–1883. These were acute enough to divert considerable public attention from the demand for administrative reform, despite the way in which the assassination of President Garfield dramatized the need for civil-service reform. The shooting of Garfield by a disappointed office seeker stirred the country to indignation at the current method of hiring nonelective government personnel, and Senator Pendleton's civil-service measure was enacted; but the commotion was not enough to still completely the clamor for economic reform.

In 1882 the business cycle was again carrying the national economy downward. The entire economic machinery seemed to be out of gear, as heavy gold exports contributed to raise the price level, as surpluses of goods caused unemployment and lower wages, and as farmers suffered the additional misfortune of widespread crop failures. At the same time surpluses were mounting in the federal treasury, largely because of revenue collected through duties on imports. Many people, including politicians in both parties, believed that lowering the tariff wall would cause money to flow into the stream of business instead of into the federal treasury. President Arthur took the initiative, and the first result was the creation of a tariff commission to conduct a "scientific" study of the situation and make recommendations.

Before the work was completed, the 1882 congressional elections brought a landslide victory to the Democrats. The voters showed that they were restless and angry because the Republicans had failed to prevent or alleviate the hard times and had sustained a grotesque patronage system that resulted in the assassination of a president. The election changed the Democrats' House minority of nineteen into a majority of seventy-seven.[33]

[33] Scott, "Political Career of William R. Morrison," loc. cit., 155; Josephson, Politicos, 325–26; O. M. Hall to Ignatius Donnelly, May 13, 1884, in Donnelly MSS.

Then followed an interval in which the Republican Lame-Duck Session tackled the tariff problem. Public clamor mounted; the Tariff League was active. Free-trader J. Sterling Morton became increasingly excited. Illinois congressmen received from a conclave of Illinois farmers a communication declaring "that this meeting of farmers . . . desire to join their voices with the common expression of all other classes in favor of relief from the excessive and inequitable burden of the present tariff." [34] In March, 1883, just before the Democratic majority took office, the Lame Duck Session passed the so-called "Mongrel Tariff." This measure had started on its legislative logrolling travels as a bill to revise the rates downward, but by the time it became law it was definitely high-protectionist.

Democratic tariff reformers thereupon redoubled their efforts to make their crusade an important issue in the 1884 presidential election. It was clear, however, that not all Democrats were for free trade or even for lower rates. Tariff-reformer Joseph Medill of the Chicago *Tribune* was among those skeptical over the possibility of the Democracy uniting on the issue. William F. Vilas tried to induce Medill to abandon the protectionist Republican party and join the Democracy, but the Chicagoan perceived "so many sheep in the Democratic flock astray on the free trade question that I hardly know which way it is tending. The next session of Congress may cast light on its position on the tariff question. I like to look before I leap." [35] Medill knew whereof he spoke, for that same month, May of 1884, eastern Democrats foiled Illinois' William R. Morrison in his attempt to push a moderate tariff-reform measure through the Democratic House. Forty-one Democrats, led by Pennsylvania's Samuel J. Randall, voted with the Republicans to defeat the measure.[36]

---

[34] Chicago *Tribune*, February 16, 1883.
[35] Joseph Medill to William F. Vilas, May 17, 1884, in Vilas MSS.
[36] Scott, "Political Career of William R. Morrison," *loc. cit.*, 157–58.

With "Randall and his Forty Thieves" aligned on the side of Republican protectionists, tariff reformers faced a stiff battle if they wanted to commit the national Democracy to their cause for the 1884 presidential campaign. Because this required a combined western-southern challenge to eastern Democratic leadership, Bourbons of the William F. Vilas type now had to show how determined they were to fight for a principle in the face of their eastern brethren's opposition. They did not choose to fight. A few free-trade apostles like J. Sterling Morton pleaded to make the cause a part of the campaign bid, but they confronted a stone wall of opposition. Vilas turned Morton's pleas aside,[37] and only a few Democrats participated in the movement to push Morrison for the presidential nomination.[38] Middle-western Bourbons bowed weakly to the New York Bourbon leadership.

Men like Vilas had slight chance of political advancement within their own states unless they became champions of the masses, and they therefore pinned their political hopes on the patronage which would be forthcoming if the eastern-led national Democracy captured the presidency. The New York Democracy was traditionally the chief post–Civil War spawning area of Democratic presidential nominees. Many middle-western Bourbons were impressed by the value of making concessions to New York's large and doubtful electoral vote. Individual Bourbons knew that if they did not co-operate with the New York leadership, they would be left out in the political cold in the event of a national victory, at which time the victorious Empire State Democracy would start distributing spoils to its hinterland colonials. The New York Democracy, whenever it had a plausible candidate for the presidency, was thus the best potential

[37] J. Sterling Morton to William F. Vilas, February 24, 1884; *id.* to *id.*, March 6, 1884; and William F. Vilas to J. Sterling Morton, March 22, 1884, in Vilas MSS.; Olson, *Morton*, 293–94.
[38] Nevins, *Cleveland*, 147, 151.

patronage band wagon. In 1868 there had been former Governor Horatio Seymour; in 1876 there had been Governor Samuel J. Tilden; and now there was Governor Grover Cleveland.

Most middle-western Bourbons could see no impelling reason to curry favor in their home states by insisting on tariff reform if they could get a slice of the national patronage melon by shouting the praises of eastern Bourbon Grover Cleveland; so many middle-western tariff-reformers and protectionists alike shoved the issue into the background and looked toward the eastern leaders. Along with the eastern leaders, the middle-western Bourbons cast an increasingly friendly eye toward Governor Cleveland—who said truthfully and frankly that he was ignorant on the tariff question.

Morton, one Bourbon still more devoted to his pet cause of free trade than to patronage, was unable to keep his Nebraska Bourbon associates in line. While Morton was in Washington, Dr. George L. Miller and James E. Boyd won Nebraska's convention delegates to the course of following New York's lead.[39] Nor was William R. Morrison able to dominate the scene in Illinois. Chicago's Mayor Carter H. Harrison, bowing to the wishes of Chicago industrial interests and defying Morrison, forced the state convention to side-step the tariff issue. Harrison won the gubernatorial nomination and went to the national convention as a Cleveland supporter.[40]

Grover Cleveland, aside from being an important figure in the politically strategic New York Democracy, possessed personal qualities that made him a good candidate for the Bourbons. He could be counted upon to hold the line while

[39] Olson, *Morton*, 294–95.
[40] Chicago *Tribune*, July 3, 1884; Bogart and Thompson, *Industrial State*, 146–47; Carter Henry Harrison, *Stormy Years, The Autobiography of Carter H. Harrison, Five Times Mayor of Chicago* (New York, 1935), 37.

individualism went rampantly forward within the existing framework. He had climbed the political ladder from a position as sheriff and later as mayor of Buffalo to that of governor of New York without raising an eyelash in the direction of regulatory legislation. His reputation as a political reformer fitted the current individualistic conception that any governmental change should be in the direction of administrative reform. He was honest, and he believed in honest administration.

The business world, as Tilden had discovered, was becoming more and more incensed at corrupt and inefficient government. An admixture of anger and moral indignation over the financial burden which such government entailed caused substantial and enlightened people to crusade for administrative reform. The stolid Cleveland had risen to prominence on the wave, fought Tammany, and at the same time made known his conviction that business should be well represented in the councils of government. Daniel Manning, the political lieutenant of Tilden, banker, newspaper-owner, and Democratic boss of Albany, was in the forefront of the movement which, in 1882, placed Cleveland in the governorship.

The new governor had a common-touch appeal to the voters, but he did not hesitate to veto a bill designed to lower the fare on the New York City elevated railroads. He said that the measure impaired the obligation of contract.[41] Nor did he neglect asking a banquet audience of the potent New York Chamber of Commerce whether enough care was being taken to send champions of this all-important interest to the legislature.[42] In January, 1884, a Bourbon lumber operator in Wisconsin observed that the laborers in his company opposed Cleveland because of his antilabor policy, and later he was overjoyed to discover that many Repub-

[41] Josephson, *Politicos*, 351–55.   [42] Nevins, *Cleveland*, 137.

lican businessmen approved the New York governor.[43] Indeed, Cleveland was a safe man for Bourbons everywhere.

At the national Democratic convention, over which Wisconsin's William F. Vilas ably presided, Boss Manning quickly achieved the nomination for Grover Cleveland. Second place on the ticket again went to Indiana's urbane Thomas A. Hendricks, who supposedly might carry his doubtful home state. Administrative reform was the keynote of the convention drive for Cleveland. Middle-western delegates not of the Bourbon clan were appealed to on the basis of Cleveland's onslaught upon the hated Tammany. A Wisconsin delegate, General E. S. Bragg, forgot his recent fight against the Bourbons on the currency issue as he saw the Cleveland forces whip the Tammany machine. The excited Bragg arose in the assemblage and dramatically proclaimed that the young men of Wisconsin "love Cleveland for his character, but they love him also for the enemies he has made." [44]

Certainly if the masses voted for the Democracy with enthusiasm, it would have to be because of hate for the Cleveland enemies of administrative reform, for the national platform turned out to be the usual collection of verbiage. Its tariff plank was a confusing wordage; each could interpret as he saw fit the endorsement of a "tariff for public purposes exclusively." [45]

The ensuing campaign was marked by considerable mudslinging and rumor-spreading regarding the public immorality of Republican candidate James G. Blaine and the private immorality of Cleveland. While Democrats reiterated the Mulligan Letters episode, which revealed the glamorous Blaine's pecuniary reward for obtaining a land grant for an

[43] John Knight to William F. Vilas, January 15, 1884; and *id.* to *id.*, July 13, 1884, in Vilas MSS.
[44] Plumb, *Badger Politics*, 74; Nevins, *Cleveland*, 153.
[45] Josephson, *Politicos*, 361.

Arkansas railroad, Republicans advertised the fact of bachelor Cleveland's illegitimate child.

All the while, both parties were obtaining huge sums to spend on the show. The flow of money into the respective party coffers revealed the high reputation of both parties in the business world. The usual interest in patronage motivated some individuals to contribute, and there was evidence that some corporations contributed to both parties to ensure friendship regardless of the winner. But consideration of the tariff question and administrative reform determined the direction in which considerable money flowed. Tariff reform was not an open issue in the campaign; but there was a widespread feeling that a Democratic victory might eventually result in lower tariffs and that a Republican triumph would ensure the protectionist *status quo*. Some merchants, the western railroad interests, and a few industrialists supported the Democracy. James J. Hill, St. Paul railroad magnate, began to take an active interest in Democratic politics. He inquired of corporation lawyer Samuel J. Tilden, "What about this man Cleveland?" Upon receiving Tilden's reply, "He is all right," Hill sent five thousand dollars to Daniel Manning and telegraphed his associates in the West to "get busy" for Cleveland.[46] Merchant Levi Leiter of Chicago contributed ten thousand dollars, and dry-goods prince Isidor Straus also rendered financial assistance. East-coast iron manufacturers Edward Cooper and Abram S. Hewitt swelled the Democratic fund with contributions totaling about seventy-five thousand dollars. Handicapped by the distances to the western ore fields and by the tariff on imported ore, these two eastern industrialists favored tariff reform and hence the Democracy. On the other hand, the Republicans were well supplied with funds.

[46] Joseph G. Pyle, *The Life of James J. Hill* (Garden City, 1917), I, 426; "Contributions to the Campaign Fund of the National Democratic Committee, 1884," a list dated February 5, 1885, in Grover Cleveland MSS., Library of Congress.

Eastern railroad operators such as William K. Vanderbilt and Jay Gould and eastern financiers and industrialists such as Andrew Carnegie and Stephen Elkins contributed heavily to the Republicans.[47]

The Democracy profited from the business world's interest in administrative reform. Many entrepreneurs were weary of the scandalous reputations which many of their clan had received through such exposures as the Mulligan Letters, and they were weary of the financial burden entailed in deals with politicians. An ethical code was gradually taking shape within the business realm, and James G. Blaine represented the shameful past. The New York *World* reported that "representatives of four large firms in New York" had told solicitors of funds for the Republican campaign that "they couldn't stand Blaine" and had therefore each given five thousand dollars to the Democrats.[48] The Republican boss of Iowa later declared that "it was Republican business men voting against their party who defeated it in New York, Connecticut, and New Jersey."[49]

The expenditures of effort and money were, as usual, greatest in doubtful states like Indiana and New York, but the normally Republican, agrarian Middle West was also well sprinkled with money and insatiable party workers.[50] An Illinois Democratic campaign manager, editor H. A. Clendenin, later said: "The most trouble I had was to keep the Democratic ward heelers of Chicago under control. They were demanding more money than it was possible to give them."[51]

[47] Robert McElroy, *Grover Cleveland, The Man and the Statesman* (New York, 1923), I, 98; William C. Hudson, *Random Recollections of an Old Political Reporter* (New York, 1911), 241; Josephson, *Politicos*, 362–64.

[48] New York *World*, October 2, 1884, as cited in Josephson, *Politicos*, 372.

[49] *Nation*, XLVII (July 26, 1888), as cited *ibid.*

[50] Thomas A. Hendricks to William F. Vilas, October 8, 1884, in Vilas MSS.

[51] Clendenin, *Autobiography*, 169.

In northern Wisconsin a Democratic candidate for the legislature, John H. Knight, noted great Republican activity in his county. Reporting optimistically to his business associate, William F. Vilas, candidate Knight at first felt that his Superior Lumber Company "alone can change one hundred and fifty Republican votes." Later he discovered that the Republican zeal was too much for him. In commenting on his defeat Knight emphasized the effect of having many new settlers in the country—the population having jumped from eight thousand to twenty-five thousand during the preceding three years. Knight said that "the Land Department at Washington sent a man by the name of Samuel Lee, who spent three weeks" looking after "every pre-emption and homesteader, and threatening them with the loss of their lands unless they voted the straight Republican ticket." On election day the Republicans "had two men at the polls in Ashland all day from somewhere—evidently shoulder hitters and experienced manipulators of elections." These men shepherded the voters to the polls in squads, "principally Swedes and Norwegians, thirty and forty in numbers and voted them solid." Knight had never seen "such a spectacle." [52]

The majority of middle-western voters found nothing in the campaign of sufficient interest to jar them from their traditional Republican allegiance. A few campaigners, like William F. Vilas, talked long and hard on tariff reform,[53] but voters interested in that movement could find no hope for action in the Democratic platform or ticket. Nor did many voters like the free-trade notion expounded by overzealous theoretical crusaders. Farmers and laborers could be sold on moderate tariff reductions, but they had a horror of free-trade competition with peasant farmers and low-wage laborers of Europe. In the eyes of many, men like

[52] Knight to William F. Vilas, August 20, 1884; and *id.* to *id.*, November 6, 1884, in Vilas MSS.

[53] Madison *Democrat*, September 19, 1884.

J. Sterling Morton were overdoing a good thing and turning the Democracy into a dangerous nest of visionaries.
Most campaigners of both parties chose to steer clear of
the widely misunderstood and prejudice-ridden tariff question. Most of them lacked the type of patience and ability
exhibited by William R. Morrison in his extended educating
of constituents in his Illinois congressional district.

Disillusioned Henry Adams, writing to an English friend,
said:

"We are plunged in politics funnier than words can ex-
press. Very great issues are involved. Especially everyone
knows that a step towards free trade is inevitable if the
Democrats come in. For the first time in twenty-eight years,
a Democratic administration is almost inevitable. The public
is angry and abusive. Everyone takes part. We are all doing
our best, and swearing at each other like demons. But the
amusing thing is that no one talks about real interests. By
common consent they agree to let this alone. We are afraid
to discuss them. Instead of this the press is engaged in a
most amusing dispute whether Mr. Cleveland had an illegitimate child, and did or did not live with more than one
mistress, whether Mr. Blaine got paid in railway bonds for
his services as Speaker. . . . I have laughed myself red with
amusement over the letters, affidavits, leading articles and
speeches which are flying through the air. Society is torn
to pieces. . . . Yet when I am not angry, I can do nothing
but laugh." [54]

In the Middle West party fealty carried the day for
Blaine; in the South it carried the day for Cleveland; in the
East the vote was divided. Cleveland, apparently largely
through the "Rum, Romanism, and Rebellion" label attached to Blaine, carried New York and hence obtained
the victory in the final count. By a national plurality of but

[54] Henry Adams to C. M. Gaskell, September 21, 1884, as cited in
Worthington C. Ford (ed.), *The Letters of Henry Adams, 1858–1891*
(Boston, 1930), 360.

twenty-three thousand votes, the Bourbons at last established a candidate in the White House.

In the Middle West the economic front remained in its
pre-election doldrums. One farmers' leader, writing to
Ignatius Donnelly, said: "Cleveland is elected . . . yet I
do not look for much relief for the masses, for the same
monopolies that run the Republican party run the Democratic party." [55]

[55] J. E. Fullerton to Ignatius Donnelly, November 27, 1884, in Donnelly MSS.

Chapter Nine

Serving God, Big Business, and the Democratic Party 1885-1888

> *In a change of government, the poor seldom change anything except the name of their master.*
>
> —PHAEDRUS

DURING THE first Cleveland administration the nation gestured toward the application of nineteenth-century liberalism. President Cleveland strove to prevent dishonest and extravagant spending of the people's tax contributions and to protect the citizenry against legislative interference with individual efforts. Cleveland's approach constituted a more consistent attempt to follow individualism than had that of his Republican predecessors, for he eventually came to believe that no government action should deliberately provide special economic privileges to any group. Big business, according to Cleveland, should not have the special governmental aid of a high protective tariff. All pursuers of profit were to stand on their own— free to suffer or prosper within the sacred framework of laissez-faire economics.

To ensure the continuance of the twin dogmas of honest government and laissez-faire economic life, and to fortify his own position, President Cleveland relied upon political organization. The Cleveland era was thus dedicated to honesty, *laissez faire*, individualism, and Democratic politics;

in practice it consituted an effort to serve God, big business, and the Democratic party. For the masses the result was unhappy. Honesty—the Cleveland conception of godliness in government—was a narrow and negative medium for ensuring the equality of man. Nor was this limited concept of the millennium conspicuous in the actual administration; it was greatly overshadowed by service to big business and the Democracy. It was inconceivable that the little man would be joyous over governmental indifference to exploitation by corporate interests. The Middle West had long been in colonial subservience to those interests, and in such it continued.

The Cleveland administration found it conveniently easy to serve both the Democratic party and big business, using the patronage as a major link between these two institutional interests. Upon the accession of Cleveland to the presidency there was already at hand a well-prepared list of Democratic office seekers who could be counted upon to be loyal both to the Bourbon Democracy and to big business. This list was assembled by, and carried in the memory of, New York's wealthy and shrewd Daniel Manning. Ever since the Samuel J. Tilden presidential sortie Boss Manning had been perfecting a nationwide network of loyal political associates. With the rise of the Grover Cleveland star Manning simply transferred his entourage to the front man. President Cleveland had that list and of course combined it with the one taking shape in his own mind. Sifting the collection of names, Cleveland was careful to eliminate anyone whose reputation was tainted with unlawfulness. His really sincere devotion to honest government precluded the admission of known grafters to the party's inner circle. He also carefully considered all aspirants in the light of their political value to the party, for as a practical politician he did not intend to discard the party fence just because it contained rotten rails like the Tammany leaders. He was, observers concluded, trying to serve God while serving his political and business friends.

President Cleveland's over-all blueprint for political fence building consisted of patronage dispensation along regional lines and therefore called for regional representation on his cabinet. The middle-western Democracy was slated for a cabinet post. The choice fell to railroad attorney William F. Vilas of Wisconsin, and the position was the patronage-dispensing postmaster-generalship. Ever since the Tilden campaign Vilas had been in close relationship with the Empire State Democratic leaders; and at the same time he had built up a widely recognized reputation as an attorney, an eloquent political orator, and an alertly intelligent parliamentarian. As permanent chairman of the 1884 national convention, he had greatly enhanced his reputation,[1] and Thomas H. Hendricks was moved to remark that Vilas should have been selected as second on the ticket instead of himself.[2] The Cincinnati *Commercial Gazette*, in reporting Vilas' keynote speech, noted that "he made such an impression some newspapers claimed that if the convention had grown tired" he would have been the presidential nominee.[3] As chairman of the committee appointed to officially notify the New York governor of his nomination, Vilas made a very favorable impression on Cleveland.[4]

Following the election there was much political specula-

[1] Omaha *Herald*, July 10, 1884, and Chicago *Chronicle*, July 8, 1895, in "Scrapbook of William F. Vilas," Library of the State Historical Society of Wisconsin; Milwaukee *Sentinel*, January 1, 1885; Madison *Democrat*, July 10, 1884; New York *Herald*, July 10, 1884; Ignatius Donnelly and Minnesota Democratic congressmen to Grover Cleveland, November 27, 1884, in Donnelly MSS.; Henry Vilas to William F. Vilas, July 14, 1884; Thomson to *id.*, July 13, 1884; John C. Spooner to *id.*, July 14, 1884; and Melvin McCohen to *id.*, July 14, 1884, in Vilas MSS.

[2] Alexander Barclay to William F. Vilas, February 24, 1885; and Charles H. Vilas to *id.*, July 13, 1884, in Vilas MSS.

[3] Cincinnati *Commercial Gazette*, as cited in Milwaukee *Sentinel*, January 1, 1885.

[4] George Frederick Parker, *Recollections of Grover Cleveland* (New York, 1909), 80; Nevins, *Cleveland*, 196.

tion and wirepulling before President-elect Cleveland designated Vilas as the middle-western regional boss. Vilas made
no open gestures of soliciting a cabinet post, but "band-
wagon jumpers" and friends kept him well informed on
developments.[5] One revealing bit of information reaching
Vilas was an account of Iowa's National Committeeman M.
M. Ham's visit with President-elect Cleveland. Vilas was
informed, indirectly, that after a desultory discussion of a
general nature, Cleveland asked the Iowan for information on Vilas. "He is generally popular everywhere," Ham
reportedly announced, "and particularly with the best element. . . ." As a high-ranking lawyer Vilas had "charge
in Wisconsin of the interests of the great Northwestern
Railroad Company." Ham added, "Of course there is a small
granger element still existing in the west which always op-
poses an officer of a corporation for any position, but it has
little weight or influence now, is not much considered in
our politics and ought not to be." Cleveland brushed the
Granger factor aside, remarking that Vilas' railroad connections were "simply a matter of business." It is the duty
of an attorney, continued Cleveland, "to seek the best
clients and remain faithful to them, and use all honorable
means to enhance his emoluments and increase his experience
and his fame in the profession to which he devotes the best
years of his life. I have noticed that great corporations always secure if possible the best legal talent to protect their
interests and in this they show much shrewdness and economy." [6]

[5] Ignatius Donnelly (Minnesota) to William F. Vilas, November 19,
1884; *id.* to *id.*, December 13, 1884; J. C. Black (Illinois) to *id.*, January
6, 1885; P. H. Kelly (Minnesota) to *id.*, December 30, 1884; B. G. Caul-
field (Dakota Territory) to *id.*, January 30, 1885; Doolittle (Wisconsin)
to *id.*, January 30, 1885; J. Sterling Morton (Nebraska) to *id.*, January
30, 1885; M. M. Ham (Iowa) to *id.*, January 31, 1885; L. M. Fay (Oregon)
to *id.* (telegram), February 16, 1885; Barclay (Minnesota) to *id.*, February 20, 1885; and *id.* to *id.*, February 24, 1885, in Vilas MSS.; Madison
Democrat, December 13, 1884, January 30, February 3, 7, 21, 24, 1885.

[6] J. F. Bates (of Iowa, reporting on Ham's conversation with Cleveland)
to William F. Vilas, January 29, 1885, in Vilas MSS.

An Ohioan informed Cleveland that he found "that among the staunch business men, Merchants and Manufacturers alike, there is a very strong desire that Col. William F. Vilas be tendered a Cabinet position."[7]

No other middle-western Democrat possessed enough prominence to outweigh the qualifications of Vilas. Nebraska's Dr. George L. Miller, however, had the temerity to make a bid for a cabinet position. Unlike his fellow Nebraskan J. Sterling Morton, with whom he was currently at odds, Dr. Miller had for several years followed the lead of the New York Democracy. In 1868 he had served as a leading preconvention promoter for New York's Horatio Seymour; in 1876 he had done the same for New York's Samuel J. Tilden; and in 1884 he had been one of the first on the band wagon of New York's Grover Cleveland. Now he was out to collect his reward—and even made an eastbound trip to talk with Daniel Manning and other eastern Bourbons.[8] Meanwhile, however, his old associate J. Sterling Morton, whose lack of enthusiasm for Cleveland had been too pronounced for him to entertain hopes of a cabinet post for himself, announced his preference for Wisconsin's Vilas.[9]

Another cabinet possibility was Alexander Mitchell, who earlier had been a bulwark of strength in keeping the Wisconsin Bourbon Democracy from being overwhelmed by the Granger and Greenbacker scourges. New Yorker John Livingston, president of the Railway Shareholders Association, in urging Cleveland to select this Wisconsin tycoon, pointed out that Mitchell was "president of the Milwaukee

[7] James Reynolds to Grover Cleveland, February 13, 1885, in Grover Cleveland MSS.

[8] Bates to William F. Vilas, January 29, 1884; Ham to id., January 3, 1885; and Kelly to id., December 30, 1884, in Vilas MSS.; Mrs. K. Donnelly to Ignatius Donnelly, March 13, 1885, in Donnelly MSS.; Madison Democrat, February 24, 1885; Olson, Morton, 317–19.

[9] Clipping from Cheyenne (Wyo.) Democratic Leader, February 22, 1885, and A. C. Campbell to Cleveland, February 23, 1885, in Cleveland MSS.; J. Sterling Morton to William F. Vilas, January 30, 1885, in Vilas MSS.; Olson, Morton, 318.

and St. Paul—the largest Railway System in the United States. . . . He is the greatest man, and the ablest and wealthiest, west of the Alleghany range." The president of the Honest Money League of the Northwest, George W. Allen, wrote to Cleveland from Milwaukee that Mitchell was "a very able, safe, conservative man—known as such at the East as well as the West." Most Bourbons, however, recognized that the mantle of the Wisconsin Bourbon leadership now belonged to the younger William F. Vilas.[10]

Upon being ensconced in the cabinet, Postmaster General Vilas immediately tackled the prodigious task of sprinkling the nation with Democratic postmasters and operating his department as much like an efficient business concern as political conditions afforded. A New York *Herald* writer characterized him as "a western man," and said that "in the quaint vernacular of his section he is known as a 'hustler.' " [11] Vilas received hearty co-operation from the President and, in fact, became Cleveland's most favored personal friend on the cabinet. This co-operation was nevertheless somewhat of a handicap at times, for President Cleveland had the unexecutive habit of personally going over with Vilas stacks of applications even for minor posts.[12] Nonetheless, a great number of appointments rapidly came out of the mill. Cleveland had promised to replace officeholders upon expiration of their four-year terms, which would mean a house cleaning of the Republican incumbents before the President's term expired. The process was hastened by Vilas' policy of firing many Republicans before they had served four years, because they had shown "offensive partisanship." Thus ensued a job turnover at a rate which seemed slow only to patronage-starved Democrats.[13]

[10] John Livingston to Cleveland, January 3, 1885; and George W. Allen to *id.*, February 4, 1885, in Cleveland MSS.
[11] New York *Herald*, September 10, 1888. See also New York *Times*, as cited in Madison *Democrat*, February 28, 1889.
[12] Nevins, *Cleveland*, 196–97, 314–15.
[13] Josephson, *Politicos*, 380. See also William F. Vilas to Daniel Lamont,

In perfecting his patronage organization Vilas did not forget his and the Bourbon Democracy's admiration for big business. He was particularly solicitous of the railroad interests. In the middle-western Democracy, railroad officials and friends of the railroads possessed a priority on favors.[14] Railroad interests were not reluctant to ask, and Vilas was not reluctant to give. Even before Vilas was chosen for the cabinet, he received a request from W. P. Clough, St. Paul counsel for the Northern Pacific Railroad. Lawyer Clough asked his fellow railroad attorney to favor the "officers of the Company" by exerting his "influence to prevent the removal of Mr. N. H. Owens, Secretary of the Washington Territory." Owens was but recently appointed, and the Northern Pacific people did not wish him removed "prior to the expiration of his term." [15]

Railroad lobbyist J. Sterling Morton, despite his pre-election coldness toward Cleveland, managed to obtain some postmasterships for friends. This was accomplished while Morton was in Washington working against the congressional moves toward interstate-commerce regulation. Employing him was the Chicago, Burlington, and Quincy Railroad. Morton's rival for Nebraska patronage,[16] Dr. George L. Miller, also obtained some appointments for friends. Miller was not without railroad connections; otherwise he would not have paid a visit to Jay Gould in the fall of 1886. The Omaha *Bee* assumed that the prime object of the conversation was to plan the defeat of the antimonopolist Republican, Senator Charles H. Van Wyck.[17]

March 21, 1885; Lamont to William F. Vilas, April 2, 1885; and William F. Vilas to O. D. Conger, February 6, 1886, in Cleveland MSS.

[14] Josephson, *Politicos,* 380.

[15] Clough to William F. Vilas, February 14, 1885, in Vilas MSS.

[16] George L. Miller to Lamont, April 5, 1885; and *id.* to *id.,* March 24, 1887, in Cleveland MSS.

[17] Olson, *Morton,* 325–28; Marie U. Harmer and James L. Sellers, "Charles H. Van Wyck—Soldier and Statesman," *Nebraska History Magazine,* XII (October–December, 1929), 342; Omaha *Bee,* October 14, 1886, as cited *ibid.*

A flagrant example of Bourbon Democratic machinations was the patronage support granted a railroad–city machine combination in Minnesota. Directing the railroad-political combination was the Kelly-Doran-Hill triumvirate. Irish-born Patrick H. Kelly was a St. Paul wholesale grocer who became a Democratic national committeeman. Irish-born Michael Doran was a St. Paul banker and a well-known political manipulator. Neither Kelly nor Doran could claim great popularity with the electorate, for Kelly had never held an elective office, while Doran could boast only of his brief 1875–1879 service in the state senate.[18] James J. Hill, third member of the triumvirate, was a St. Paul railroad tycoon who was then in the process of combining old and building new railroad lines into the gigantic system that was to become the Great Northern Railroad. "Empire Builder" Hill, as this dynamo of railroad promotion came to be known, had jumped abruptly upon the Cleveland band wagon when it appeared that the Democratic nominee was headed for the White House. Assurance from Samuel J. Tilden that Cleveland was "all right" resulted in Jim Hill's contributing five thousand dollars to the campaign and ordering his railroad subordinates to "get busy." [19] With victory, Hill proceeded, and continued for many years, to use his position to advise Cleveland on matters of policy and patronage. Routine matters of organization and appointments were left to Kelly and Doran, but Hill exerted his influence and tendered advice and information whenever it struck his fancy to do so.[20]

[18] Kelly to William F. Vilas, December 30, 1884; and Alexander Barclay (Kelly's secretary) to *id.*, February 3, 1885, in Vilas MSS.; Martin W. Odland, *The Life of Knute Nelson* (Minneapolis, 1926), 82; *Minnesota Biographies* (*Collections of Minnesota Historical Society*, Vol. XIV [St. Paul, 1912]), 183, 395; Madison *Democrat*, February 3, 1885.

[19] Pyle, *Hill*, I, 426; Josephson, *Politicos*, 362–63, 380; "Contributions to the Campaign Fund of the National Democratic Committee, 1884," a list dated February 5, 1885, in Cleveland MSS.

[20] James J. Hill to Kelly and Michael Doran, August 1, 1885; *id.* to

Some Minnesota Democratic leaders had great difficulty in believing that Kelly and Doran were on the inside track in patronage dispensation. This was doubtless due to the situation of Kelly and Doran's lack of any marked prestige in the party and the public's initial unawareness of either the five thousand dollars contributed by Kelly to the national Democratic committee campaign fund in 1884 [21] or the behind-the-scenes activity of Jim Hill. Two months after the Cleveland administration took office, a prominent Minneapolis lawyer and Democratic leader, E. M. Wilson, said that "Mr. Kelly by his boasting of supreme intimacy with Secretary Vilas, and his statement that he has received a letter from one member of the Cabinet approving the 'boss plan,' has led many Democrats who do not know Mr. Vilas to wonder if he can be so poor a politician and so bad a judge of human nature." [22]

Ignatius Donnelly and his friends realized that the triumvirate had influence in Washington, but most of these anti-monopolists were slow to realize that the Kelly-Doran-Hill trio had a monopoly on Minnesota patronage. Ignatius Donnelly discovered the bitter truth when soliciting jobs for himself and his friends. The Sage of Nininger had taken an active part in the 1884 election, after having sat out the 1882 campaign. In 1882 he had refused to run for Congress on the Democratic slate. "Count me out," he had said. "While I was converting Republicans," other Republicans would be "buying up the Democrats." [23] In the Cleveland campaign Donnelly was the Democratic nominee for Congress in his district and received much more than the usual minority

---

Cleveland, July 7, 188[6?]; *id.* to Lamont, May 5, 1888; and many letters during Cleveland's second administration, in Cleveland MSS.

[21] "Contributions to the Campaign Fund of the National Democratic Committee, 1884," a list dated February 5, 1885, *ibid.*

[22] E. M. Wilson to Ignatius Donnelly, April 23, 1885; and *id.* to *id.*, May 8, 1885, in Donnelly MSS.

[23] Ignatius Donnelly to J. M. Bowler, August 17, 1882, *ibid.*

vote. Thereupon he exerted considerable effort in the drive
to obtain a cabinet position for Vilas, following which he
made a job-seeking visit to Washington.[24] Mrs. Donnelly
was somewhat discouraged over his prospects, telling her
optimistic husband, "It looks to me as if there is always to be
a railroad or millers ring in some shape standing in the way
and choking you off." [25] Others were more hopeful, even
to the extent of contributing money to help pay the Sage's
Washington expenses—for he was going there partly to secure positions for them.[26] In Washington he found Postmaster General Vilas very friendly and was entertained at
his home. Mrs. Donnelly received optimistic reports from
her husband and in reply expressed the hope that he wore
his "dress suit for dinner" when a guest of the elegant
Vilas.[27] Despite the optimism exuded by Donnelly as a result of his "relations with Mr. Vilas," [28] the Sage of Nininger and his friends received nothing.

For a time Donnelly even entertained the hope of aid
from Kelly, asking him for a supporting letter to Secretary
of the Interior L. Q. C. Lamar. To this request Kelly expressed regret that he could not comply. "Having consulted with the leading Democrats of our state," wrote
Kelly, "I find that your appointment as Surveyor General
would bring about more disaffection and trouble than I care
to encounter." But he did offer to assist in obtaining for
Donnelly a mission abroad. With a red pencil Donnelly

[24] Id. and Minnesota Democratic congressmen to Cleveland, November
27, 1884; Mrs. K. Donnelly to Ignatius Donnelly, November 8, 1884; William F. Vilas to id., November 22, 1884; id. to id., December 13, 1884; and
id. to id., May 14, 1885, ibid.; Ignatius Donnelly to William F. Vilas, November 19, 1884, in Vilas MSS.

[25] Mrs. K. Donnelly to Ignatius Donnelly, March 11, 1885, in Donnelly
MSS.

[26] Ignatius Donnelly to G. E. McAllister, March 16, 1885; W. P. Chris-
tensen to Ignatius Donnelly, March 23, 1885; and P. H. Rahilly to id.,
May 8, 1885, ibid.; St. Paul Pioneer Press, May 17, 1885.

[27] Mrs. K. Donnelly to Ignatius Donnelly, March 14, 1885, in Donnelly
MSS.

[28] Ignatius Donnelly to McAllister, March 16, 1885, ibid.

scrawled at the end of Kelly's letter, "How can a man be worthy of a mission abroad and not worthy of a little place at home?" And he sent the communication on to President Cleveland.[29]

The triumvirate continued on its merry way.[30] Although in the spring campaign for the St. Paul mayoralty it failed to prevent the nomination of Edmund Rice, it did act soon enough to defeat in the final election this "uncontrolled" enemy of its special railroad interests.[31] General R. W. Johnson of St. Paul wondered "what sort of a Democrat" Pat Kelly was, who voted "against the nominees of his party." [32] H. H. Fuller, St. Paul alderman, called a mass meeting to promote the ousting of Kelly from power. Fuller had the backing of Mayor Albert A. Ames of Minneapolis, but Kelly's control of patronage continued.[33] The St. Paul *Pioneer Press* announced that W. M. Campbell of the "Kelly-Doran crowd" had left for Washington to get a "United States Marshalship, and ruin Donnelly in patronage disposal." [34] Lawyer J. J. Thornton said that job-seeking Campbell "is a lobbyist of Jim Hill, and a pliant tool of Kelly and Doran." The disgusted Thornton added, "A protest of twenty thousand people in southwestern Minnesota could be obtained against Campbell on account of grossly deceiving the people in selling out to Jim Hill the charter to the St. Cloud, Austin and Mankato Railroad, for which it is said he received $7,000." Previously, a citizens' protest from that area had kept "Governor Hubbard from appointing him Railroad Commissioner." [35]

Ignatius Donnelly could do nothing to sever the Kelly-Doran-Hill patronage pipeline from Washington. In the

[29] Kelly to Ignatius Donnelly, April 2, 1885, in Cleveland MSS.
[30] Rahilly to *id.*, April 30, 1885, in Donnelly MSS.
[31] Ignatius Donnelly, Jr., to *id.*, April 25, 1885, *ibid.*
[32] General R. W. Johnson to *id.*, April 25, 1885, *ibid.*
[33] H. H. Fuller to *id.*, June 15, 1885; and *id.* to *id.*, June 25, 1885, *ibid.*
[34] St. Paul *Pioneer Press*, May 17, 1885.
[35] J. J. Thornton to Ignatius Donnelly, May 19, 1885, in Donnelly MSS.

fall of 1885 he protested directly to President Cleveland, writing that the Minnesota Democracy "is going to the devil . . . with P. H. Kelly at its head," for the party could not poll 75 per cent of the vote it received the preceding fall. "Our people do not altogether blame you," he informed Cleveland, "for they know you rebuked Kelly for advertising for office-seekers last spring." Nevertheless, "good Democrats like Judge Flandrau, H. H. Sibley, General R. W. Johnson, O. C. Merriam and E. M. Wilson are ignored." [36] All was without avail, and soon the antimonopolists of Minnesota were pushing an incipient third-party movement and co-operating with the more friendly Republicans. It was a matter of supporting the bad against the worse, for as one Minnesota agrarian leader remarked, "The millers ring runs the Republican party and the railroad ring runs the Democratic party." [37] And P. H. Kelly in 1887 made plans to send President Cleveland a wedding present consisting of two musk-ox robes. [38]

Although there was no room in the Minnesota Democracy for serious and determined enemies of the monopolists, there remained opportunity for demagogues. This was made clear in the 1886 election when Mayor Albert A. Ames of Minneapolis captured the governorship nomination. Ames was a demagogue of the first rank. He had the bearing and the personality of a good vote catcher, having a commanding soldierly figure—tall and erect—and eyes that drew people to him. He possessed considerable cordiality, generosity, and loyalty, but he was extremely vain, a poor judge

[36] Ignatius Donnelly to Cleveland, October 21, 1885, *ibid*. See also Kelly and Doran to *id*., August 1, 1885; Ignatius Donnelly to *id*., May 1, 1885; *id*. to *id*., November 3, 1885; *id*. to *id*., December 3, 1885; newspaper clippings dated April 24 and November 21, 1885; C. H. Chadbourne to Ignatius Donnelly, April 21, 1885; and Mrs. J. N. Castle to John R. Fellows, October 18, 1886, in Cleveland MSS.

[37] C. Canning to Ignatius Donnelly, September 11, 1886, in Donnelly MSS.

[38] Kelly to Lamont, July 1, 1887, in Daniel Lamont MSS., Library of Congress.

of men, and weak in self-control, especially when near a bottle of spirits. Three times he had been elected mayor of Minneapolis, twice as a Republican and the last time as a Democrat; but during his third term, this genial doctor had become deeply involved in corrupt practices. In 1886, largely through the aid of old soldier friends, he obtained the Democratic nomination for governor. His campaigning was marked by travel over the state in a special train and boasts to audiences of his poverty. To emphasize his identity with the common people, he boasted of being in debt and reiterated that he was "a ring-buster, not a ring-maker." There were almost enough voters disgusted with the Republicans or convinced of Ames's superiority to bring him victory in the election. The returns brought victory to the Republican opponent by a mere 2,397 votes, and there was considerable justification in the charge that Ames was cheated out of the office by corruption in the balloting. But not even masterful demagoguery was able to unseat the masterful monopolists.[39]

Throughout the Middle West railroad interests or wealthy Bourbons friendly to railroads controlled the patronage. It was not everywhere so openly obvious and direct as in Minnesota, because opponents elsewhere could be spanked more quietly than Ignatius Donnelly and his embattled farmers. In Iowa, where National Committeeman M. M. Ham could feel elated over backing William F. Vilas for a cabinet post, the Democracy was temporarily able to fix voter attention on the liquor question.[40] Not until the next presidential election did it become obvious in Iowa that railroad influence was greater in the Democracy than

[39] Zink, *City Bosses*, 336–42; A. A. Ames to Ignatius Donnelly, October 25, 1882, in Donnelly MSS.

[40] Cyrenus Cole, *I Remember, I Remember, A Book of Recollections* (Iowa City, 1936), 115–17; Herman Clarence Nixon, "The Populist Movement in Iowa," *Iowa Journal of History and Politics*, XXIV (January, 1926), 27–28.

in the Republican camp. In Nebraska there was no hiding the fact that railroad interests were turning more and more to the Democrats to rescue them from antimonopolist Charles Van Wyck, Republican United States senator.[41] In Wisconsin the Democracy was securely held in the palm of William F. Vilas.[42]

It was President Cleveland's dictum that "public officials are trustees of the people," and the situation in Illinois now illustrated what the Democracy considered "the people." It was, as elsewhere, "the right people." In accordance with the prevailing urban-middle-class view, President Cleveland was correctly incensed over the plundering activities of city political machines. With less claim to enlightenment he was anxious to replace the rapacious Tammany type of leaders with substantial citizens who did not raise questions about the evils inherent in the "lawful" means that sustained the "right people" class. Change rulers, yes; change the law, no!

In Illinois the Cleveland reform crusade centered on the thrice-elected mayor of Chicago, Carter H. Harrison. Democrat Harrison had plugged hard for the nomination and election of Cleveland. At the national convention he was accused, but he publicly denied the charge, of packing the galleries for Cleveland. He also responded to the Cleveland managers' request that as a good Catholic he address the delegates, with a denial of Tammany hints that the New York governor was anti-Catholic. In the election Harrison was re-elected mayor with a vote much larger than Cleveland's Chicago vote, but the ensuing events on the federal-patronage front were not so pleasing for the Chicagoan. Although Mayor Harrison was a magnetic figure, a graduate of Yale, and a widely traveled and well-read man, Presi-

[41] Harmer and Sellers, "Van Wyck," loc. cit., 342; Olson, Morton, 326.
[42] W. H. Foster to Ellis B. Usher, August 29, 1885; and E. C. Wall to id., May 12, 1888, in E. B. Usher MSS., Library of the State Historical Society of Wisconsin; Milwaukee Sentinel, March 25 and April 13, 1893.

dent Cleveland would have none of him. The fact that the
mayor was a political-machine boss and a demagogue with
a large popular following in the lower element was enough
to persuade honest President Cleveland against embracing
Carter Harrison. Cleveland did not turn matters over to
Illinois congressman and tariff-reformer William R. Morrison, who had a large following in the state; he turned instead to the so-called "silk-stocking" Bourbons of Chicago.
Railroad attorney William C. Goudy was in the favored
group, as were wealthy Bourbons like Erskine M. Phelps
and S. C. Judd.[43]

Most politically influential in the Chicago Bourbon group
was attorney Melville W. Fuller. For a long time urbane
Fuller, along with his bank president father-in-law, W. F.
Coolbaugh, had been active in Illinois politics. Fuller, like
many Bourbons of the Middle West, had never sought an
elective office. He was too busy with his lucrative law practice of about thirty thousand dollars a year. President Cleveland offered him various positions, including a place on the
Civil Service Commission, but not for some time did he accept anything beyond helping with the patronage chore.
Then, in 1888, Fuller obtained the enviable plum of chief
justice of the United States Supreme Court. It was a great
victory for the entire Bourbon cause, for the new chief
justice could be relied upon. Fuller, according to the Philadelphia *Press*, was the most obscure man ever appointed
chief justice.[44] He was emphatically conservative in outlook. On the bench he could always be counted on to protect property interests and the sanctity of contracts, and to
oppose strict regulation of corporations—and he was destined to be chief justice for twenty-two years.

The Cleveland administration's desire to keep on friendly

[43] Harrison, *Stormy Years*, 37; Nevins, *Cleveland*, 475–76; Chicago
Tribune, March 27, 1887; H. A. Hurlbut to Cleveland, March 8, 1888, in
Cleveland MSS.
[44] Nevins, *Cleveland*, 250–51, 445–46.

and helpful terms with the trilogy of Deity, dollars, and the Democratic party at times resulted in distortion. Bolstered by the logic of Darwinian evolution, some business leaders and Democratic leaders were operating on the premise that God was interested exclusively in material progress.

Some men close to Cleveland blandly used their positions to throw wide the gate of "progress." A striking example was the diligence of cabinet member William F. Vilas. Late in 1887 Cleveland promoted Secretary of the Interior L. Q. C. Lamar to the Supreme Court, and he soon transferred Vilas to head the Interior Department. There Vilas applied the same undoubted efficiency and honest devotion to progress that had marked his command of the Post Office Department. But his impatience with the impediments of bureaucratic red tape resulted in some by-passing of certain traditional departmental regulations.

In transferring plots of timberland from Indian ownership to white entrepreneurs, the legal regulations called for the approval of the commissioner of Indian affairs. A certain Indian agent in northern Wisconsin, James T. Gregory, had the habit of overlooking this requirement when allowing timber-hungry operators to cut the trees. Nor did Gregory insist upon enforcement of the bothersome, hampering regulations calling for the use of Indian labor in the logging process. A result of this efficiency was a very marked increase in lumber production in the area. That was "progress." Unorthodox reformers and Republican enemies of the administration found reasons for censuring Agent Gregory and the higher-ups who condoned his actions. Singled out for a large portion of vitriol was Secretary Vilas. Agent Gregory had been appointed at the behest of Vilas and subsequently was defended by Vilas for his logging-contract activities. A Senate "Select Committee on Indian Traders" investigated the matter. Headed by Republican

William E. Chandler of New Hampshire, this committee sought to connect the interests of the Superior Lumber Company with the contracts. Vilas was a heavy stockholder and Gregory a former employee in the company. But after many months of assiduous work, accompanied by much publicity in Republican newspapers, the committee felt compelled to admit that there was no financial connection between the company and the timber contracts.[45]

In the end the administration had reason to feel self-righteously that it had been subjected to a political smear and that no one in the Cleveland entourage had forsaken the puritan creed of simple honesty and the business-world creed of swift efficiency. It was for the good of advancing civilization—and the popularity of the Democracy among the logging operators—that the Cleveland administration had circumvented outmoded and hampering minor departmental regulations. Conservation of timberlands and the protection of Indian-owned property in the interest of the red men would be pure folly. After all, as Vilas later enunciated, God had planned that the pine trees be used only in the initial stages of progressing civilization.[46]   And of course Indians were expected to learn the lessons and the ways of progress—survival of the fittest. By such logic and means did the Cleveland administration effect a wedding between purity and progress. But some thought that the offspring were more expedient than ethical.

While middle-western Bourbons busied themselves with patronage and progress, they followed President Cleveland's theory and example of leaving legislative matters to the

---

[45] *Select Committee on Indian Traders* (50 Cong., 2 Sess., Senate Report No. 2710 [Washington, 1889]), *passim; Annual Report, Secretary of Interior,* 1888 (Washington, 1888), 43–45; Madison *Democrat,* March 8, 22, 24, April 7, 12, 21, June 13, July 4, 1888, February 24, March 1, 1889; Milwaukee *Sentinel,* March 6, 16, 1888; George B. Shaw to William F. Vilas, February 4, 1889, in Vilas MSS.; Usher to John P. Hume, April 10, 1888; and Hume to Usher, April 13, 1888, in Usher MSS.
[46] Vilas, "State of Wisconsin," *loc. cit.,* 688.

legislative branch. The Bourbons in the government service were primarily in the appointive administrative branch, not the legislative. In fact, most of them had never held an elective office or even accepted nominations. Although they left legislation to Congress, they nevertheless reserved an outsider's interest. They did what they could to discourage legislation inimicable to business, and in that respect they were more successful with Democratic legislators than with Republicans. The Bourbon party managers were aided by their patronage domination and by the Democratic "principle"—or excuse—of leaving government primarily to the local and state units.

Public clamor and manufacturers' pressure forced Congress to bestir itself on the important matter of railroad regulation. In the Wabash Railroad decision of 1886 the Supreme Court removed the power of states to regulate interstate commerce. Farmers, who suffered from high rates, and certain industrial shippers, provoked by the railroads' practice of favoring other, rival shippers with railroad rebates and secret rates, turned to Congress with demands for reform. Before the Cleveland administration took office, Congress was well on its way toward passing legislation on the matter. Democrats in the House, true to their state-rights heritage, passed the mild Reagan bill, which would place the regulatory process largely in the hands of federal attorneys and the courts. The Senate passed the Republican-sponsored Cullum bill, which would create a supposedly effective federal commission to prevent abuses. After breaking this legislative deadlock early in 1887, Congress passed, and Cleveland signed, a mild measure based on the Republicans' Cullum bill.[47]

This move, which resulted in the establishment of the Interstate Commerce Commission, was nonpartisan in its final form. Most certainly it was not the product of pur-

[47] Nevins, *Cleveland*, 355–57; Josephson, *Politicos*, 385–86, 388–89.

poseful and united leadership on the part of Democratic bigwigs. President Cleveland recognized the need for legislation, but his only role in the matter was signing the measure. No middle-western Bourbons had been in the vanguard of the movement; in fact, J. Sterling Morton had lobbied against even the mild Reagan proposal.[48] Many citizens would also remember that in Minnesota Democratic legislators had combined with reactionary Republican legislators to defeat United States Senator William Windom in his 1883 bid for re-election. And Windom, ever since the Granger days, had been an outstanding leader in the drive for federal interstate commerce legislation.[49]

A few Republicans, on the other hand, had been agitating for congressional action on the subject since the early seventies. They represented agrarian and manufacturing interests and were unmoved by consideration of state rights. The Republican party, because of its connections with protectionist manufacturers, was less under the control of railroad barons than was the Democracy. But the nonpartisan vote on the final measure made it impossible for either party to use it for election-campaign purposes.

Nor was the Interstate Commerce Act a great boon to the mass of voters. The many loopholes in the measure, together with court decisions from reactionary judges, nullified the effectiveness of the newly created commission within a few months. Certainly the voters had no great cause to feel grateful to Congress.[50]

The mass of middle-western voters likewise could not be expected to demonstrate enthusiasm over the action of Congress and President Cleveland on the Pacific railroad scandal. Senator Thurman's 1878 funding measure had proved inadequate for collecting money due the government from the

---

[48] Josephson, *Politicos*, 389; Olson, *Morton*, 291.
[49] Hall, *Political Contests*, 211.
[50] Josephson, *Politicos*, 394, 447–48; Shannon, *Farmer's Last Frontier*, 178.

Pacific railroads. An insistent public clamor finally caused Congress to create, in 1887, a Pacific Railway Commission. The majority report of the commission called for a generous time-spread in the payment of the debt, while the minority report reflected the agrarian sentiment by demanding that the government foreclose its mortgages on the roads and revoke their land grants.[51]

Behind the scenes there seemingly developed some political dealing with railroad barons. Republican J. S. Clarkson of Iowa reported to his close associate Senator William B. Allison that the Democrats were showing undue friendship toward the railroads. Reporting in July, 1888, Clarkson said, "There are many things to show that the Democrats are in this deal" to push the generous Outhwaite funding bill. The Democratic reward was to be "help out of it for the party in the campaign." Clarkson also asserted: "The same is true of the Western Union Company. I *know* that Gould is with the Democrats, and we know, from undoubted authority" that another party to the deal "gave the Democratic National Committee $10,000 last Saturday." The Iowan concluded his revelations with an insistence that "there is no mistake in any of these conclusions."[52]

President Cleveland, along with the majority in Congress, gave his blessing to the plan calling for mild treatment toward the Pacific railroads. The President unquestionably acted in good faith and showed political courage in taking this unpopular stand. But his position also showed that he was without a true understanding of the manner in which these railroads were receiving undue favors at the expense of the public weal. Only in dealing with petty legislative matters was Cleveland consistently outspoken in his de-

[51] Nevins, *Cleveland*, 350–54.
[52] J. S. Clarkson to William Allison, July 31, 1888, in William Allison MSS., Iowa Department of History and Archives.

votion to his concept of government as a "trustee of the people." He wisely vetoed the invalid-pension act, which was a John A. Logan plundering scheme amounting to fifty million dollars. This and his veto action on numerous individual pension bills for veterans were as wise as they were politically dangerous.[53]

With much less wisdom Cleveland vetoed, in 1887, the Texas seed bill. He would be lenient with corporations but not with drought-stricken farmers seeking a small appropriation for seeds. The President announced in vetoing the bill that he did "not believe that the power and duty of the General Government ought to be extended to the relief of individual suffering which is in no manner properly related to the public service or benefit." To him, "the lesson should constantly be enforced that though the people support the Government the Government should not support the people." [54] Government support, apparently, should be extended only to railroad corporations.

President Cleveland's action on the tariff issue proved an exception to his general policy of leaving initiative on legislative matters to the legislative branch. He had not been elected as a tariff reformer, and not until he issued his third annual message to Congress in December, 1887, did he take action on the issue. In this unheralded foray into legislative matters Cleveland delivered a long and well-considered attack on the existing high tariff rates. He had been concerned, along with others, over the continually mounting surplus in the Treasury—a surplus which kept much needed money out of circulation and constituted a temptation to Congress for making wasteful pork-barrel appropriations. President Cleveland studied the tariff question and arrived at the conclusion that reduction of the rates would remove unjust privileges maintained by certain producers and relieve the Treasury surplus. Politically, the President was

[53] Josephson, *Politicos*, 390.   [54] *Ibid.*, 391.

aware that no effective tariff-reform measure could pass
the Republican Senate, but he reasoned that his message
and the action of the Democratic House would place his
party on record for a tariff battle in the 1888 presidential
campaign.[55]

The House promptly responded with the Mills bill, a
measure sponsored by the chairman of the House Ways and
Means Committee, Roger Q. Mills of Texas. It called for
reductions from the average level of about 47 per cent to
about 40 per cent. On the free list were placed wool, flax,
hemp, salt, lumber, and tin plate, but rates were left on so
many items that it was doubtful if the net result would reduce the Treasury surplus. The Republican Senate offered
the Allison bill, a measure promoted under the leadership
of the chairman of the Committee on Finance, Iowa's William B. Allison. It ensured a maintenance of the general high
rates but foreshadowed a reduction in the Treasury surplus
by lowering excises and the sugar duty. Both parties thus
went on record without having to pass a compromise measure before the approaching presidential campaign.[56]

The effect of this Democratic tariff strategy could not
possibly be widespread enthusiasm. Certainly it was no way
to handle middle-western voters. The move came too late.
The Democratic record of dealing with the tariff question
by fits and starts and then ending up with results far different from promises made had the effect of confusing and
disgusting the voters. More important, middle-western farm
voters were traditionally in favor of tariff protection when
confronted with a showdown choice between protection
and free trade. Many—for reasons running the gamut from
simple patriotism to personal economic hopes and fears—
favored protection for "infant industries." They also enter-

[55] *Ibid.*, 396–400; McElroy, *Cleveland*, I, 268–72; Nevins, *Cleveland*,
368–80.
[56] Nevins, *Cleveland*, 388–94; Josephson, *Politicos*, 402–404; McElroy,
Cleveland, I, 273–74.

tained a horror of competition with European-peasant food producers. Just as industrial monopolies resulted in part from fear of destructive competition, so protective tariffs on food-stuffs had come about out of that same fear. Wage laborers, fearing that lower wages and unemployment would come if their employers were not protected against foreign low-wage producers, shared the farmers' horror of foreign competition. The farmers and laborers were not at all sure that they could trust the Democrats to use "discretion" in lowering the tariff schedules, and Republicans were not slow in reminding them of the free-trade sentiment within the Democracy. Farmers also observed, or were reminded, that the Democracy's Mills bill included on the free list some agricultural products—wool, flax, and hemp. It was also very much a question whether the Mills bill would reduce the Treasury surplus and thus relieve the currency shortage.

Then, too, many Republicans leaders in the agrarian districts of the Middle West showed just as much interest in reforming the tariff as did the Democrats. Republican state platforms in this area indicated growing interest in the issue. In 1887 the Minnesota Republican convention went on record for "a simplification and reduction of the customs revenues"; in Nebraska the Republicans declared that "the business of the country now demands a revision of the tariff"; the Iowa Republican platform demanded that "the tariff should be revised and reduced." Over and against this, the voters could place the record of forty Democrats voting against the Morrison low-tariff measure of 1884, and thirty-five Democrats voting against an improved Morrison bill in 1886.[57] Indeed, it appeared to many friends of tariff reform that the Republican party was the sounder vehicle for tariff legislation. With the disunited, straddling, inconsistent Democracy at the helm the result might be no reform

[57] Nevins, *Cleveland*, 370; Scott, "Political Career of William R. Morrison," *loc. cit.*, 157.

—or the other extreme of free trade. The party could not be trusted.

Protectionist Republicans, through the almost frenzied concern of wealthy protectionist industrialists, had a valuable source of campaign funds and workers. Protectionists, when aroused, even proved capable of dealing with tariff-reformer William R. Morrison of Illinois. In the 1886 campaign the secretary of the American Tin-Plate Association, John Jarett, arrived in Morrison's congressional district. He was weighted down with money, which he alleged was supplied by a Pittsburgh "working-man's tariff club," but which apparently came from the American Iron and Steel Association. Secretary Jarett won the support of the Knights of Labor and of many of the operatives in the tariff-protected industries of Alton, Belleville, and East St. Louis. Morrison, who had served in Congress since 1872 as an active tariff reformer, was this time defeated.[58]

Democratic tariff reformers, understanding the middle-western voters better than President Cleveland—who understood the region not at all—were concerned over their vulnerability on the question. They recognized the necessity of pursuing a consistent and persistent educational program among the voters. Nebraska's J. Sterling Morton said that Cleveland's tariff message came too late, for the "term of school has been too short for teaching economics to 60,000,000 people." [59] Early in 1888 Vilas instructed his Wisconsin Democratic chairman, Ellis B. Usher, on what tactics to use. "People go to hear speakers of note with their teeth set, usually," said Vilas. He believed that such speakers "stir up the other side almost as much as their own. The trumpet that sounds the note of battle, not only inspires its friends, but awakes its enemies." A better approach was

[58] Scott, "Political Career of William R. Morrison," *loc. cit.*, 142–43; Chicago *Daily News*, November 4, 1886.
[59] Olson, *Morton*, 329.

"school district speaking," which "is the simple ingratiation of sound education." It would, insisted Vilas, "tell for the gain of more voters," if intelligently, fairly, and wisely pushed, "than all the rest of the campaign work together. Indeed, all the rest is simply to 'dress the ranks.'" [60] But he was too late and too much alone, and he was operating in a party too inconsistent and too out of touch with the real Middle West. Upon the subsequent defeat of the middle-western Democracy, State Chairman Usher of Wisconsin said, "I think the expression was one of timidity and that in reality the West is for lower taxes but they were frightened by the free trade howl. Education is what they need. . . ." [61]

The Bourbons were likewise in grave need of "education," for they continued to sabotage every basic economic-reform movement except the tariff. While the Democrats were in power in Washington and using patronage to perfect their party machinery in the hinterland, the bad economic condition among the farmers and wage earners was driving many citizens toward independent political action. Among the farmers, those of the wheat-growing area were the most bitter. Wheat prices were as discouragingly low as freight costs were disgracefully high. The Interstate Commerce Commission did not relieve the railroad-rate situation; on the contrary, freight charges on carrying wheat to the Atlantic Coast actually increased during the decade 1885–1895. The cost was about ten or twelve cents per bushel, compared with the five- or six-cent rate after 1900.[62] Thus in the wheat-growing sections, which were located chiefly in Nebraska, Iowa, Minnesota, and states further west, there was a strong disposition to protest loudly against the "do nothing" Cleveland Democrats and the "done noth-

[60] William F. Vilas to Usher, March 20, 1888, in Usher MSS.
[61] Usher to William F. Vilas, November 21, 1888, *ibid.*
[62] Nevins, *Cleveland,* 593; Shannon, *Farmer's Last Frontier,* 313–14, 417.

ing" Republican leaders. Even in the less-stricken farm areas there was widespread disgust. A farmer in southern Minnesota, for example, said: "We are not quite as badly in the pinch as the farmers in the northern part of the State, we keep more cattle and hogs, and follow a more mixed kind of farming generally. Still I think that an agitation would bring them right out." [63]

The chief medium through which the discontented protested was the Farmers' Alliance. The northern branch of this organization had been founded back in 1880 by the editor of a Chicago farm journal, Milton George. Because George's *Western Rural* had been primarily antirailroad in character, the organization which he founded was immediately branded as antirailroad. The Alliance movement spread by a series of local groups, and when the number of these reached a goodly total, a state Alliance was organized. Although there was no spectacular rise of the movement during the first Cleveland administration, there were evidences of real political strength in the Alliance. It had earlier shown its effectiveness in Nebraska politics, and in 1886 it was active in Minnesota and Iowa.[64]

Ignatius Donnelly, who was in the Minnesota Alliance, pondered the question of how best to utilize the organization in the 1886 Minnesota election. In midsummer, thinking in terms of Alliance-Democratic relations, Donnelly expressed belief that "as a third party movement, it depends upon the Democrats themselves whether it will help or hurt them." Donnelly's hope was for a "coalition with the Democrats, provided Kelly, Doran and Jim Hill are relegated to the rear. The Democracy will be compelled at its next State Convention to choose between sustaining that corrupt ring of plunderers and accepting overwhelming defeat at the

[63] Seth Bottomley (of Martin County) to Ignatius Donnelly, March 26, 1886, in Donnelly MSS.
[64] Hicks, *Populist Revolt*, 98; Shannon, *Farmer's Last Frontier*, 312–13.

polls; or on the other hand, throwing them overboard, and forming a combination with the Alliance and working-men. . . . If the third party is reduced to choose between Republican thieves and Democratic thieves, they, being largely Republicans, will prefer the rascals of their own kidney; and who can blame them?" [65]

The Kelly-Doran-Hill triumvirate proved to be firmly entrenched in the Democracy; and, in accordance with Don-nelly's prediction, Alliance members aided in the Repub-lican campaign. The Republican party, which endorsed many of the Alliance demands, won the election. Among the victors were a number of Alliance candidates running on either the Republican or the local Alliance ticket. Don-nelly himself was elected to the state assembly as an Al-liance candidate and gave every indication of at last being completely fed-up with co-operating with the Democ-racy.[66] Soon Jim Hill, apparently aware of the rising Al-liance influence within the Republican party and mindful of the strong possibility of the Republicans' capturing the presidency, began to rethink his political affiliation. It was time to smoke the antimonopolists out of the Republican party. By the time of the 1888 election campaign railroad-baron Hill had changed his gray granite fortress in St. Paul from a Great Northern Railroad and Democratic head-quarters to a Great Northern Railroad and Republican den. It was widely repeated that Hill was making fabulous fi-nancial offers to the Republican campaign managers in re-turn for the promise of naming a member of the cabinet.[67] The railroad mogul had discovered the convenience of hav-ing a railroad friend in the Democratic cabinet, so why

[65] Ignatius Donnelly to MacDonald, August 12, 1886, in Donnelly MSS.
[66] *Id.* to *id.*, October 6, 1886, in Donnelly MSS.; St. Paul *Dispatch*, November 20, 1886; John D. Hicks, "The Political Career of Ignatius Donnelly," *Mississippi Valley Historical Review*, VIII (June–September, 1921), 107–108; Folwell, *History of Minnesota*, III, 170–73.
[67] Josephson, *Politicos*, 488.

not prepare for the same advantage with the Republicans.

In Iowa the Farmers' Alliance and farmers in general threatened the reactionary Democratic and Republican parties. In 1887, operating through the traditional parties, the angry farmers delivered a telling blow on the political chins of conservatives. The final score was an antirailroad majority in the legislature. Forty-nine of the one hundred members of the Iowa House of Representatives were farmers, and Republican Governor William Larrabee gave active support to the farmer movement. The main force of the blow fell on the Republican party. The Democracy managed to side-step the full fury of the movement, partly because it was too weak to command much voter interest and partly because it sought shelter behind a smoke screen of antiprohibition agitation.[68]

Even such a compromiser as Senator William B. Allison, while declaring the railroad problem to be the burning issue of the day, was unable to control the Iowa Republicans in the legislature. A drastic regulatory act was rushed through the legislature and signed by Republican Governor Larrabee. Chauncey Depew, renowned railroad attorney of New York, was greatly shocked at this "extreme of radical legislation" and advised "capitalistic" New York Republicans to erase Senator Allison's name from the list of possible presidential candidates. Depew was angry over Allison's failure to control the situation "which threatens the investment in securities" of Iowa railroads. To him, "that makes Allison impossible." [69]

The railroad interests immediately turned with determination to build the Iowa Democracy into a medium for driving the antimonopolist Republican scamps out of office. In the 1888 election the railroad forces expended consider-

---

[68] Nixon, "Populist Movement," *loc. cit.*, 35–36.
[69] Chauncey M. Depew, *My Memories of Eighty Years* (New York, 1922), 131–32; Nevins, *Cleveland*, 289.

A HEAVY LOAD TO CARRY

How the High Tariff Serves the Monopolist, the Farmer, and the Laborer

In *Puck*, XXIII (June 27, 1888), 308.

able money and energy to defeat the entire slate of Iowa Republican candidates. Iowa's Republican leader Charles Beardsley reported that "one prominent railroad president has offered to bet that the Republican state ticket will be defeated, and he has always been a Republican." [70] This proved an underestimate of the agrarian fury, for the railroadized Democracy was badly mauled in the election.

While the middle-western farmers were on the march, wage earners likewise attacked the politico-business partnership which exploited the masses. The Bourbon Democracy of the Middle West, as one segment of this bulwark of defense against the people, tried to ride out the storm of a labor upheaval which gripped the region and the nation until it petered out in 1887. Membership in the Knights of Labor and trade unions leaped forward, to reach a combined total in 1886 of nearly a million. The Knights of Labor membership, consisting chiefly of unskilled workers, reached 700,000, as compared with its 28,136 of six years before. Trade-union membership, mostly of skilled workers, was at least 250,000. This unprecedented growth of labor organizations had the aspect of a genuine class movement. The concept of labor solidarity had taken hold in a positive manner, and a wave of boycotts and strikes swept the nation. The workers wanted such reforms as the eight-hour day, decent wages, and legislation against immigration of alien contract laborers. The most dramatic incident in the general upheaval was the bomb explosion in Haymarket Square, Chicago, on May Day of 1886, which was attributed to the few but combative "Chicago Anarchists." This incident aroused public feeling against organized labor; and that factor, combined with labor's inexperience in mass organization, caused the general upheaval to subside in 1887.[71]

[70] Charles Beardsley to Allison, July 31, 1888, in Allison MSS. See also *id.* to *id.*, February 22, 1888; *id.* to *id.*, September 7, 1888; *id.* to *id.*, September 20, 1888; and Clarkson to *id.*, October 20, 1888, *ibid.*
[71] Perlman, *Trade Unionism*, 83, 91–94.

For the Bourbon Democracy of the Middle West and for
the Cleveland administration, the labor upsurge brought a
structural weakening. The city-machine Bourbon wing was
the most vulnerable. Despite the efforts of ward heelers and
bosses, independent labor parties emerged and acquired recruits from among the erstwhile Democratic voters.

In Wisconsin industrial centers a militant Workers' party
under the direction of Robert Schilling of Milwaukee,
threatened the Bourbon Democracy. The Bourbons were
confused as to how to handle the situation. Wealthy Alexander Mitchell and his Milwaukee cohorts favored fighting
the Workers' party and stirring up dissension within it.
Others, like Vilas, favored making concessions with the aim
of absorbing the upstart party, a method that involved brib-
ing the labor leaders with positions in the Democratic organization and controlling them afterwards. Still others
favored a fusion effort with the Republicans in such danger
spots as Milwaukee. The Bourbons proved unable to agree
on the matter. In the 1886 election the Democratic candidate for governor, G. M. Woodward, surprised the Bourbons by coming out in the campaign against the policy of
attacking labor with the veiled excuse of resistance to order.
Mitchell immediately ordered his Milwaukee gang to withdraw all support of Woodward. The Republicans, who had
been encouraging the Workers' party as a means of drawing off laborers from the Democracy, won the election by
a huge majority.[72] Thereafter the Bourbons could count
very much less than usual on their old city-machine Bourbon partnership in Milwaukee. At the same time they faced
the rising tide of farmer unrest moving in from the Alliance-
ridden states to the west and finding the Republican party

[72] T. E. Dodge to Usher, August 6, 1887; C. W. Graves to *id.*, September
14, 1887; Wall to *id.*, November 11, 1887; William F. Vilas to *id.*, December 15, 1887; John E. Wright to *id.*, April 11, 1888; Usher to William
F. Vilas, April 18, 1888; *id.* to *id.*, July 5, 1888; *id.* to E. S. Bragg, April
18, 1888; *id.* to H. H. Gray, August 7, 1888; and *id.* to William F. Vilas,
December 12, 1887, in Vilas MSS.; Plumb, *Badger Politics*, 86.

a much better medium than the railroadized Democracy.

Another example of Bourbon trouble with organized-labor activity was in Chicago, where the Union Labor party refused to kowtow to the unsavory ward-heeling Democrats and Bourbon bigwigs. The labor party at first entertained hopes of co-operating with the Democracy in electing a congressman, but the Democratic choice for a candidate was more than the third party could swallow. The editor of the Chicago *Knights of Labor Weekly*, G. E. Detwiler, said that Democratic candidate Taylor was in no position to serve the workers. "Taylor will promise anything," said editor Detwiler, "but is in the hands of a gang of heelers who will make him powerless to keep his promises. He is a very good man himself, but is surrounded by the worst lot of toughs I ever knew." [73] The Union Labor party decided to continue with their own separate offering —antimonopolist writer Henry Demarest Lloyd.[74]

Chicago was normally the core of the Bourbon strength in Illinois, as was Milwaukee its center in Wisconsin. There was trouble ahead for the Illinois Bourbons, and the Republicans did what they could to give it momentum. The Democrats were not even able to save themselves by choosing former Republican John M. Palmer for the 1888 gubernatorial race. The enlightened Palmer boldly denounced the system of hiring Pinkerton detectives to quell labor uprisings and said that because of these private standing armies the "State has become an object of contempt." His Republican opponent, Joseph Fifer, countered with reference to recently enacted prolabor legislation in Illinois and assured the voters that the legislation would be well enforced. The Republicans won.[75]

[73] G. E. Detwiler to Henry Demarest Lloyd, October 27, 1888, in Henry Demarest Lloyd MSS., Library of the State Historical Society of Wisconsin.

[74] *Id.* to *id.*, September 6, 1888; *id.* to *id.*, September 19, 1888; *id.* to *id.*, October 27, 1888; and E. Stewart to *id.*, September 7, 1888, *ibid.*

[75] Bogart and Thompson, *Industrial State*, 175–78.

Against the background of four years of Bourbon pandering to big business and machine politics occurred the presidential election of 1888. There was no disputing Cleveland's renomination, for his control of patronage, his well-earned reputation for simple honesty, and his kindness to many fat-purse business leaders rendered him a safe guardian of the entrenched political and economic orthodoxy of the day. Nor was the choice of Ohio's Allen Thurman as vice-presidential candidate an event to upset the conservative tenor of the Democracy. There was, however, one note of liberalism, in the nineteenth-century sense of that term: the inclusion in the platform of a vigorous statement calling for lower tariffs. The Democracy was standing on the ground prescribed in the Mills bill, which called for lower tariff rates and placed some items on the free list.

The Republican national convention's final choice for the presidential nomination was Indiana's Senator Benjamin Harrison. He had a spotless, although virtually empty, political record, and thus could not be attacked for his record. Favorite-son Harrison had the additional political good fortune of being from doubtful Indiana and of also being the grandson of President William Henry Harrison. For second place the Republicans chose New York banker Levi P. Morton. In their platform the Republicans took a firm stand in favor of protective tariffs, denouncing the Mills bill and declaring for "the entire repeal of internal taxes, rather than the surrender of any part of our protective system." [76]

For the first time since pre-Civil War days the Democracy entered a presidential campaign as the party of the "ins," so the Cleveland candidacy had to stand on its record; and once again the national Democracy stood in clear-cut contrast to its opponents on an economic issue—the tariff. In neither instance was the Democracy's position

[76] Josephson, *Politicos*, 420.

among the mass of middle-western voters. President Cleveland and the advisers surrounding him had dealt with the voters of the region as though they were subject peoples of a foreign ruling clique. At no time during the four years of the Cleveland administration had a farmer or a wage earner been able to read with satisfaction the newspaper accounts of Democratic appointments made and legislation passed.

On the tariff issue, the Republicans had the advantage of unusual financial and propagandic support from worried industrialists, together with the Democratic failure to start an "education program" until after Cleveland's 1887 tariff message. The situation on the tariff was well summed up by Republican editor Joseph Medill of the Chicago *Tribune*. Writing to Senator Allison late in September, tariff-reformer Medill reported: "We have lots of Republicans deeply dissatisfied with that rabid, unrepublican . . . plank, but they have been kept from bolting by the strength of old party ties and the vigorous assaults that have been made on certain sections of the Mills bill and the scare cry of free trade against the Democrats, and they have barely concluded to vote for Harrison on the assurance that the Republican Senate was framing a better reform bill than the Democratic House had done." [77]

Taken together, the four-year record and the campaign promises of the Democrats were not conducive to changing party allegiance in the normally Republican Middle West. The region, as usual, cast its majority vote for the Republicans.

In the Cleveland administration's attempt to serve God, big business, and the Democratic party, only big business emerged with any marked reward. President-elect Harrison thought that God had turned his blessings to the Re-

[77] Medill to Allison, September 23, 1888; and *id.* to *id.*, September 24, 1888, in Allison MSS.

publican party, for he jubilantly proclaimed that "Providence has given us the victory." [78] Perhaps the day would come when Providence or some factor would cause the voters to arise in earnest against the hierarchy of both old parties. There were already ominous signs of an upsurge of the incipient antimonopolist sentiment among the little men.

[78] Josephson, *Politicos*, 433.

Chapter Ten

Bourbon Victory Casts Its Shadow 1889-1892

> *To a new truth there is nothing more hurtful than an old error.*
>
> —GOETHE

SHORTLY AFTER the election defeat of Cleveland the Bourbon Democrats of the Middle West found themselves subjected to a mounting tempest of economic discontent and social cleavage. The drabness of middle-western farm life, accented by increasing economic frustration, was bringing farmer patience to the breaking point. Emotional feelings of inferiority, bred of futile toil, hunger for excitement to relieve the loneliness of unremitting labor, and outright indignation at the leaderless drift of affairs, combined to cause a tense political situation in farm areas. Life among the wage earners, many of them recently arrived from immigrant ships, was likewise one of worry. The constant threat of unemployment, low wages, and long, dull working hours caused great unrest in labor circles.

Among farmers and wage earners alike, instability in the noneconomic aspects of this socially unsettled region made for cleavages on moral and religious questions. Various groups, their sensitiveness, suspicion, and intolerance accented by a sense of financial insecurity, were fearful lest other social mores than their own should prevail in the community and the state. There ensued outbursts of nativism, to be met with counterblows from touchy nonpuritans. Basically, the great need of the masses was to acquire a reasonable slice of the prosperity being monopolized by the capitalists.

Especially disheartened and embattled were the farmers of the wheat belt, where economic conditions had been rapidly growing worse. To these farmers, already suffering from oppressive mortgages and high freight rates, came in 1887 the first in a series of crop failures and lower prices for wheat.[1] Farmers in other parts of the Middle West were also in dire plight. The *Iowa Agricultural Report* for 1890, after reporting on the low price of corn, asked: "Why not have a cheap and suitable stove that corn may be used for fuel?" [2] It also pointed out that hogs were selling at a lower price than at any time since 1879 and, in comparison with the price of corn, at a lower price than they had ever brought.[3]

The farmers reacted to their hard times by entering into direct political action against railroad excesses, gold currency, and high tariffs on industrial products. They swelled the ranks of the Farmers' Alliance, exerted pressure on the old parties, and finally formed the so-called "Populist party." In the eary stages the Alliance was the focal point of farmer political action. In some places Alliance groups offered independent tickets in elections; in other places they invaded the old parties and gained influence; and in still other areas professional politicians scrambled to endorse the demands of the upsurging Alliance.

Despite the momentum of the new farmer outburst, the Bourbon Democrats stubbornly refused to retreat. For a considerable time they succeeded in hanging on to the party reins and even in turning the general unrest to their

---

[1] Hicks, *Populist Revolt*, 31, 154.

[2] *Iowa Agricultural Report*, 1890, p. 50, as cited in Herman Clarence Nixon, "The Economic Basis of the Populist Movement in Iowa," *Iowa Journal of History and Politics*, XXI (July, 1923), 388.

[3] Nixon, "Economic Basis of the Populist Movement," *loc. cit.*, 388.

own political advantage. Outside the wheat-growing prairie area, the core of discontent in the North, the Bourbons even managed for a long time to forestall the Alliance threat; in Wisconsin and Illinois the farmers were especially slow to rebel. Throughout the Middle West, moreover, Republican actions were arousing many voters to anger against that party, and the Bourbons made capital of these. In state Republican parties the focal point inviting Bourbon attacks was the nativist upsurge; in Nebraska, Iowa, and Minnesota it was prohibition; in Wisconsin and Illinois it was the parochial-school curriculum.

In the national Republican party the fury of the voters centered chiefly on the McKinley tariff bill, which was passed in October, 1890. This was the highest protective measure in the nation's annals. The Republicans apparently hoped that their passage, in the same year, of the Sherman Antitrust Act and the Sherman silver purchase act would provide a backlog of public good will sufficient to allow general acceptance of a high protective measure. But these measures were too innocuous, and the McKinley Tariff too drastic, to checkmate effective opposition.

The first test of Bourbon strength in the Middle West following Cleveland's defeat came, however, before the debate over the McKinley Tariff, for in 1889 Iowa held a state election. In the middle eighties Iowa's Republican Congressman J. P. Dolliver found most people agreeing with his statement that Iowa "would go Democratic when hell went Methodist." [4] Soon this son of a Methodist circuit rider was exhibiting "a profound silence as to the spiritual condition of Satan's realm"—for in 1889 Iowa went Democratic and anti-Methodist.[5] A year before the election some Iowa Republican leaders showed signs of uneasiness. Republican Joseph M. McDill was especially concerned over the "extreme views and methods of the temperance men" and ob-

4 Cole, *I Remember*, 176.   5 *Ibid.*, 177.

served that the Republican prohibition record had "cooled the ardor not only of German citizens but of all who are not extremist." He was also concerned over the effects of the recently passed "drastic" railroad-regulatory measure, which "some cannot help regarding as unjust and oppressive" and which also resulted in the "railroad men . . . not feeling happy." And to top it off, the "laboring people are discontented." [6] Despite these ominous signs of impending doom the Iowa Republicans managed to carry the state in the 1888 presidential election, but in the following year they were in real trouble. The temperance movement was going full tilt, and the "railroad men" were bent upon ousting the party which had passed the "drastic" regulatory measure.

The Iowa Bourbon Democrats were in an optimistic mood, except when pondering the question of whom to nominate for the governorship. Ever since Civil War days professional vote catchers had avoided getting tied to the Iowa Democratic millstone. So in 1889 the Bourbon Democrats looked far and wide for a suitable candidate. Finally they stumbled upon and nominated Horace Boies, a lifelong Republican who had recently left the Republican fold because he disliked that party's position on prohibition and the tariff and was now quietly practicing law. In Boies, the Democrats reasoned, they had a candidate who would capture the German antiprohibitionist vote simply because he was on the Democratic ticket and who at the same time would not be personally offensive to other elements in the populace.[7] He was a "good man who did not drink whiskey, nor use tobacco," and apparently "no vulgar or profane words ever passed his lips." Moreover, this "good man" was an arresting personality. Audiences at political rallies liked the little man, with his Prince Albert coat and a "Mona

[6] Joseph M. McDill to Allison, September 21, 1888, in Allison MSS.
[7] Nixon, "Populist Movement," *loc. cit.*, 41.

Lisa smile on his affidavit face." Then, too, the railroad barons supplied ample funds to the enterprising Bourbon campaign managers. The outcome was victory for Boies and enough Democratic strength in the legislature to bring about the selection of a Democratic speaker. The Republicans, however, retained enough strength to maneuver successfully for the return of Allison to the Senate.[8]

In the next year's elections the Republicans received a drubbing on a national scale. The congressional elections resulted in victory for 235 Democrats, 9 Farmers' Alliance or Populist candidates, and 88 Republicans. The agrarian Middle West, coupled with areas farther west and with the South, delivered the hardest punch in this assault upon the Republicans. For the first time in its history Nebraska was graced with a Democratic governor. Wisconsin Democrats swept almost all Republicans out of office. In Minnesota the Democrats and the Populists each captured two of the state's four congressional seats. Democrats made gains in Illinois, adding five to their previous congressional delegation of seven and chalking up enough strength in the legislature to send John M. Palmer to the United States Senate.[9] Originally a Democrat, Palmer had played an important part in organizing the Illinois Republican party and in 1868 had been elected governor as a Republican. His distaste for federal extension of power and his anti-Grantism had propelled him into the Liberal Republican movement in 1872, and finally back into the Democratic camp.[10]

The role of the Bourbons in this middle-western tidal wave was one of fighting in two directions—lambasting the

[8] Cole, I Remember, 172–77, 194; Haynes, Third Party Movements, 197; Nixon, "Populist Movement," loc cit., 41; Jean B. Kern, "The Political Career of Horace Boies," Iowa Journal of History, XLVII (July, 1949), 215–21.

[9] Hicks, Populist Revolt, 153, 180–81; Bogart and Thompson, Industrial State, 179–80; Chicago Tribune, January 14, March 7, 13, 1891.

[10] Allan Westcott, "John McAuley Palmer," in Johnson and Malone (eds.), Dictionary of American Biography, XIV, 187–88.

Republicans and warding off farmers' independent parties. The Bourbons raised a terrific din against the puritan and high-tariff colorization of the Republican party. Their protest achieved the double purpose of discrediting the Republicans and diverting the attention of farmers from the antimonopoly, antirailroad, and free-silver issues. Where that was not enough, the Bourbons found themselves forced to witness Democratic candidates' endorsing at least part of the Populist demands.

In this election the insurgency of the farmers did not penetrate deeply into the Middle West. In Minnesota the Bourbons maintained their control of the state party machinery. There the Democrats had real strength in the combination of railroad baron Jim Hill's power and that of the anti-nativist voters. There were many German and Scandinavian farmers in Minnesota who were opposed to the current anti-liquor and anti–parochial school agitation. The large Irish Catholic parochial-school element of St. Paul embraced the same sentiment and constituted a formidable popular backing for the city machine headed by Jim Hill's cohorts Michael Doran and Patrick Kelly.

In vain the Alliance men attempted to push their crusade out of the wheat belt into eastern Minnesota. Not even the golden oratory of benign-countenanced Ignatius Donnelly was equal to the task of diverting the mass of "foreigners" from social questions to economic issues.

One Alliance worker, Joseph Penner, complained of the difficulty in combating the proclivity of nonpuritans to join the Democratic party. The "town where I got 38 members," lamented Penner, is "troubled with 'church on the brain,' mostly German Catholics; and that 'Brohibition Blank in der blatform' also bothers them. Some of the Swedes are also troubled with church; but if all of the Cranks would throw Dogma to the Devil, and try and better their worldly condition, they would be better off." [11]

[11] Joseph Penner to Ignatius Donnelly, May 1, 1890, in Donnelly MSS.

WHAT IT COSTS A FARMER TO DINE
AT A FIRST-CLASS CHICAGO RESTAURANT

In William H. Harvey, *Coin's Financial School* (Chicago, 1894), 115.

The power of corporate interests was illustrated in a letter received by Ignatius Donnelly from Dr. W. W. Mayo of Rochester, Minnesota. Dr. Mayo, while pioneering in the medical field, was also a challenger of the *status quo* in political affairs. He wrote to his long-time cohort Donnelly:

> I do not meet with any success about getting any body of men or Church to take hold of your lecture. You as well as myself are under the ban of the Chicago and North Western Railroad. This town is the headquarters of the Railroad and Wheat ring and these corporations hold us with an iron grip. They have an influence upon every church and every organization that has taken hold of the Lecture business. About one half of the town, the money lenders and merchants are violently opposed to me for my action against the Railroad and Wheat ring. The working men are with me to a man.

Mayo concluded that Donnelly would have to act for himself, or through the county Alliance chairman, to obtain sponsorship in the Rochester area. Mayo added, regarding his own position with the Alliance: "So far I am apparently ignored by them as none of the members come to see me. . . . I must move slowly so as not to give offence. For some years I have been alayed [*sic*] with the Democratic party. This makes the Republican farmers suspicious of me. . . . Southern Minnesota is ripe for action." [12]

Nebraska Bourbons, under the direction of George L. Miller and James E. Boyd, did not neglect the liquor question. And aiding them in their efforts was the magnetic young William Jennings Bryan. Included in the state Democratic platform was a statement submitted by Bryan declaring that "we regard with distrust the various forms of sumptuary legislation and accept a well-regulated and carefully guarded license law as the most peaceful solution of the liquor question." Aided by the liquor interests of Omaha,

[12] Mayo to *id.*, May 20, 1890, *ibid.* See also Mayo to *id.*, November 8, 1890; and "Donnelly's Diary," June 21, 1890, *ibid.*

which city boasted the third largest distillery in the nation, the Democrats succeeded in electing Omaha's James E. Boyd to the governorship and William Jennings Bryan to the congressional seat of the district embracing Omaha. The Republicans retained the other state offices, but the Alliance's Independent party captured the state legislature and a congressional seat. The Nebraska Bourbons had done better than usual, and soon they had the satisfaction of witnessing Governor Boyd's veto of a railroad-regulatory measure. But they also soon became concerned over the doings of neophyte Bryan, who showed an inclination to neglect tariff reform in favor of the free-silver heresy.[13]

The Wisconsin Democratic landslide was the most clear-cut Bourbon victory in the Middle West. No concessions were granted to farmer groups as William F. Vilas and his henchmen systematically traveled the highways and byways to castigate the Republicans. They divided their tub-thumping between attacks on the highly protective McKinley Tariff and the anti–parochial school Bennett law. The Wisconsin Republicans had recently enacted the Bennett measure, which made it mandatory for parochial schools to use English in teaching basic subjects. Lutherans and Catholics feared that this was a move to destroy their parochial schools, and the Democrats certainly did nothing to quiet their laments.[14]

Vilas set an active pace in the campaign, talking much on his pet subject of tariff reform but not neglecting the Bennett law. Repeatedly, as he stumped the state, Vilas asked audiences what difference it made whether a person said "two and two make four" or "zwei und zwei machen

[13] Paxton Hibben, *The Peerless Leader, William Jennings Bryan* (New York, 1929), 122–25; Olson, *Morton*, 331, 339; J. Sterling Morton to Lamont, May 8, 1893, in Lamont MSS.

[14] H. C. Payne to Rusk, December 2, 1890; and J. Spooner to *id.*, December 28, 1890, in Rusk MSS.; Spooner to G. O. Jones, July 27, 1890, in John C. Spooner MSS., Library of Congress; Wall to William F. Vilas, innumerable letters on the nativist issue, 1890–1895, in Vilas MSS.

vier." [15] The state's most important Republican, United States Senator John C. Spooner, thought Vilas' talk was a lot of harmless nonsense. Spooner, noting a newspaper synopsis of a Vilas outburst, remarked that it was mostly on the tariff "and not very strong either." And on the Bennett law Spooner thought that Vilas' comments were "simply puerile." He could not believe that "such stuff would do us much harm." [16] But it did do harm to Senator Spooner and the Republican officeholders in general, for the Democrats made almost a clean sweep of the election. Spooner said that the Republican defeat was "not because of the Farmers' Alliance at all, but the Bennett law." [17] He thought that "the tariff hurt us some" [18] but that the parochial-school issue had been the determining factor: "The school law did it—a silly, sentimental and damned useless abstraction. . . ." [19]

The Democratic gubernatorial candidate, editor-humorist George W. Peck, was swept into office. This was a real Bourbon victory, for in naming the quaint author of *Peck's Bad Boy* the Vilas organization had chosen a rank amateur at politics and thus a good front for the really "bad boys." The Democrats also captured the state legislature and eight of the state's nine congressional seats, including the one held since 1885 by young Robert M. La Follette. It was the only time in his career that earnest and able La Follette was rejected by Wisconsin voters. He had made the mistake of voting "regular" on the McKinley bill and had not as yet started pulling the beards of stalwart Republicans.[20]

[15] William F. Whyte, "The Bennett Law Campaign in Wisconsin," *Wisconsin Magazine of History*, X (June, 1927), 386. See also William F. Vilas, "The 'Bennett Law' in Wisconsin," *Forum*, XII (October, 1891), 197.
[16] Spooner to Payne, September 22, 1890, in Spooner MSS.
[17] *Id.* to S. H. Hunt, February 7, 1891, *ibid.*; W. C. Goudy to Cleveland, September 14, 1892, in Cleveland MSS.
[18] Spooner to N. T. Martin, November 19, 1890, in Spooner MSS.
[19] *Id.* to H. M. Kutchin, November 18, 1890, *ibid.*
[20] Wall to William F. Vilas, January 6, 1892, in Vilas MSS.; Whyte, "Bennett Law Campaign," *loc. cit.*, 386.

The Wisconsin Democratic victory was clearly a Bourbon victory, and immediately the Bourbon party managers began to consolidate their position. Former state Democratic chairman Ellis B. Usher aided in pushing a friend of the railroads, James J. Hogan, into the speakership of the lower branch of the legislature. Usher solicited the aid of the general manager of the Soo Railroad, whose office was in Minneapolis: "I want you to put in all the aid you can for [Hogan], but don't write any of your garrulous friends that he is your candidate." Usher emphasized the need of caution by adding, "We want no Granger market as the Minnesota plan. Spare us the publicity of your active assistance." [21] The Bourbons also made a successful drive to place Vilas in the United States Senate seat hitherto occupied by John C. Spooner.

The middle-western Bourbons, although maintaining control of their state organizations throughout the hectic 1890 election, were far from being clear of the Populist movement which was sweeping toward them from the western prairies and the South. The hard times causing the upsurge became more acute. There came a nationwide slump as the business cycle, beginning in 1890, gained momentum in its downward course. Big business men reacted by becoming increasingly adamant in their determination to guard their holdings against a cheapening of the currency, which supposedly would lower the money value of their holdings. They also continued with their traditional theory that sound money was the only currency policy conducive to a sound economy. As an adverse foreign-trade situation and gold hoarding pulled specie from the government surplus, the worried magnates of business redoubled their efforts to ensure a sound currency. At the same time, a growing number of desperate farmers joined the silver miners in

[21] Usher to B. G. Lennox, January 8, 1889; and *id.* to F. D. Underwood (of Minneapolis), December 4, 1890, in Usher MSS.

demanding cheap currency through free coinage of silver. By 1891 the cleavage between the goldbugs and the silverites threatened to push other issues into the background.[22]

The gold, or sound-money, element concentrated on repeal of the Sherman silver-purchase act. This measure, passed in 1890 as a sop to the silver-mining states, provided for an increase in currency based on silver. In the eyes of sound-money men this procedure dangerously drained the nation's gold accumulations out of circulation. Reasoning that the Sherman Act rather than the business cycle was at the root of the nation's sad economic plight, the sound-money leaders demanded repeal of the measure. The Republican Congress, which had been badly mauled in the 1890 election, bestirred itself to act before the new Congress took over. In its Lame Duck Session early in 1891 the Republican Senate almost voted a majority for repealing the silver-purchase act. The Republican House, on the other hand, took the opposite tack by reversing its past position and almost passing a free-coinage bill.[23] Pressure from the public had undermined the sound-money leadership of even the Republican party, despite the leaders' control of patronage and campaign funds. And sound-money men envisaged greater inflationary moves from the incoming Democratic Congress. A year previously Republican Senator John C. Spooner of Wisconsin had remarked that the Democrats in Congress would not vote for free silver if they thought it would pass.[24] But now the public pressure was more intense, and unless firm party discipline was applied, the silverites would certainly get out of hand.

Amid this fear and confusion former President Grover Cleveland stepped forward to bolster the Bourbon sound-money faction in his party. Since his retirement from the

[22] Josephson, *Politicos*, 462.
[23] *Ibid.*, 480–81.
[24] Spooner to H. H. Camp, May 8, 1890; *id.* to C. K. Wills, June 25, 1890; and *id.* to A. A. Arnold, July 5, 1890, in Spooner MSS.

White House in 1889 Cleveland had been practicing corporation law in partnership with a group closely associated with Wall Street nabobs, and through stock-market speculations he had become moderately wealthy. If anyone had ever doubted his devotion to Wall Street, there was certainly no doubting his position now. Many of the Wall Streeters considered him the only hope for salvation from the fanatical silverites. Many looked upon the stouthearted, stubborn Cleveland as a better bulwark against financial chaos than public-pacifier President Harrison, who had submitted to the Sherman silver-purchase measure. They would back Cleveland for a return engagement at the White House. It was no surprise to Wall Street operators when Cleveland, in February of 1891, issued a forthright public letter in the interest of sound money. With knowing nods of approbation they received Cleveland's pronouncement against "the dangerous and reckless experiment of free, unlimited, and independent silver coinage." [25]

Bourbon Democrats the nation over were much pleased and relieved when Cleveland spoke forth, for they were now provided with a focal point for their political activity and a promise of security for their private economic holdings. Politically, the Bourbons had in Cleveland a presidential candidate whose chances of replacing the unpopular Republican incumbent were good, and general knowledge of that fact served to draw patronage-seeking Democrats to his standard. Middle-western Bourbon leaders thus were given aid in keeping their party workers in line.[26]

Bourbons in the trans-Mississippi wheat belt sought to have their party ignore the silver issue, while those in the more conservative sections made gestures toward endorsing sound money. Most aggressive in endorsement of sound money was the Bourbon-controlled Wisconsin Democracy,

[25] Nevins, *Cleveland*, 468; Josephson, *Politicos*, 489.
[26] Josephson, *Politicos*, 489–90.

where Vilas was anxious to please his friend Cleveland and keep the lid on radical notions. Vilas' response to Cleveland's silver letter had been enthusiastic, and he "felt better" than usual when complimenting the former president on having "let the fools have it direct." Vilas thought the letter "great, big, sound, wise politics." [27] His Democratic legislature apparently had a similar view, for that body shortly passed a resolution against free silver.[28]

As weeks stretched into months without the free-silver storm reviving in Congress or elsewhere, middle-western Bourbons became more optimistic. In the spring of 1891 Vilas reported boastfully to an old colleague of the Cleveland cabinet, William C. Endicott of Massachusetts. After remarking that Cleveland's silver letter "has saved us from an extreme peril," Vilas added that the Wisconsin Democratic legislature's resolution against free silver "ought to help restrain the talk about the position of the west on that question." [29] In midwinter Congressman E. S. Bragg of Wisconsin wrote optimistically to his state party chairman. Apparently he still loved Cleveland "for the enemies he has made," as he had so colorfully said at the nominating convention of 1884. For now he declared that "Cleveland and the tariff will be the next battle cry, and 'unlimited silver coinage' . . . will soon be recognized as a 'fallacious bubble.' " [30]

The Bourbon cabal around Cleveland, notwithstanding Congressman Bragg's assumptions, seemed most indifferent to issues that would appeal to the Middle West. The generally prevailing eastern Bourbon attitude was one of making no concessions to middle-western voters which might impair the Democratic chances in the East; for the eastern

[27] Nevins, *Cleveland*, 469.
[28] Copy dated February 19, 1891, in Anderson MSS.
[29] William F. Vilas to William C. Endicott, May 10, 1891, in Cleveland MSS.
[30] Bragg to Wall, July 31, 1891, in Vilas MSS.

Bourbons felt that victory in the East, added to the supposedly inevitable triumph in the Solid South, would carry
the day. This was clearly set forth in a letter written by
Governor William E. Russell of Massachusetts, who expressed conviction that Cleveland's stand was a happy political stroke. Russell thought that "a wise party policy will
look to Democratic support from New Hampshire, Connecticut, Rhode Island, Massachusetts, and New York,
rather than to Iowa, Kansas, and the Western States." "We
can," said Russell, "afford to let those States be Republican,
provided that we hold our own in the East and South. The
only danger we now see is free coinage. I am sure that if the
Democratic party stands united for that measure it is going
to drive off from us the independent support that we have
won in the East." [31]

On the tariff issue, the Bourbons remembered that the
tariff-reform campaign of 1888 had not broken the Republican hold on the Middle West and had done the party
damage in the East. Ardent talk on the subject seemed simply
to invite the free-trade bugaboo—which frightened too
many important industrialists and lesser people. The Cleveland inner circle, with their eyes trained on the eastern vote,
preferred to exhibit an air of stolid devotion to soundness
in all things touching on big-business activity. They would
spread the impression that Cleveland and his friends were
just as safe on the tariff as on currency. Industrialists would
thus be less insistent in their fight against the Democratic
bid; and, in view of their anxiety over President Harrison's
signature on the silver-purchase act, some of them might
even support the Cleveland cause. The big-business element
wanted that measure repealed, and it appeared that Cleveland was of the same opinion.

Cleveland Bourbons were pleased to discover kindly

[31] William E. Russell to W. L. Wilson, April 10, 1891, as cited in
Nevins, *Cleveland*, 469.

words coming from Republican protectionists. In April, 1893, no less a person than industrialist Andrew Carnegie wrote to the former president: "You know that for several years my chief anxiety in public matters had been in regard to the 'silver question' and that I stated in the North American Review that if I were called upon to vote for a Free Trade Democrat who supported sound money, or a Tariff Republican who was not sound upon money, I should vote for the former."[32]

The key figure in managing the Cleveland cause was wealthy, sagacious William C. Whitney of Wall Street. During Cleveland's first term Whitney had demonstrated unusual ability as a political manager, just as he showed remarkable acumen in forming monopolies in whisky, tobacco, and street railways. He proved equal to the task of stamping out every anti-Cleveland movement appearing in the eastern Democracy, even pricking the presidential bubble of New York's Democratic boss, Senator David B. Hill. Demagogue Hill had gone so far as to endorse bimetallism in order to capture public approval; but Whitney spent his own money on a newspaper campaign, consisting of accounts of Hill's underhanded methods in obtaining delegates favoring his candidacy. That quickly disposed of Hill. In preparing for the national convention, which was scheduled for early June, Whitney astutely called a secret conference of Bourbons to set up a cabal to work in Cleveland's behalf. This inner-circle group of twelve planners from various parts of the nation included such friends of Cleveland as William F. Vilas of Wisconsin, Don Dickinson of Michigan, and F. L. Stetson of New York.[33]

At the convention, which was held in Chicago, the Whitney machine operated like clockwork in securing the nomination of Cleveland. Comparitively few delegates had the

[32] Andrew Carnegie to Cleveland, April 22, 1893, in Cleveland MSS.
[33] Josephson, *Politicos*, 493–95.

audacity to throw away their chances for patronage by voting against "sure-thing" Cleveland. On the first and only
ballot Horace Boies, low-tariff enthusiast and victor in the
1889 Iowa gubernatorial race, obtained 103 votes, and New
York's boss, David B. Hill, collected 114 votes; but Cleveland chalked up an impressive 617⅓. He would have needed
but 607 to obtain the nomination. The silver element was
given a pacifier in the selection of Illinois currency-reformer
Adlai Stevenson as the vice-presidential candidate.[34]

The Whitney machine was less fortunate when trying to
dictate the composition of the platform. On the silver question, a vague, impractical resolution was adopted after
fierce disputation. On the tariff question, erstwhile tariff-
reformer Vilas, in conjunction with Whitney, vainly attempted to gain acceptance of a mild measure which the
two men had written and which Cleveland sanctioned.
Their resolution called for a judicious revision of existing
rates which would not injure "any domestic industries" and
which would be "at every step regardful of labor and capital." [35] This proposal, which was the traditional Republican
position, was too much for tariff reformers. Kentucky editor Henry Watterson and Congressman Tom L. Johnson
killed it in committee. Watterson later reported, in reference
to candidate Cleveland's attitude, that "over the protest of
Whitney, his organizer, and Vilas, his spokesman, I had
forced him to stand on the gospel [of tariff reduction]. He
flew into a rage and threatened to modify, if not to repudiate, the plank in his letter of acceptance." The plank which
was finally adopted, and which Cleveland so much disliked,
denounced the McKinley Act as "the culminating atrocity
of class legislation" and called for duty-free raw materials
and lower rates on manufactured goods.[36]

[34] Nevins, *Cleveland*, 489–91; McElroy, *Cleveland*, I, 340–41.
[35] Josephson, *Politicos*, 497.
[36] Mathilda Gresham, *Life of Walter Quinton Gresham* (Chicago,
1919), II, 266–67; Henry Watterson, *"Marse Henry," An Autobiography*
(New York, 1919), II, 133–34; Josephson, *Politicos*, 497–98.

The platform was thus not entirely to the industrial capitalists' liking, but with the nomination of Cleveland many business leaders felt that they had proof enough that the Democracy was in safe hands. New York banker Jacob H. Schiff felt that the current good leadership and responsibility exhibited in the Democracy were sufficient to destroy any fears that "Democratic ascendancy may become a threat to the prosperity of the country." [37] Industrialists could not fail to be pleased with comments on the tariff question which Cleveland presented in his letter of acceptance: ". . . we wage no exterminating war against any American interests . . . we contemplate a fair and careful distribution of necessary tariff burdens rather than the precipitation of free trade. . . ." [38]

In the ensuing campaign the Cleveland forces faced two political parties—the listless Republican party and the enthusiastic Populist, or People's, party. The Republicans, expediently unwilling to admit their past mistake in advancing Harrison, halfheartedly renominated the uninspiring Indianian. More spirited and enlightened was the Populist party, with its bold challenge to the traditional parties and to economic *laissez faire*. This third party was primarily an agrarian offering, for wage earners were busily giving vent to their wrath through such labor-union activity as the Homestead Strike.

The Populist party was a stage in the organized farmer protest rooted in the Farmers' Alliance movement and in independent parties. In the spring of 1891 a mass convention of farmers formally organized the Populist party on a national basis; and early the next year it held a delegate convention at St. Louis, where a platform was adopted. Four months later the Populists held a spirited national nominating convention at Omaha, where they chose Iowa's

[37] Cyrus Adler, *Jacob H. Schiff: His Life and Letters* (New York, 1928), I, 304.
[38] Josephson, *Politicos*, 515.

James B. Weaver for their presidential candidate and adopted a platform. They carried over from the St. Louis convention, with slight alterations, the preamble which had been written and read by gifted Ignatius Donnelly. It declared:

> . . . we meet in the midst of a nation brought to the verge of moral, political, and material ruin. Corruption dominates the ballot-box, the legislature, the Congress, and touches even the ermine of the bench. The people are demoralized. . . . The newspapers are largely subsidized or muzzled; public opinion silenced; business prostrated; our homes covered with mortgages; labor impoverished and the land concentrating in the hands of the capitalists. The urban workmen are denied the right of organization . . . a hireling standing army, unrecognized by our laws, is established to shoot them down. . . . The fruits of the toil of millions are boldly stolen to build up colossal fortunes for the few. . . . We have witnessed . . . the struggles of the two great political parties for power and plunder. . . .

In the specific reforms called for in the platform, the issues of currency, transportation, and land were most emphasized. The existing banking and credit system, which operated with appalling inadequacy for the farmers, was challenged by a demand for currency inflation. The Populists were convinced that the capitalist-politico partnership dominating the government had artificially raised the value of the gold dollar and thereby enhanced its own wealth and brought distress to the debtors. The Populists thus demanded that the circulating medium "be speedily increased to not less than fifty dollars per capita." The means for accomplishing this should be either direct issuance of paper money or "free and unlimited coinage of silver at the ratio of sixteen to one," or both.

On the transportation issue the Populists went farther than the preceding Granger and Greenbacker revolts. Since regulatory legislation had not sufficed to solve the problem, the Populists advocated government ownership and operation of the nation's railroad, telegraph, and telephone systems. On the land issue they gestured toward conservation by demanding that "railroads and other corporations" be required to return to the government all lands obtained "in excess of their actual needs." The platform, in addition to these three main demands, endorsed the Australian ballot, the initiative and the referendum, direct election of United States senators, a single term for the president and the vice-president, and the "Subtreasury Plan." The last-named scheme called for the establishment of national warehouses wherein farmers might store nonperishable produce as collateral for loans of currency issued on this nonmetallic wealth.[39]

Within this national political framework the middle-western Bourbons fought valiantly to maintain control of their state organizations and deliver the vote to Cleveland. For the most part it was a lone fight, because the national Democratic campaign committee was hesitant about investing money and effort in what seemed a poor gamble. But fortunately the region's Bourbons did possess the political leverage of potential patronage, and consequently they succeeded quite well in convincing state-convention delegates that it would be smart to adopt platforms and name candidates in harmony with the wishes of the Bourbon wise men of the East.

When it came to the actual campaign, there was considerable Democratic deviation from the program outlined at the national convention. It was obvious to politically wise Democrats that the voters had wearied of the confusing, unrewarding Democratic claptrap on the tariff question. The voters had listened to that noise in the 1890 election and had subsequently seen the Democrats' failure to do anything about the tariff situation even after getting a House

[39] Hicks, *Populist Revolt*, 230–32, 238, 256–57.

majority in the election. Hence, in the most depressed areas, determined-to-win candidates concentrated on making free-coinage-of-silver promises. In the less impoverished states the fare included strong doses of antinativist bitters.

In Iowa the election for state offices had taken place in 1891 and had resulted in the re-election of Governor Horace Boies. His victory rested on a pledge to continue his efforts to achieve repeal of the Iowa prohibition law, his opposition to Republican protectionism, and his excellent record in office. In the congressional contests of the following year, according to editor Cyrenus Cole, "what the Democrats did . . . was to give the Populists a mortgage on their party." [40] The voters were not ready to accept free silver, so they voted Republicans into office in ten of the eleven congressional contests and delivered the electoral vote to Harrison. [41]

The 1892 Minnesota contest centered on the three-way gubernatorial race between Populist Ignatius Donnelly, Republican Governor Knute Nelson, and lawyer-Democrat Daniel W. Lawler. It was a battle over personalities, Populist doctrines, racial-religious considerations, tariff reform, and railroad influences. Governor Nelson supposedly had a strong hold on the large Scandinavian population, but many of this element in western and northern Minnesota forsook him for the Populist cause because of his tariff straddle and his alleged affiliations with railroad magnate Jim Hill. Irishman Ignatius Donnelly, who supposedly had considerable strength among his fellow Irishmen, was handicapped by the presence in the race of St. Paul's Irish Catholic Daniel W. Lawler. Sage of Nininger Donnelly believed that the Lawler nomination had been engineered by Jim Hill in an effort to draw Irish Catholic support from the Populist candidate. [42] A Populist editor reported to Donnelly that

[40] Cole, *I Remember*, 194.
[41] *Ibid.*, 194; Nixon, "Populist Movement," *loc. cit.*, 58, 64–65.
[42] Folwell, *History of Minnesota*, III, 196; Hicks, *Populist Revolt*, 258; Odland, *Nelson*, 165.

"the corporation element apparently had absolute control in the Democratic convention . . . and ruled things with an iron hand." [43] The outcome was a general Republican victory. Unsavory activity within the machine-controlled Democracy continued. In selecting a United States senator the Democrats, charged the St. Paul *Pioneer Press*, conspired to stop the re-election of Senator C. K. Davis.[44] The Democratic legislators and a few Republicans were supposedly involved in a bribery deal to defeat Davis. But Davis was re-elected—although by a margin of victory much smaller than had been generally anticipated.[45]

The free-silver and tariff battles in Nebraska supplied the most drama and brought out in sharpest outline the Bourbon-Populist cleavage in the 1892 middle-western campaign. Nebraska, along with the newly admitted Dakotas, the western border states, and the silver-mining region, constituted the area of most intense northern Populist activity. In a sense this Populist area, like the Granger Northwest of the seventies, was a unit in itself; but at the same time it blended into the other sections where the agrarian bitterness had not as yet reached such a high pitch. In another sense the mixed farming of Nebraska made the state a bridge between the older and newer agrarian Wests, just as increasing industry in parts of Illinois and Wisconsin blended the agrarian Middle West into the still more industrialized states to the east.

Nebraska Democrats, caught in an intense pulling from two directions, found it impossible to compromise their differences. On the one hand were the Bourbons, backed by railroad barons, liquor distillers, and scattered interests representing moderate or more than moderate wealth. The Republican hierarchy drew its support from the same economic level. The railroad interests were the chief bulwark of both the Bourbons and the Republican bigwigs. Pulling

[43] H. B. Martin to Ignatius Donnelly, August 4, 1892, in Donnelly MSS.
[44] St. Paul *Pioneer Press*, January 13, 1893.
[45] Hall, *Political Contests*, 185–88.

from the other direction was a sizable mass of angry debtor and near-debtor farmers, many of whom, in disgust, had joined the Populist party or remained in the old parties to bore from within.

The Bourbon Democrats of Nebraska had met with surprising success in the 1890 election. The Republican McKinley Tariff and the prohibition agitation had landed Omaha's James E. Boyd in the governor's chair. He was a wealthy real-estate operator and friend of the railroads and the distillery interests, and he shared with George L. Miller the pleasurable job of dispensing considerable federal patronage for President Cleveland. The Miller-Boyd machine had gradually pushed aside the anti-Cleveland tariff reformer J. Sterling Morton. But the 1890 Democratic victory, together with a newly acquired conviction that only Cleveland could win for the Bourbon Democrats in 1892, caused the disgruntled Morton to patch up his differences with the Miller-Boyd machine. It thus appeared that the 1892 Democratic campaign, as in the days before the Cleveland election in 1884, would be a show directed by the Morton-Miller-Boyd trio.[46]

Before the Morton-Miller-Boyd combination could be certain of complete control of the Nebraska Democracy, it had to make certain of co-operation from William Jennings Bryan, popular young lawyer-politico of Omaha. This young Illinois-born spellbinder had arrived in the state in 1887, bringing with him a letter of introduction to J. Sterling Morton. Bryan, then but twenty-seven years old, made a favorable impression on Morton and became a frequent visitor at Morton's Arbor Lodge home at Nebraska City. On one occasion, in 1888, Bryan came to Nebraska City to speak in behalf of his new friend's bid for a seat in Congress. This moved Morton to record in his personal journal that "Bryan . . . is a remarkably promising man. He has gifts.

[46] Hibben, *Bryan*, 123–25; Olson, *Morton*, 336–38.

He will be, with good habits and right directions, a bene-
factor to good government." In 1890 Bryan utilized his
remarkable oratorical ability and instinct for determining
the public mood to his own political advancement. He was
elected to Congress, after a campaign that pleased tariff
reformers and was not displeasing to his Omaha distillery
backers and the antiprotectionists. Upon Bryan's nomination for Congress, George Miller had asked J. Sterling Morton: "Who the hell is Bryan?" He had received assurance
that "Mr. Bryan is able, eloquent and of most pure and un-
tainted character. His election, which I consider quite probable will do honor to every citizen in this District. And to
elect him I am doing all that is in my power to do." [47]

Before long, however, Morton had reason to wonder if
he had been discreet in backing young Bryan—for this new
congressman was a free-silver advocate. He wrote a free-
silver plank into the 1890 state platform. The Bourbons felt
no great concern then, because the campaigning was confined principally to the issues of tariff and prohibition. Even
Bryan had no opportunity to use the silver question to gather
votes, for his Republican opponent held free-silver views.
But soon the free-silver boom was in full swing, and Bryan
was in its midst. When the Nebraska Democrats met to
select delegates to the 1892 national convention, Bryan made
an eloquent and almost successful plea for passage of a
resolution endorsing free coinage. And he nearly succeeded
in sweeping the delegates into an endorsement of Iowa's
Horace Boies for the presidency.

At the state nominating convention, held four months
later, Bryan again threatened to upset the political apple-
cart of the Morton-Miller-Boyd machine. But the Bourbon
trio managed to soft-soap Bryan by persuading him, temporarily, that his great forte was tariff reform. The Bourbon
chieftains even had him deliver the main convention speech

---

[47] Olson, *Morton*, 331-32.

—on the tariff. The Bourbons managed to squeeze through
the convention without free silver being mentioned in the
platform, and they obtained the nomination of J. Sterling
Morton for the governorship. Governor Boyd was satisfied
with one term only—partly, it would seem, because of the
unpopularity which he had engendered by vetoing a measure prescribing maximum railroad-freight rates.[48]

The railroad barons, as usual, had no reason to fear Morton. In fact, testimony of his continued friendship for the
railroads was present in the quiet but fruitless movement of
railroad men to secure his appointment to the Interstate
Commerce Commission, where less-safe Democrat William
R. Morrison was already ensconced. In the autumn of 1891
a Chicago railroad president urged a member of Harrison's
cabinet to use his influence in behalf of Morton's appointment. To this railroad executive, Morton was "a fair man
for all interests, and his experience has been such as to enable him to approach the questions coming before the Commission with some considerable previous preparation of
study and practical dealing." [49]

Bourbon Morton, although adept at practical dealing in
connection with railroads, proved inadequate to the task of
nullifying the Populists' clamor and William Jennings
Bryan's attempt to get re-elected to Congress. Bryan broke
from the Bourbon leash and campaigned for free silver.
With refreshing candor he practiced democracy, instead of
merely paying lip service to the theory or distorting its true
meaning. He frankly and disarmingly told voters: "I don't
know anything about free silver. The people of Nebraska
are for free silver and I am for free silver. I will look up the
arguments later." [50]

In contrast, gubernatorial candidate Morton took the

[48] *Ibid.*, 335, 338–39.
[49] R. Miller (of Chicago) to Rusk, September 4, 1891, in Rusk MSS.
[50] Omaha *World-Herald*, September 28, 1892, as cited in Hibben, *Bryan*,
145; Olson, *Morton*, 344–45.

hard, futile course of directly bucking the free-silver storm. He tried to interest the voters in tariff reform, sound money, and the defects of the popular Populist gubernatorial candidate, Charles H. Van Wyck. At the same time Morton refrained from attacking his Republican opponent, Lorenzo Crounse, whom he liked and considered a man worthy of the governorship. So apparent was Morton's avoidance of attacking Crounse and his onslaught upon Van Wyck that it appeared to many that he was merely "playing the role of tail to Crounse's kite." In the final count Morton went down in the worst defeat of his political career, coming in a poor third to the victorious Crounse. Bryan was re-elected to Congress, with his district giving him a plurality of 140 votes and his "colleague" Morton a terrific drubbing.[51]

The Bourbons then carried their battle into the state legislature, in an effort to obtain a United States senatorship for Morton. If party lines meant anything, the seventeen Democratic legislators held the balance of power. The Republicans showed a willingness to co-operate, but only five of the Democrats were Bourbons. The remainder of the Democrats united with the large Populist delegation and sent able Populist William V. Allen to the Senate. Bourbon control of the Nebraska Democracy, and reactionary dominance of the state in general, had been placed on the skids.[52]

The Democrats of Wisconsin and Illinois followed a different course and were much more successful than their Nebraska cousins. Wisconsin and Illinois voters were not obsessed with the silver craze and were kept clear of succumbing to it by a carefully fostered campaign built around concentration on social cleavages. Nativism, finding expression in the parochial-school issue, provided the excitement for the 1892 election, with a dash of tariff reform thrown in

[51] Olson, *Morton*, 342–44, 345–46.
[52] Addison E. Sheldon, "Nebraskans I Have Known: 1. William V. Allen," *Nebraska History Magazine*, XIX (July–September, 1938), 191–206; Hicks, *Populist Revolt*, 281–83; Olson, *Morton*, 350–51.

for good measure. In Wisconsin the Republican-sponsored Bennett law, which interfered with parochial schools, was still rankling in the minds of German Lutherans, Scandinavian Lutherans, and Catholics. In Illinois the Republicans had in 1889 enacted a school law which was fundamentally the same as the Wisconsin measure. This Illinois law, the Edwards act, provided for compulsory eduction of children up to twelve years of age and contained some slaps at the parochial schools. Lutherans and Catholics resented the provisions that reading, writing, arithmetic, history, and geography must be taught in English and that state truant officers must inspect both public and parochial schools.[53] The emergence of a large nativist secret society, the American Protective Association or A.P.A., as it was called, added to the uneasiness of the foreign element and correspondingly added fuel to the antinativist crusade. By the time of the 1892 campaign the Democrats had decided that it would be an excellent focal point for their election bid.

The central political figure in the Wisconsin-Illinois antinativist campaign was Wisconsin's Democratic state chairman, Edward C. Wall. There was nothing amateurish or sentimental in the political approach of Chairman Wall. An efficient and enterprising businessman without being in the mogul class, Wall managed the Wisconsin Democracy with devotion to system and thoroughness. He maintained friendly relations with political competitors, even to the extent of causing the rumor to spread that he and state Republican Chairman H. C. Payne managed Wisconsin politics jointly. Wall and Payne had offices in the same building, were both involved in the Milwaukee electric utilities, and were poker-playing cronies of long standing.[54] Neither had an abiding personal desire to champion crusades against the monopolists, but they engaged in friendly rivalry of a poker-politics variety.

[53] Clendenin, *Autobiography*, 188.   [54] Plumb, *Badger Politics*, 102.

Determined to outsmart Republican Payne and at the same time to increase his own prestige in politics and the business world, Democrat Wall focused his attention on the nativist issue. His experiences in heavily German Milwaukee and his remarkable success in directing the party organization during the 1890 Bennett law furor deepened Wall's conviction that continued use of the issue might well place the state permanently in the Democratic column. Following the 1890 election Republican Chairman Payne lamented that the "worst feature of the situation is the almost hopeless task of getting back our German Republicans without whose help it is impossible to carry Wisconsin." [55] Democrat Wall, with his eye fixed on that same cold fact, discussed little else than the nativist issue in the ensuing five years of reporting political affairs to his chief, William F. Vilas.

So thorough was Wall that he rounded out his program to embrace the foreign element of neighboring Illinois. He utilized every opportunity to bring about a united Wisconsin-Illinois front on the issue. There was a close connection between the "foreigners" of these states, because of their church ties, foreign-tongue newspapers, and anti-parochial school laws in both states. It was thus highly desirable that the kindred spirits of both states be treated to a clear-cut and united propaganda front which left no room for confusion and disagreement. This was brought about through extensive correspondence between Wisconsin and Illinois political managers and through such means as working in harmony to effect the friendship of foreign-language newspapers edited in centers like Milwaukee and Chicago.[56]

Wisconsin's Wall did not overlook the obtainment of adequate funds for the campaign, and for this task he found

[55] Payne to Rusk, December 2, 1890, in Rusk MSS.

[56] Wall to William F. Vilas, February 27, 1892; *id.* to *id.*, May 17, 1892; *id.* to *id.*, July 20, 1892; *id.* to *id.*, September 5, 1892; and *id.* to *id.*, September 8, 1892, in Vilas MSS.

aid and comfort in the person of money-laden Henry Villard and in a fund collected and distributed by the New York *World*. Villard, erstwhile journalist and currently a mighty railroad promoter and president of the Northern Pacific Railroad, was drawn to Wall by a combination of circumstances. For one, the fact that Villard had been an immigrant from Germany gave him a particular interest in the large German population of the Middle West. He also had a financial stake, along with Democratic Chairman Wall and Republican Chairman Payne, in Milwaukee electric utilities. In fact, Villard's interest in electricity extended to giving Thomas A. Edison a helping hand and founding, in 1889, the Edison General Electric Company.

The main cause of Villard's interest in the middle-western political situation was his determination to see Grover Cleveland back in the White House, where he could lead the battle to repeal the Sherman silver-purchase act and establish the gold standard in its place. As a holder of securities and the agent of powerful German banks which held American securities, Villard was determined to do all in his power to make sure that these holdings would continue to be payable in gold. He was convinced, after an 1891 tour of his Northern Pacific Railroad, that a depression was not far off and that western radicals were aggravating the situation and endangering the chances of financial interests' finding a haven in sound currency. Farmer-legislators, he observed, were spreading "an epidemic of dishonesty . . . manifesting itself in the most outrageous legislative violence to railroads and the free coinage of silver infatuation." Thus did Villard bend every effort to elect Cleveland to the presidency, and thus did a portion of his private campaign fund land in German constituencies of the Middle West.[57]

As early as the spring of 1892 Chairman Wall of Wis-

[57] Josephson, *Politicos*, 488–91; William W. Wight, *Henry Clay Payne, A Life* (Milwaukee, 1907), 58.

consin was interesting Villard in the possibility of delivering the German vote to Cleveland. In March, Wall received
word from Villard's private secretary that "I have your
confidential note. Of course, we [the local company] are
not in a flourishing condition, and do not feel like spending
much money. Still, we can see the desirability of being on
good terms with your political friends. If you will please
indicate the minimum amount you think would be acceptable, we will let you hear from us." [58] Wall also made it a
point to work in harmony with the New York operator on
the free-silver question, conferring personally with Villard on a suitable currency plank for the Wisconsin Democracy. Villard requested Wall "to draw one that he could
submit to Mr. Cleveland" for possible correction. That was
done, and the resulting plank was, according to Wall, "very
gratifying indeed to Villard," who henceforth had "more
than usual interest in Wisconsin." The New Yorker had
the Wisconsin sound-money platform, as corrected by
Cleveland, printed in pamphlet form and circulated.[59] The
Wisconsin Democracy's currency stand which thus emerged
was "We denounce the Republican legislation on this subject, more particularly the Sherman Act of 1890 as a cow-
ardly makeshift and an inexcusable waste of the national
resources in the purchase and storage of seven tons of silver
bullion per day, and as a menace to the maintenance of a
sound and stable currency; and we demand the repeal of
that act." [60]

To ensure results in the Wisconsin Democracy's crusade,
interested parties, especially in the East, contributed generously. Villard sent $40,000 and included Wisconsin in the
area to be served by his "German Bureau." The plan of this

[58] C. A. Spofford to Wall, March 12, 1892, in Villard MSS., as cited
in Josephson, *Politicos*, 490–91.
[59] Wall to William F. Vilas, April 21, 1890; *id.* to *id.*, April 27, 1890; *id.*
to *id.*, April 29, 1890; and *id.* to *id.*, November 30, 1892, in Vilas MSS.
[60] Copy sent by *id.* to *id.*, May 23, 1892, *ibid.*

bureau, embracing in its activities the states of New York, Indiana, Illinois, and Wisconsin, included stationing one or two German experts in each of these states and setting up a literary department headed by a man to be imported directly from Germany. The Wisconsin Democracy also obtained over $70,000 from the mysterious New York *World* fund, which was used in part to maintain the friendship of foreign-language newspapers. The "*World* people" sent $15,000 for Wall's "special purpose," getting control of the German-language newspaper the Chicago *Germania,* but the money came too late in the fall to save it from slipping into Republican clutches.[61] Home-state people also aided the Wisconsin Democracy, the Milwaukee brewers' contribution being $21,500. Milwaukee's Congressman John Mitchell, son of wealthy banker Alexander Mitchell, contributed to the cause; Ashland's John Knight, a northern Wisconsin lumber operator and an associate of Senator Vilas, also added to the campaign fund.[62] The national Democratic campaign committee, however, sent no money into any middle-western state. Not until late in July, when trouble with the New York Hill machine threatened the Democracy with defeat in New York, did the national campaign managers look with interest toward the Middle West. They then discovered that Wisconsin and Illinois might be carried, thereby offsetting the possible loss of New York.[63] But before they could send any money to those states, the New York situation cleared up; and they continued to confine their spending to the eastern campaign.

The actual campaigning in Wisconsin was a still hunt. Senator Vilas, as a national leader, helped his eastern cohorts in the areas considered more important, and Wisconsin was

[61] *Id.* to *id.,* July 20, 1892; *id.* to *id.,* August 12, 1892; *id.* to *id.* (telegram), August 13, 1892; *id.* to *id.,* September 8, 1892; and *id.* to *id.,* November 30, 1892, *ibid.*

[62] *Id.* to *id.,* May 27, 1892; and *id.* to *id.,* October 14, 1894, *ibid.*

[63] Cleveland to *id.,* July 24, 1892; and Wall to *id.,* August 12, 1892, *ibid.*

left without any important figure to stump the state thoroughly. Local and state leaders did personal-contact work with the voters. Much was done indirectly through Wall's recruitment of Catholic and Lutheran editors and clergy. There was also considerable activity on the part of office seekers. In one congressional district, for example, E. S. Bragg made an eight-day house-to-house campaign in the interest of a congressional candidate; and in the same district many other Democrats worked assiduously. To that district Wall "sent 5,500 personal letters" and $100; Congressman John Mitchell sent $500; and John Knight, $100. Such activity resulted in a Democratic victory in the November election.[64]

For the first time since before the Civil War Wisconsin went Democratic in a presidential election. Cleveland was given the electoral vote; six of the ten congressional seats went to Democrats; and the state legislature had a Democratic majority which subsequently sent Milwaukee's John Mitchell to the United States Senate.[65] The outcome prompted former Senator Thomas F. Bayard to write his friend Vilas: "Allow me to raise my hat to Wisconsin— Martin Luther deserves a new statue—now his pupils turn against religious bigotry in the 'far west.' "[66] The parochial-school question, the tariff issue, hard times, ample campaign funds, and excellent party management had combined to bring the victory.

Vilas, whose inner-circle rule in the Cleveland machine placed him at the patronage font, was the real boss of the Wisconsin Democracy. This he soon demonstrated by forcing the selection of banker John Mitchell as junior senator from the state. Many Democrats did not want this son of Alexander Mitchell as senator, because they realized that

---

[64] Wall to *id.*, May 23, 1892; and *id.* to *id.*, November 30, 1892, *ibid.*

[65] *Id.* to Don Dickinson (of Michigan), November 23, 1892, *ibid.*

[66] T. F. Bayard to William F. Vilas, November 15, 1892, *ibid.* See also Wall to Cleveland, June 12, 1893, in Cleveland MSS.

he was but a Vilas tool, who would take orders from his chief on patronage matters and at the same time would add nothing to Democratic popularity with the voters. A faction of discontented Democrats rallied around colorful and popular E. S. Bragg and tried to deliver the senatorship to him. It appeared that many Republican legislators would join in this anti-Vilas, pro-Bragg effort.[67] In order to check this move Vilas wielded the whip, instructing his friend Colonel John H. Knight to bury his own ambitions for the post and switch his personal following to Mitchell. In January, 1893, Colonel Knight reported to "Boss" Vilas that he had "strained the charitable side of my nature and carried out your wishes." Despite his own personal ambition for the position, and although fully convinced that the selection of Mitchell meant victory for the Republicans in the next election, Knight carried out the orders from above. Perhaps he realized that his chances were slim. "There got to be a danger of Bragg's nomination," reported Knight, "and before I withdrew I had to take my men in hand individually and appeal to them to vote for Mitchell. A considerable majority of them were for Bragg but I finally got fourteen to agree to vote for Mitchell and he is now nominated." But before delivering these votes Knight made Mitchell "agree to the following . . . in writing: 1. Be loyal to Cleveland; 2. Be loyal to Vilas. 3. That the northern [Wisconsin] Democrats should have their just and fair share of patronage and the industrial interests of that section receive his constant care. [4.] That he would recommend [Vilas'] selections of Democrats in the northern part of the state to have offices." [68]

The final selection of Mitchell for the senatorship did not quiet the Bragg supporters. The Vilas clan had reason to wish that they had brought about an earlier suggestion of

[67] Bryant to William F. Vilas, January 23, 1893, in Vilas MSS.
[68] Knight to id., January 23, 1893, ibid.

Wall's, that Bragg be given a foreign post so as to get him "out of the way and have his followers satisfied." Wall reported in June that the Mitchell victory "created a most unfriendly feeling throughout the state within our ranks, so we should get Bragg a good appointment." Wall further observed that there was a "strong feeling in Milwaukee that he was badly treated, and this grows as you go into the state; and the result is feeling against Milwaukee." [69] It appeared that boss Vilas had overplayed his hand and was thus heading his Bourbon machine into trouble.

In neighboring Illinois the Democratic campaign effort was in one notable aspect similar to that of Wisconsin Democrats—the prominence given the parochial-school question.[70] Responsibility for making use of this issue was due largely to the Wisconsin Democrats' influence on Illinois Democratic leaders and foreign-element spokesmen, the campaign efforts of gubernatorial candidate John Peter Altgeld, and the energetic activity of campaign-manager Congressman Benjamin T. Cable. The initial impetus came from the Wisconsin Democrats, for Wall had been concentrating on the parochial-school question since the 1890 campaign, at a time when some Illinois Democrats were even showing a favorable attitude toward the anti–parochial school Edwards measure. For a long time Wall was very disgusted with the Illinois Democrats' failure to make more of their opportunity to concentrate on the question. In May, 1892, he felt that what support the Illinois Democracy had among the German Lutherans was due to the Wisconsin-engendered agitation; and he pointed out that Wisconsin Lutherans Hurth, Schlerf, Ernst, Notz and Schutte had worked in Illinois "for weeks on minister friends." And as late as July Illinois' state chairman Erskine M. Phelps was so inactive

[69] Wall to *id.*, September 4, 1893; and *id.* to *id.*, June 30, 1894, *ibid.*

[70] Goudy to Cleveland, September 14, 1892; J. L. Ulrich to *id.*, September 15, 1892; and G. A. Asche to *id.*, September 16, 1893, in Cleveland MSS.

and bumbling that "everything is at sixes and sevens in Illinois." [71]

Chairman Phelps, who even had the notion that the national Democratic committee would come to the rescue with about a hundred thousand dollars, finally relinquished management of the campaign to aggressive Congressman Benjamin T. Cable. This well-educated and wealthy young socialite was thought to have his sights set for a foreign post. And equally ambitious was his brilliant and beautiful wife, who was a granddaughter of Thomas H. Benton. Cable stepped forward in the campaign to direct affairs. Between fifty and one hundred thousand dollars was collected.[72] The money raising, if Altgeld's later assertion was correct, was really done by Bourbon Judge Lambert Tree, and Cable merely did the spending and took the credit.[73] In any case, this spirited Bourbon activity and the popularity of Cleveland among big business men aided the new manager in overcoming the financial handicap of radical blemishes on the state party shield. The majority of delegates at the state convention had shown free-silver leanings and had nominated "unsafe" Altgeld for the governorship. Moreover, Illinois' Congressman Adlai Stevenson, vice-presidential candidate, was a free-silver advocate.[74] This kept the Illinois Democracy from receiving outright financial backing from easterners like Henry Villard. The expenditure of eastern money on middle-western foreign-language newspapers, through Wisconsin's Wall, nevertheless brought indirect aid from the East; and the German Bureau included Illinois in its plans.

One candidate in the Illinois campaign, Altgeld, early

[71] Wall to William F. Vilas, May 17, 1892; and *id.* to *id.*, July 20, 1892, in Vilas MSS.

[72] *Id.* to *id.*, September 5, 1892; and *id.* to *id.*, September 8, 1892, *ibid.*

[73] John Peter Altgeld to Cleveland, July 12, 1893, in Cleveland MSS.

[74] Edward M. Shepherd to *id.*, September 10, 1892; and Cleveland to Shepherd, September 14, 1892, *ibid.*

demonstrated that he needed no aid from the Cleveland organization. Born in Germany in 1847, he had grown up in Missouri, where, during the antimonopoly upsurge of the early seventies, he had championed the Granger cause. In 1875 he moved to Chicago to practice law and there soon demonstrated an interest in politics. In 1884, running as a Cleveland Democrat, the personable Altgeld made an unsuccessful bid for Congress. Soon afterward he became interested in the chaotic labor conditions in Chicago, and in 1886 he submitted an essay to the Chicago *Mail*, pleading for compulsory arbitration of labor controversies. Later he became a municipal judge and took an active part in real-estate operations. All the while his sympathy for the underdog grew apace, and he wrote a pamphlet called *Live Questions* which revealed him as favoring a more enlightened and liberal treatment of the wage earners.

His personality and his record for fair play on the bench brought him much favor among the lower social strata of Chicago. "King Mike" McDonald, a power in the Cook County Democracy, took a fancy to Altgeld and decided to give his fellow Chicagoan a political boost. During 1891 an Altgeld-for-governor boom was thus put in motion, and in the following spring the Cook County Democratic convention endorsed Judge Altgeld for the governorship. At the state convention, where he was quickly nominated, his cause was aided by the mistaken belief among the delegates that Altgeld had made a million-dollar fortune in an office-building-construction venture and hence would spend a considerable amount of his own money in the campaign.[75]

Altgeld carried on an active election campaign, in which he spent most of his private fortune of about a hundred thousand dollars. He made a shrewd "just folks" tour of the state, visiting an amazingly large number of individuals

[75] Harry Bernard, *"Eagle Forgotten," The Life of John Peter Altgeld* (New York, 1938), 148–55.

and conducting himself in a manner that called forth a statement by the Chicago *Inter-Ocean:* "Judge Altgeld has visited more families, kissed more babies, inspected more dairies and helped set more hens than any man before who wanted to be Governor." Candidate Altgeld also made it a point to call on leading businessmen in the various towns and chat with them about his real-estate project and how he had spent years as a judge in the enforcement of laws.

Algeld's shrewdest tactic was his handling of the parochial-school question. He administered a blistering attack on his opponent, Governor Joseph Fifer, for signing the anti–parochial school Edwards act. In this Altgeld was unfair, because not only had nearly as many Democrats as Republicans voted for the measure in the legislature but Altgeld himself had been almost as active in urging its passage as had Fifer. However, the opposition learned of German-born Altgeld's part in the passage of the Edwards act too late to use the information in the campaign. A big majority in Chicago tipped the scales for a general Democratic victory.[76]

Nationally the Bourbons won the election count. They not only defeated the Republicans but demonstrated that they could win without making concessions to the middle-western farm voters. The combined Cleveland victories in the East and the Solid South were great enough to ensure Cleveland's election, and they made unimportant the almost unsolicited electoral votes from Wisconsin and Illinois. Middle-western Bourbons could feel emotionally elated over carrying two states and could look forward to such patronage rewards as they had received during Cleveland's previous term in the White House.

The middle-western Bourbons needed all the enthusiasm

[76] *Ibid.,* 156–61; Bogart and Thompson, *Industrial State,* 183–86; Wall to William F. Vilas, September 5, 1892, in Vilas MSS.

and patronage which they could wring from the Cleveland victory, for there were signs of trouble ahead. They were threatened with loss of their perch on the party lid in the region. Farmer discontent with economic conditions was growing in intensity, and through the free-silver crusade it was finding an outlet which Bourbons could not easily bury by the sham battle over tariff reform and fleeting up-surges of religious and racial issues. Popular and determined leaders were emerging to threaten the Bourbon machine, even within the Bourbon-monopolized Democratic organization itself. The activities of Nebraska's Bryan and Illinois' Altgeld had shown that able leadership rooted in popular sentiment was equal to the task of booting the Bourbons out of party control. The Populist party was threatening the Bourbon Democracy from without. Populist presidential candidate Weaver had collected over a million votes. Most of these were outside the Middle West, but the Populist strength was creeping into that area. Weaver's percentage of the presidential vote was about 40 in Nebraska, 11.5 in Minnesota, 4.5 in Iowa, and 2.5 in Wisconsin and Illinois.[77] Populist doctrines were creeping into the Democratic party leadership as men like Adlai Stevenson, Horace Boies, and William Jennings Bryan demonstrated friendship for the free-silver panacea.

The greatest Bourbon danger lay in the nature of the 1892 victory. Because the eastern Bourbons had not needed electoral votes from the Middle West, they would doubtless continue their political policy of no concessions to any middle-western demand which might impair the Bourbon majority in the East. This was made more certain by the presence of Grover Cleveland at the helm, for this stubborn and honest champion of the eastern brand of laissez-faire liberal capitalism certainly would not bow to radical ideas

[77] Hicks, *Populist Revolt*, 263.

from the agrarian West. Political and economic factors had brought victory to the eastern Bourbons and a mood of revolt to the agrarians. Only a sudden turn toward prosperity or compromise could head off a widening of the cleavage—and such a turn was not in the nature of the current economic-political system and its current Bourbon guardians.

Chapter Eleven

Damnably Mauled
1893-1896

> *To laud Clevelandism on Jefferson's birthday is*
> *to sing a Te deum in honor of Judas Iscariot on*
> *Christmas morning.*
>
> —JOHN PETER ALTGELD

DURING THE second Cleveland administration the Bourbon Democracy outdid itself in effrontery and finally collected its just reward. Ever since the Civil War the Bourbons, along with the Republican hierarchy, had ridden the wave of a rampant and unhumanized brand of capitalism. Seldom had the Bourbons been bowed into public office, but never had they been left without control of the national Democratic organization. With dominance over the national party machine the Bourbons had what they and their partners in economic exploitation wanted most—insurance against a massed democratic onslaught from the unhappy, dispossessed agrarians and despoiled wage laborers. Bourbon practices had helped add to the nation's wealth and had brought many conveniences, but the material rewards which the Bourbons collected and the sacrifices and risks which they asked of the less fortunate were not in keeping with a humane concept of responsible leadership. Some of the Bourbons' failure to be worthy stewards of the people could be laid to incompetence bred of innocent ignorance; some was a product of ivory-tower dogmatism; some resulted from sheer cupidity; all added up to a need for their removal from political leadership.

The fortunes of politics chanced to place the Bourbons in national power at a time when their cherished system of exploitation and monopolistic capitalism ran amuck—and with economic consequences more dire than at any previous depression in the post–Civil War period. Within two months after Cleveland assumed office for his second term, the great panic of 1893 was delivering serious deflationary blows at the national economy. Onward it swept, all the time gaining momentum and inflicting untold suffering and financial ruination. By the end of 1894, 642 banks had closed, 22,500 miles of railway were in receivership, and a fourth of the heavy industries were moribund. The government's gold reserve dwindled rapidly. Unemployment among the wage earners was appalling. The farmers' plight became steadily worse. Between 1891 and 1895 the farmers' returns, based on estimates of the ten leading crops, shrank each year: in 1891 the crop value per acre averaged $14.70; by 1895 it had dropped to $9.71. In 1893 and 1894 the farmer received only thirty to forty cents for a bushel of wheat which cost him at least fifty cents to produce. And all the while—despite the existence of the Interstate Commerce Commission—freight charges on hauling grain rose. The angry people gave very pointed vent to their desperation through politics, strikes, demonstrations, and all manner of agitation. Along the way occurred such episodes as the Chicago Pullman strike and the march on Washington by Coxey's Army of unemployed, a living petition for reform.[1]

James J. Hill wrote several times to Cleveland, describing conditions in the hinterland and suggesting remedies. In the middle of June, 1893, he reported that he had made "careful inquiry along over five hundred miles of our lines as to the ability of the farmers to find the necessary money to pay for their binding twine, and the little they need for harvest help." And the result of the survey was "that but

---

[1] Nevins, *Cleveland*, 591–94; Josephson, *Politicos*, 538, 560.

A WESTERN PROTEST

In Harvey, *Coin's Financial School*, 91.

very few of the farmers have any money, and the local banks are unable to aid them." A year later Hill informed Secretary Daniel Lamont that on the labor-business front, "The panic of last year is nothing, compared with the reign of terror that exists in the large centers. Business is at a standstill, and the people are becoming thoroughly aroused. Their feeling is finding expression about as it did during the War of the Rebellion." [2]

Against the background of panic the Cleveland administration sternly adhered to the precepts of laissez-faire economics. The men Cleveland gathered around him were Bourbons. The legislative, administrative, and political program that was forthcoming from the President and his Bourbon cohorts was a stubbornly consistent defense of all the things which the Bourbons had stood for during their three decades of ignoring public demands for economic reform. There was no truckling to the people, no new ideas. Three Bourbons having particular importance for the Middle West were J. Sterling Morton, William F. Vilas, and Richard Olney. These Cleveland lieutenants worked harmoniously in the interest of laissez-faire business and were socially very congenial. Morton often vacationed at the Olney summer place at Falmouth, Maine. Morton and Vilas dined frequently at the Olneys' Washington home, where it became a tradition for the trio to join forces on Sunday evenings to partake of meals which included boiled onions.[3] Bostonian Olney served the onions as a concession to the middle-western tastes of his guests—and did so with the New England regularity usually applied to baked beans.

The occasion for Morton's presence in Washington was not his usual one of lobbying for railroad barons but rather of carrying on his cabinet duties as secretary of agriculture.

[2] Hill to Cleveland, June 15, 1893, in Cleveland MSS.; *id.* to Lamont, July 7, 1894, in Lamont MSS. See also *id.* to Cleveland, April 4, 1893; *id.* to *id.*, July 4, 1893; and *id.* to *id.*, May 5, 1894, in Cleveland MSS.

[3] Olson, *Morton*, 354-55.

President Cleveland, generously overlooking Morton's past criticisms of the first Cleveland administration, had been impressed by his fight to keep the Nebraska Democracy from falling prey to Bryan and the Populists. The result was the selection of the Nebraskan as the middle-western representative on the cabinet.[4] Friends of Wisconsin's Democratic chairman, E. C. Wall, had attempted to secure a cabinet post for the Milwaukean, but the task of looking after Wall was finally turned over to Henry Villard, who steered considerable law business in Wall's direction. Wall found that serving as a receiver in connection with the Northern Pacific Railroad was lucrative compensation for his services to the party.[5] A movement to place William R. Morrison on the cabinet was nipped in the bud. Apparently either Henry Villard or Jim Hill, or both, disapproved of Morrison's record on the Interstate Commerce Commission and therefore prevailed upon Cleveland to overlook him.[6]

Certainly neither Wall nor Morrison could have equaled Morton as a caustically outspoken enemy of Populism in all its aspects. As secretary of agriculture he proved to be efficient, hard-working, economical, and genuinely interested in civil-service reform; as a spokesman for the Cleveland Democracy he delivered a headlong and headstrong flailing at the Populist opposition. His first public address as secretary, delivered in October, 1893, opening the Congress of Agriculture held in connection with the Chicago World's Fair, was a startling insult to agrarian leaders. "The most insidious and destructive foe to the farmer," said the tactless Morton, "is the 'professional' farmer who, as a 'promoter' of granges and alliances, for political purposes, *Farms the Farmer*. . . ." He also offered a solution to the farmer's problems, recommending that each farmer assiduously study

[4] *Ibid.*, 349–50, 352.
[5] Wall to William F. Vilas, January 20, 1893; *id.* to *id.*, January 23, 1893; and *id.* to *id.*, December 20, 1896, in Vilas MSS.
[6] Scott, "Political Career of William R. Morrison," *loc. cit.*, 166.

Adam Smith's *The Wealth of Nations*, which he characterized as being "to political economy as the New Testament
is to the Christian religion." He also urged as solutions the
careful daily reading of a newspaper "from a great city,"
fighting for free trade, and allowing no restrictions upon
private accumulation of wealth. The response was widespread anger among farmers and approbation from other
quarters. The National Grange passed a resolution demanding his removal from office; editor Walter Hines Page induced him to write an amplification of the Chicago address
for publication in the *Forum*. The *North American Review*
published a similar Morton outburst.[7]

In handling patronage Morton failed to show, with a few
exceptions, any real interest. And he discovered before very
long, as did the entire Cleveland cabal, that the patronage
device was not equal to the task of keeping many middle-
western officeholders in line and that it alienated many disappointed office seekers. At the outset he turned the Nebraska patronage dispensation over to two loyal Bourbon
politicos. One was national committeeman Tobias Castor,
trouble shooter for the Burlington Railroad; the other was
state party chairman Euclid Martin, wealthy Omaha paint
manufacturer. These men worked assiduously to fortify
the Nebraska Democracy against the influences of William
Jennings Bryan. Free-silverite Bryan, despite his being the
only Nebraska Democrat in Congress, was granted no patronage to distribute,[8] so the Morton-Castor-Martin machine had a distinct advantage. In preparation for the 1893
state convention, which was to select a Supreme Court
nominee, they called a conference of all endorsees for important postmasterships in order to bring about "a very
thorough understanding" of the course to be pursued at the
state convention. At the convention hope of acquiring fed-

[7] Olson, *Morton*, 367–71.
[8] George L. Miller to Cleveland, March 20, 1893, in Cleveland, MSS.

eral appointments kept the delegates in line, and Bryan was quickly voted down on every score. Despite Bryan's threat to bolt the party, the convention accepted a resolution demanding repeal of "that vicious law, the Sherman silver act" and nominated pro-Cleveland Frank Irvine for the Supreme Court.[9]

During the ensuing campaign Bryan remained a Democrat in name but endorsed the Populist Supreme Court judgeship candidate, Silas A. Holcomb. Bryan hoped eventually to drive the Bourbons from control of the Democracy and thereby to lure the Populists into the de-Bourbonized Democracy. The Bourbons made a bold effort to acquire a vote large enough to impress the Democrats with Bourbon popularity among the voters. Secretary Morton wrote to the president of the Burlington Railroad, Charles Perkins, and to its general manager, George W. Holdrege, beseeching their aid in the crusade to overwhelm Bryan and the Populists by an avalanche of votes. But Bourbon candidate Irvine came in a poor third, and the victory went to the Republicans.[10] Most important was the continued determination of boy-orator Bryan to drive the Bourbons out of the Nebraska Democracy—and Bryan was a formidable foe.

Though Morton had reason to be concerned, he could continue to eat boiled onions with Olney and Vilas without feeling that he was the only Bourbon in trouble back home, for his friends were also fighting a losing battle with the middle-western mob. Richard Olney had entered the Cleveland cabinet as attorney general without a previously known political record as far as the public was concerned but with many admirers among wealthy easterners. Hard-crusted Olney had served big-business interests well in his capacity of corporation attorney, and big-business men were grateful

[9] Olson, *Morton*, 377–79; George L. Miller to Lamont, October 5, 1893, in Lamont MSS.; William Jennings Bryan to Frank Irvine, October 10, 1893, in Cleveland MSS.
[10] Olson, *Morton*, 379–82.

to learn that he was head of the government agency charged with prosecuting industrial and railroad monopolies. The Sherman Antitrust Act was in safe hands. An odd circumstance in connection with the negotiations preceding his acceptance of the attorney-generalship was Olney's inquiry of President Charles Perkins whether it would be "to the true interest" of the Burlington Railroad if he accepted the appointment.

In Olney's early days as attorney general, he sent information to corporation leaders concerning where to "spend some money" in bringing about repeal of the silver-purchase act. This was in the form of a list of "doubtful Senators, who ought to be persuaded to see the thing in the right light." [11] Olney also did valiant service in the interest of restoring order among angry railroad workers and strikers, by using the injunction device and creating scores of United States deputy marshals.

Bulldog Olney brought particular satisfaction to President Cleveland and corporate interests through his legalistic military handling of the Chicago Pullman strike. In the spring of 1894 the Pullman Company laid off a third of its men and cut the wages of the rest from 30 to 40 per cent. At the same time the company continued its old rent scale on company houses used by the employees and did not lower prices in its company stores. The workers protested by striking. The company remained adamant; the strikers were on the verge of starvation. Then Eugene V. Debs brought his American Railway Union to the workers' rescue, and soon virtually all railroad traffic between Chicago and the West was paralyzed. The national government, at the direction of Attorney General Olney, stepped into the picture and with the use of troops broke up the strike. This was done over the head of Illinois' Governor Altgeld, who asserted that such federal interference was a violation of state-

[11] Josephson, *Politicos*, 523–26.

rights jurisdiction of the dispute. Olney justified his action on grounds of protecting the flow of United States mail. He also used the injunction device, which resulted in a jail sentence for strike-leader Debs.[12]

The immediate political result for the Cleveland administration was great unpopularity among wage earners and many other citizens and the wrathful enmity of Altgeld. Altgeld, who had already won plaudits among the working class for pardoning the Haymarket anarchists, was now completely disgusted with Bourbon Democrats. He decided to take an active part in national politics, aiming straight at driving the Cleveland element out of the Democratic hierarchy. Illinois representatives on the Democratic national committee were Bourbons, and Illinois patronage was in Bourbon hands; but Altgeld had strong influence on the state central committee and enormous popularity among the rank and file. By the spring of 1895 he was ready to act.[13]

Olney was able to render additional aid to the Bourbon cause after he was transferred to head the State Department, following the death of Secretary Walter Q. Gresham in the spring of 1895. President Cleveland was having an argument with the British over the Venezuela boundary, and Secretary Olney advised the twisting of the British lion's tail. Perhaps the new secretary of state thought it a good chance to direct public attention from really serious domestic ills. At any rate he was encouraged along those lines by Congressman Thomas Paschal of Texas, who wrote Olney:

> You are right, now go ahead. Turn this Venezuela question up or down . . . and it is a "winner" . . . morally, legally, politically, or financially: Your attitude at *this* juncture is the trump card. It is, however, when you come to diagnose the country's internal ills that the possibilities of "blood and iron" loom up immediately. Why, Mr. Secretary, just

[12] *Ibid.*, 570–80; J. R. Commons and others, *History of Labour in the United States* (New York, 1918–1935), II, 501–508.
[13] Barnard, *Altgeld*, 321–23, 351–52.

think of how angry the anarchistic, socialistic and popu-
listic boil appears on our political surface, and who knows
how deep its roots extend or ramify. One cannon shot
across the bow of a British boat in defense of this principle
will knock more pus out of it than would suffice to inoculate
and corrupt our people for the next two centuries.[14]

The ensuing belligerent Cleveland message to Congress, inspired by Olney, caused a momentary anti-British saber-
rattling among the citizens, but this soon petered out when
the matter was placed in the hands of an arbitration commission. The final settlement vindicated the English boundary claims.[15]

The other member of the Morton-Olney-Vilas boiled-
onion trio, William F. Vilas, specialized in the legislative—
or lack of legislative—program of the Cleveland administration. Senator Vilas had early prevailed upon the President
to call a special session of Congress to get started on the
Bourbon sound-money program, reversing the drain upon
the Treasury's gold supply and thereby bringing about recovery. The Bourbons would repeal the Sherman silver-
purchase act, replenish the Treasury's gold reserve by bond
sales, and have moderate tariff reductions so as to bring increased customs receipts from the increased volume of imports.[16]

The special session of Congress which convened early in
August, 1893, repealed the Sherman silver-purchase act. The
administration had withheld patronage in order to impress
the legislators with the wisdom of acceding to the repeal
proposal. In the House, the defection of fully one third of
the Democrats led by Bryan and Missouri's Silver Dick
Bland, together with the Populist members, threatened to

[14] Thomas Paschal to Richard Olney, in Olney MSS., as cited in Binkley, *Political Parties*, 314–15.

[15] McElroy, *Cleveland*, II, 173–202; Henry James, *Richard Olney* (New
York, 1923), 105, 140; Nevins, *Cleveland*, 636–43.

[16] James A. Barnes, *John C. Carlisle, Financial Statesman* (New York,
1931), 257; Josephson, *Politicos*, 531.

block the Bourbons. Bryan delivered a soaring speech for bimetallism. Throwing aside his prepared notes, this spellbinding orator continued for three hours.[17] He urged the need of a "second War of Independence" to free the nation from British financiers, and he drew a distinct line between the "haves" and the "have-nots" in his own country. On one hand, he saw the "imperious, arrogant, compassionless," moneyed, corporate interests; on the other he saw "that unnumbered throng, which gave a name to the Democratic party, and for which it has assumed to speak. Work-worn and dust-begrimed, they make their sad appeal . . . their cries for help too often beat in vain against the outer wall, while others less deserving, find ready access to legislative halls." [18] The Republicans finally came to the rescue, helping their Bourbon cousins to pass the measure through the House.

The Senate debate over repeal of the silver-purchase act caused the Bourbons considerable worry before the patronage whip turned the trick for the administration forces. In the course of the struggle Vilas wrote a friend, "The inherent difficulty lies in the fact that the majority for repeal is composed of patriotic men of two very antagonistic political parties, and the opponents of repeal are composed not only of similar elements from both of the old political parties, but with a third party which is almost, in its principles, like the advance guard of a French Revolution." [19]

But the stubborn Bourbons held the line. Through the patronage whip they even managed to get the vote of long-time soft-money advocate Senator Daniel Voorhees of Indiana.[20] T. V. Powderly, president of the Knights of

[17] Josephson, *Politicos*, 532–38; Nevins, *Cleveland*, 537–48.
[18] William Jennings Bryan, *The First Battle: Story of the Campaign of 1896* (Chicago, 1896), 113–14.
[19] William F. Vilas to E. P. Wheeler, October 19, 1893, as cited in Everett P. Wheeler, *Sixty Years of American Life* (New York, 1917), 235–38.
[20] Clark, *American Politics*, I, 322; Nevins, *Cleveland*, 541–42.

Labor, wrote a lengthy, scorching letter to Cleveland. In the course of condemning both the policy and the tactics of the administration, Powderly stated: "It is claimed, and justly, that if the Sherman Act is unconditionally repealed you will deserve the credit. It is believed that a majority of Congress was elected on a free silver platform, they have so expressed themselves since their election. . . ." But, added the indignant Powderly, "on assembling at Washington, they were confronted with an argument more powerful than the wishes of constituents or the voice of principle. That argument faces the legislator in two words—Federal Patronage. . . ." [21]

On October 30 repeal was achieved. Vilas quickly sent words of congratulations to his chief, President Cleveland. "Your personal triumph," said Vilas, "is no small part of the satisfaction I feel in it, great as is the public gain. . . ." [22]

With repeal the way was opened for a clear-cut contest between the scheme of the silverites and the Bourbon reform substitute. But there was no Bourbon reform substitute, unless the achieved return to the 1863 deflationary, inflexible banking-currency structure could be considered an enlightened advance. And that it could be was the belief of the Cleveland Bourbons. Magnate Jacob H. Schiff had asked for nothing more on the currency front and had informed the President that repeal of the silver act would "restore confidence at home and abroad . . . and insure a return to prosperity in the not far future." [23]

Many others, including some supporters of the repeal action, were not convinced that the administration should stop action at that point. Senator Voorhees made it clear to Cleveland that he did not "regard a vote for the repeal . . . as any test at all of a man's position on the question of the proper coinage and use of silver money." He as-

[21] T. V. Powderly to Cleveland, August 28, 1893, in Cleveland MSS.
[22] William F. Vilas to *id.*, November 1, 1893, *ibid.*
[23] Jacob H. Schiff to *id.*, August 29, 1893, *ibid.*

serted that the act "ought to be repealed if for no other reason, because it is a hindrance to a fair, honest and safe settlement of the silver question." [24] James J. Hill, considerably more enlightened than most business leaders of his day, suggested to Cleveland, "If it is true that the circulating medium of the country, per capita, is too low, and the provision for circulation in the National Banking Act is inoperative . . . ," it would seem wise to provide "an issue of bonds to meet a portion of the large pension appropriations." These, Hill reasoned, "would furnish a basis for National Bank circulation." He emphasized the two obvious facts that under the existing system government bonds were too high in price to make it profitable for national banks to use them for a basis for currency, and that the currency system lacked the necessary flexibility. [25]

The repeal of the Sherman Act failed, of course, to restore the business "confidence" which was supposedly the touchstone to prosperity. Treasury gold reserves continued to fall, despite government borrowing. An endless chain of gold flowed through the Treasury as bankers presented paper notes for gold redemption, reloaned the gold to the Treasury, and over and over repeated the process of withdrawal. This caused the fury of the silverites and the Populists to reach a higher pitch, and they spoke forth in angry voice at the policy of financial manipulation which brought appeasement to the bankers but no relief to the masses. And the Cleveland administration continued to shy away from basic currency-banking reform. [26]

Amid the precipitous downward spin of the entire national economic structure the administration could see nothing better than to begin debate on the tariff question. From January into August of 1894 the tariff question held sway

[24] Daniel Voorhees to id., August 14, 1893, ibid.
[25] Hill to id., July 4, 1893, ibid.
[26] Shannon, Farmer's Last Frontier, 322–23; Josephson, Politicos, 539–41; Nevins, Cleveland, 603–605.

in Congress; it finally culminated in the disgraceful Wilson-Gorman tariff. The only creditable feature of the measure was an income-tax rider, but even that was dispensed with in 1895 by the reactionary majority on the Supreme Court bench. The tariff schedules in the Wilson-Gorman measure were much more to the liking of the monopolists than to that of the consumers, being not unlike those of the unsatisfactory "mongrel tariff" of 1883.[27]

In logrolling the Wilson-Gorman Act through Congress, many legislators found opportunity to serve business interests back home. Senator Vilas, for example, saw to it that Milwaukee brewers would not have to submit to lower rates on beer.[28] But most conspicuous was the consideration given to the sugar trust. Sugar magnates Henry and Theodore Havemeyer were very successful in their demands for this trust. Henry Havemeyer had contributed to the New York Republicans' 1892 campaign and in the same year had donated ten thousand dollars to help Whitney renominate Grover Cleveland to the presidency. Havemeyer stoutly denied charges of making a deal with the Democrats, but there was no denying that he was consulted by Democratic leaders during the tariff controversy. In any case, the Wilson-Gorman tariff provided for sugar duties that transferred twenty million dollars annually from the consumers' pocketbooks to the coffers of the sugar trust. President Cleveland was angry over the new tariff measure, but his efforts to influence Congress were in vain for he had aligned himself with a group whom his honest efforts could not control. The extent of his final objection was to allow the measure to become law without his signature.[29]

As the leading middle-western Bourbon in Congress, Vilas symbolized, and had to answer for, the Cleveland administration's legislative record of service to his region. He also

[27] Nevins, *Cleveland*, 563–88; Josephson, *Politicos*, 541–55, 609–12.
[28] John L. Mitchell to William F. Vilas, May 8, 1894, in Vilas MSS.
[29] Josephson, *Politicos*, 548–49.

had to answer for his personal arrogance in dealing with his political vassals and the voters. These responsibilities proved too great a burden for him to carry, even in his long-subservient Wisconsin machine. General E. S. Bragg and his sizable Democratic following in Wisconsin sniped incessantly at Vilas.[30] When there was a sudden renewal of newspaper articles on the old timber-fraud scandal involving Vilas and John H. Knight, it was widely rumored that Bragg had inspired the new publicity. Perhaps the publishers of the Chicago *Times*, who first revived the old timber scandal, supplied their own initiative.[31] The *Times* was operated by the sons of Chicago's erstwhile Mayor Carter H. Harrison. The Harrison boys were in a bitter mood, for not only had their father recently been killed by an assassin, but they were incensed by the Cleveland administration's treatment of the family. In 1884 Mayor Harrison had aided in the nomination and election of Cleveland, but the patronage had subsequently been handed over to Melville Fuller and other Illinois Bourbons. In 1892 the Harrisons had aided the Cleveland campaign; but the patronage again went elsewhere, and an old-time enemy of the Harrison clan received the Chicago postmastership. The Harrison boys then turned with vehemence on Cleveland and his cohorts in a manner later reported by one of the sons as being "certainly on the border line of libel." Vilas was included in the general attack.[32] Other papers, including the Republican Milwaukee *Sentinel*,[33] took up the cry; and Vilas was thus given a thorough going-over.

[30] William F. Vilas to Cleveland, March 13, 1893; and Owen A. Wells to Lamont, March 13, 1893, in Cleveland MSS.; Wall to *id.*, September 19, 1893; and *id.* to *id.*, December 5, 1893, in Lamont MSS.; Milwaukee *Sentinel*, March 10, 1893.

[31] Clipping from Janesville (Wis.) *Daily Record* for May 30, 1894; R. M. Bashford to William F. Vilas, May 28, 1894; Bryant to *id.*, June 21, 1894; Wall to *id.*, June 30, 1894; and Fay to *id.*, July 8, 1894, in Vilas MSS.

[32] Harrison, *Stormy Years*, 52.

[33] Milwaukee *Sentinel*, June 20, 21, 22, 29, October 22, 1894.

There were indications of restlessness even among Vilas' political aides. Men like state chairman E. C. Wall were loyal party men and normally could be counted on to serve their chief—but only as long as he remained chief and the normal political situation prevailed. When confronted with a crisis, they did do some thinking of their own accord. Wall was doing some thinking, and he was catching the spirit of reform that was swirling about him. Wall and Lute Nieman, editor of the Milwaukee *Journal* and a Vilas lieutenant, were not satisfied merely to help the Cleveland cabal into office. They wanted to be heard on matters of policy. One thing bothering them was the Pullman strike. Early in July, 1894, Wall wrote to Vilas, "Lute and I have spent a good deal of time . . . discussing the strike, its causes and effect, and it has seemed to us that something must be done to relieve the situation in the future; and it seems plain that the man who suggests anything that is really beneficial will receive the thanks of his countrymen. . . ."

Wall and Nieman had a plan, too. And their plan was not in keeping with past Bourbon thinking. These two Milwaukeans reasoned that the powers of the Interstate Commerce Commission should "be increased to include the regulation of wages on inter-state roads, settle the disputes of railroad men and the companies on inter-state roads." Wall and Nieman could not see why the entire country should be made to suffer on account of a dispute between railroad companies and their employees. "Railroads are a public institution," they reasoned, "and it seems to us that it might be proper that their disputes should be taken in hand and arbitrated by the government." Wall, in defending the Wall-Nieman brain storm, remarked that of course he knew that the railroad companies would not willingly submit to the passage of any such scheme, "for it is their plan to fight every regulation that takes from them any of their power." But that, said Wall, was not the question at stake: "The question is fair treatment and justice. It has occurred to me lately that if the courts, where the roads are in the hands of receivers, can enjoin the men from striking . . . upon application of the receivers, that the men have the same right to apply to the courts to regulate their wages, and instruct the receivers not to diminish them. Is not this so?" Wall hoped that Vilas could see his "way clear to take a prominent part in this question." [34] But that was expecting a lot from Vilas, a crony of Attorney General Olney. Vilas took no action; but he doubtless wondered what the world was coming to, and perhaps he felt a little lonesome. His own aides were questioning the existing lordship of corporate interests, and their next step logically would be to question his service in the existing order of things.

Amid this growing public restlessness came an opportunity, in the 1894 election, for the voters to register their opinion of the Cleveland administration. The Sherman silver-purchase act had been repealed, borrowing was keeping the Treasury gold reserve from complete disappearance, the Wilson-Gorman tariff had been passed, Coxey's Army had been dispersed, and the Pullman strike had been ended through the efforts of Attorney General Olney. And the nation's economic condition was worse—much worse. The public discontent was finding expression through the silverites of both major parties, through the Populist party and through a shift to the Republican organization simply to register protest against the Cleveland administration. The middle-western Bourbons doggedly strove to arrest this general scurrying from their ranks, but nowhere did they meet with success. The most they could boast of was success in maintaining control of the greater part of the state Democratic machines of the region. But in Nebraska the Bourbons were even driven from control of their party.

Through promises of federal patronage to convention

34 Wall to William F. Vilas, July 9, 1894, in Vilas MSS.

delegates, the Nebraska Bourbons had in 1893 managed to check Bryan's bid for domination of the party. However, by the time of the 1894 convention it was a different story. Many disappointed office seekers and many of those safely appointed were in no mood to take orders from the Bourbon machine. In short order silverite Bryan captured control of the convention, and fusion with the Populists was brought about. The Bourbons called a rump session and offered a pro-Cleveland slate; they then fought a campaign battle that ended in a complete rout for them. The Bourbon gubernatorial candidate obtained 6,985 votes, the Republican nominee gathered 94,113 votes, and fusion candidate Silas A. Holcomb was victorious with 97,815 votes. Bourbonism was at long last driven from domination of the Nebraska Democracy. The Bourbons might find solace in the subsequent successful attempt of the Republican legislature to check Bryan's senatorship ambition, but Bryan also found solace in the rapid rise of his political star on the national horizon.[35]

To the east of Nebraska, middle-western Bourbons were in a more fortunate position. Anti-Cleveland Democrats were not ready to make a clear-cut break with Bourbon state leaders. It was still not plain to many what the future held for the Cleveland administration, so they were disposed to play along with the Bourbons until or unless it became apparent that no more political favors would be forthcoming from that faction. No issue, not even free silver, had caught the public fancy with enough impact to stampede the vote-wise politicos out of the Bourbon fold. Free-silver advocates were still scattered among the three parties—Democratic, Republican, and Populist. Illinois' delegates to the House of Representatives, for example, were not divided along strictly party lines on the silver question. Of the ten congressmen who had silver leanings or were outright silverites, six were

[35] Olson, *Morton*, 383–86.

Democrats and four were Republicans; of the eleven sound-money champions, five were Democrats and seven were Republicans.[36] Nor had Governor Altgeld settled upon a formula for making a clean break with the Bourbons. The majority of delegates at state Democratic conventions, not as yet certain in what direction the political wind might veer by the time of the next presidential election, demonstrated uneasiness and caution. In Iowa, for example, an incipient preconvention movement to effect a Democratic-Populist fusion on the free-silver question proved abortive. And at the Democratic convention the delegates quietly voted down, by a vote of 697 to 329, a mild resolution on bimetallism. Nor was former Governor Horace Boies willing to force a break with the Bourbons on the question, for his address as permanent chairman of the conclave was very moderate.[37]

The Populists of Illinois, as elsewhere, were still undecided as to the wisdom of concentrating on the silver issue; some of them were more interested in the antirailroad and antitrust features of their program. In 1894 the publication of Chicagoan Henry Demarest Lloyd's powerful antitrust book *Wealth Against Commonwealth* profoundly affected Populist thinking. In August Lloyd informed Judge Henry Miller of Chicago that he regarded the demonetization of the silver dollar as the "greatest act of repudiation in financial history" and an act fostered by "the greedy rich who want to add more to too much." But, said Lloyd, "if I were called upon to propose a financial scheme, I should go much farther. I hold that a civilized and moral people no more need *value* in their currency than in their promissory notes." The issue in which he was most interested, and

[36] Lewis Ethan Ellis, "A History of the Chicago Delegation in Congress, 1843–1925," *Transactions of the Illinois Historical Society*, 1930 (Springfield, 1930), 90.

[37] Haynes, *Third Party Movements*, 348, 357; Nixon, "Populist Movement," *loc. cit.*, 78.

which he believed should not be pushed aside by the free-silver clamor, was the antitrust question. He told Judge Miller that "a greater political opportunity has never within my observation been thrown away than that which the Democrats in Congress lost in not continuing the struggle with the Senate and the Sugar Trust." "They could have gone to the country," stated Lloyd, "with the clean issue of war with the trusts, an issue infinitely greater than that of a few shavings off the tariff." [38] To the editor of the Chicago *Times* he wrote the same sentiments, adding that another great political opportunity lay with the chance the Populist party had for responding to the "cry of the people for leadership." [39] The Populists tendered him the nomination for Congress in his Chicago district. He entered the race, despite his desire to leave active politics to those whom he considered possessed of "gifts for such public life much greater than mine." [40]

Although the Bourbons in Illinois, Iowa, Minnesota, and Wisconsin avoided a united silverite challenge to their continued domination of the state party organizations, they were unable to offer serious opposition to the Republicans or even to check the growth of the Populist minority. The record of the Cleveland administration, the normal reaction against the party in power at the time of an economic crisis, and the failure to find diversionary local issues were too much of a burden for the Bourbons. Illinois' G. W. Fithian, Democratic silverite congressman, remarked that although the Democracy had successfully carried many a heavy load in the past, "it cannot carry Cleveland and win this fall." [41] As early as June experienced campaign managers, like Il-

[38] Lloyd to Judge Henry G. Miller, August 17, 1894, in Lloyd MSS.
[39] *Id.* to Willis J. Abbott, August 21, 1894, *ibid.*
[40] Miles M. Dawson to Lloyd, August 11, 1894; Lloyd to Henry G. Miller, August 17, 1894; and *id.* to Abbott, October 8, 1894, in Lloyd MSS.
[41] Nevins, *Cleveland*, 650.

linois' Benjamin Cable and Wisconsin's E. C. Wall, held a
similar opinion.[42] During the same month Bourbon Senator
Vilas received word from E. E. Bryant, a Wisconsin lawyer
and friend, that "it looks from all points of view as though
we should get, as Wellington said of Blücher at Lignes,
'damnably mauled' in the next election." Referring to Vilas
in particular, but in terms equally applicable to all middle-
western Bourbons, Bryant declared that "you have to carry
a big load in Cleveland. Some have hated you because you
stood by Cleveland. Some are cold on you because you have
not used enough of your friendship with Cleveland in their
interest, and just at this time you must 'tread the wine press'
alone." Not even the regular party workers were showing
any enthusiasm.[43]

The Bourbons wanted to base their campaign on state
issues, but the voters insisted on thinking in terms of the
national scene. The Bourbons had no luck in stirring the
social-cleavage cauldron into a political ferment. The voters
seemed weary of scrapping over sin and religion, or else they
were conscience-stricken over the emotional excesses of recent elections. There were, in any case, signs of a public
willingness to compromise on the social issues. This was
evinced in the Iowa state election, held the year previously.
Twice-elected Governor Boies again received the Democratic nomination, but his party managers failed this time
to capitalize on the Republican-sponsored prohibition law.
The 1893 Republican platform urged the relaxation of
modifications in the existing law, and that satisfied the antiprohibition Republicans who had previously voted for Boies.
The result was a Republican victory, with the Cleveland
record and the depression exciting the voters more than the
liquor question.[44]

[42] Wall to William F. Vilas, June 20, 1894, in Vilas MSS.
[43] Bryant to *id.*, June 3, 1894; and *id.* to *id.*, June 21, 1894, *ibid.*
[44] Haynes, *Third Party Movements*, 352–57.

The parochial-school question had died down in Illinois and Wisconsin. Chairman E. C. Wall distributed in Wisconsin some ten thousand copies weekly of a foreign-language newspaper, the *Rundschau;* but he was unable to report that this weekly expenditure of eight hundred dollars was doing the Democratic cause any good.[45] A Wisconsin German Lutheran leader reported to Vilas, "We Germans are beginning to do in our own way what the Bennett law supporters tried to force us to do. It needs no prophetic gift to say that fifty years hence the transition will have taken place. Within the last decade our *English* Lutheran church has made wonderful strides." [46] Everything seemed to indicate that Wall and other antinativist political specialists were fighting against the current.

Without the nativist question to harp on, the Democrats had little left of a local nature to win the voters to their tickets. Not even popular Governor Boies had been able to sidetrack the attention of the voters from hard times and the Cleveland administration and Congress. In Illinois the situation was made awkward for the Bourbons by Governor Altgeld's defection. The Minnesota voters seemed satisfied to re-elect Republican Knute Nelson to the governorship.[47] Wisconsin citizens—even Democrats—showed no enthusiasm for do-nothing Democratic Governor George W. Peck. Wisconsin lawyer Burr Jones reported that he could find no enthusiasm for the state Democratic administration. "At least nine out of ten Democrats in farming districts," said Jones, "would tell you if asked that they are in favor of a new deal." [48] In Minnesota the Bourbons were so discouraged over their chances of beating either the Republicans or the Populists that they made but a weak gesture in the campaign. They nominated a colorless candidate, St. Paul's

[45] Wall to William F. Vilas, September 26, 1894, in Vilas MSS.
[46] J. Schlerf to *id.,* November 17, 1895, *ibid.*
[47] Folwell, *History of Minnesota,* III, 197.
[48] Burr Jones to William F. Vilas, August 9, 1894, in Vilas MSS.

George L. Becker, who in turn made something less than a desultory effort to gain votes.[49] A Minnesota Populist remarked late in the campaign that "the Democrats are going to pieces; some stand on the fence, some are falling into the Republican campaign, and another part into ours." [50]

When the votes were counted, the result was—as had been generally expected—a smashing Republican triumph. The Republicans captured control of the House of Representatives—gaining a two-to-one majority—and almost overtook the Democratic majority in the Senate. Nor could the Bourbons or the conservative Republicans feel too secure in their positions at party helms, for the Populist party demonstrated that it meant business. The Populists had in some cases joined forces with Republicans in the South and Democrats in the West; and where they had run independent tickets, they had chalked up a respectable total. The Populist vote was 40 per cent larger than it had been in 1892. In the Middle West the fusion with the Bryan Democrats was the greatest close-to-home blow to the Bourbons of the region. The record in Minnesota also gave the Bourbons the jitters, for there the Populists collected 87,931 votes as compared with 29,313 in 1892.[51] But the Bourbon bigwigs entertained no thought of making concessions to this people's movement.

On the economic front the deflationary process continued its devastating course, causing untoward hardship and much political restlessness. The spring of 1895 brought with it fresh evidences that the masses were ready for political change and that leaders were on hand to answer the call. The oratory of Bryan and others, along with the arresting

[49] Odland, *Nelson*, 191; W. A. Fleming to Ignatius Donnelly, October 4, 1894, in Donnelly MSS.

[50] John Jenswald, Jr., to Ignatius Donnelly, October 16, 1894, in Donnelly MSS.

[51] Hicks, *Populist Revolt*, 337–43.

and logical propaganda book called *Coin's Financial School*, contributed much toward channeling public unrest into a widespread clamor for silver coinage at a sixteen-to-one ratio. The public wanted a large supply of money in circulation so that they could once again get their hands on a little. To them the quantitative theory of money seemed a logical approach.

Among the first important political leaders to give this free-silver cause a telling forward thrust was Altgeld. Although previously he had demonstrated no enthusiasm for the silver movement, by the spring of 1895 he had settled upon it as the best vehicle for defeating the Cleveland Bourbons. In a sudden move the Altgeld-controlled state Democratic committee issued in April a call for a special party convention to meet in June to endorse free silver. This was a frightening shock to the Bourbons, for Illinois had been an important political buffer state between the western silverites and the eastern goldbugs. Now Illinois was joining forces with the enemies of Bourbonism. Important too was the influence Altgeld would have in winning wage earners to the silverite banner. This champion of the workers, because of his pardon of the Haymarket anarchists and his stand on the Pullman strike episode, was a hero capable of carrying many a wavering wage earner wherever he led. A howl went up in Bourbon circles when the special convention call was issued, and from the White House the President quickly dispatched a fighting letter to the Chicago Honest Money League. This long epistle turned out to be, as Bryan later said, an "unexpected aid" to the silver cause, for it drove many Democrats off the fence and into the silverite camp. Many Democrats who had favored free silver had been hesitant in forsaking party-leader Cleveland. But they dropped their hesitancy when Cleveland forthrightly proclaimed in his letter: "Disguise it as we may, the line of battle is drawn between the forces of safe currency and those of silver monometallism." [52]

Elsewhere in the Middle West the free-silver craze gathered momentum. E. C. Wall became greatly concerned and urged aggressive action by the gold Democrats. Wall reported in April that he was "astonished to find such growth in the silver sentiment," and he noted that *Coin's Financial School* "has attracted a great deal of attention and has done some harm to the cause of sound money." [53] Iowa Bourbons were concerned—especially after Democratic silverites held a special conference to prepare for driving the Bourbons from control of the state central committee. [54]

The Bourbon chieftains nevertheless sat tight. Senator Vilas in April advised "inaction with patience" as the safest strategy. [55] It was still not clear that the silverites could capture control of the state Democratic organizations. The Bourbons possessed a powerful leverage through their office-holding delegates to the party conventions and through the general hesitancy among party workers to break with the hierarchy unless it was clearly advantageous to do so. And of course many Democrats had strong enough gold-currency convictions to keep them loyal to the Cleveland administration.

The Bourbon policy of "inaction with patience" was given a formal test in the 1895 elections held in Iowa and Nebraska. In Iowa, despite the silverites' preconvention strategy conference, the Bourbons managed to retain the party reins at the state convention. The Bourbons went to the conclave with the state committee in their control; and when they were confronted with a free-silver resolution, their machine of federal officeholder delegates loyally re-

---

[52] Barnard, *Altgeld*, 351–54; Nevins, *Cleveland*, 675–76.
[53] Wall to Henry T. Thurber, April 19, 1895, in Cleveland MSS.
[54] Haynes, *Third Party Movements*, 352–54.
[55] Wall to William F. Vilas, undated (but refers to a letter which Wall received from Vilas on April 18, 1895), in Vilas MSS.

jected the proposition by a vote of 651 to 420. In the ensuing election, following a campaign in which the silver question cut across party lines, the outcome was not markedly different from the 1893 state election. The returns showed a moderate Republican gain and a slight Populist gain, both at the expense of the defeated Democrats.[56]

The Nebraska election was held primarily for the selection of a state supreme court judge. The gold Democrats, who had set up a separate organization after being defeated by the Bryan forces in the 1894 convention, offered a candidate. The silver Democrats and the Populists chose separate candidates. The failure of the two free-silver groups to unite, as they had in 1894, was the most significant feature of the election, for it showed that the Populists and the silverite Democrats were not ready to forswear their own organizations for a united front. Bryan wanted to absorb the Populists into the Democracy, but the Populists lacked faith in the silverites' ability to commit the national Democracy to free silver. Agrarian third-party leaders had in the past experienced too many defeats at the hands of eastern-led Bourbons and this time had no intention of walking into the trap. The result of this split brought victory to the Republicans, but the combination of the sizable Populist vote and the smaller silver-Democratic vote was larger than the Republican.[57]

As the 1896 election crept closer, the Bourbons continued their stubborn defiance of every suggestion of reform. Middle-western Bourbons continued loyally to support the eastern-Cleveland brand of politico economics, apparently not even suggesting to the eastern moguls that a few concessions were in order. Nothing out of line with the eastern Bourbons' ideas was forthcoming from middle-

---

[56] Haynes, *Third Party Movements*, 354–57; Nixon, "Populist Movement," *loc. cit.*, 78–80.

[57] Hicks, *Populist Revolt*, 347–48.

westerners like Secretary Morton of Nebraska or Senator Palmer of Illinois or Senator Vilas of Wisconsin. Palmer and Vilas had not liked the Wilson-Gorman tariff bill; but when they were called into conference by President Cleveland, they gave assurances that they would vote for it—which they did. On the silver question, Palmer showed no hesitancy in defying the popular and politically powerful Governor Altgeld of his own state, and Bourbon leaders and their machines elsewhere in the region exhibited the same independence.[58]

Suggestions of economic reforms of all sorts were summarily cast aside by the Bourbons. The gap between the static Bourbons and the fertile-minded forerunners of progress through change was typified in the correspondence between Senator Vilas and men with ideas. Vilas showed no interest in the suggestion coming from party workers Wall and Nieman that the functions of the Interstate Commerce Commission should be broadened to embrace jurisdiction over interstate labor disputes.[59] Nor was he impressed by an equally revolutionary suggestion coming from Arthur Gough, editor of a small Wisconsin Catholic paper. Haunted by the deplorable conditions in his rural community, Gough urged Vilas to put before Congress a law providing for federal assumption of farm debts, extension of the time for payment to twenty or thirty years, and reduction of the interest to 3 or 4 per cent. This, thought Gough, would "lift an enormous load off the farmers." The scheme, he added, "has been in force in nearly the same terms in the United Kingdom for fifty years and works well." [60]

Vilas responded by asking under what section in the Con-

---

[58] Nevins, *Cleveland*, 579; James A. Barnes, "Illinois and the Gold-Silver Controversy, 1890–1896," *Transactions of the Illinois State Historical Society,* 1931 (Springfield, 1931), 46.

[59] Wall to William F. Vilas, July 9, 1894, in Vilas MSS.

[60] Arthur Gough (of Chippewa Falls) to *id.,* November 29, 1895, *ibid.*

stitution such a measure could be sustained. To this, editor Gough fired back:

> I might reply in Irish fashion, by asking in return, where Congress got the right to lend hundreds of millions to the Union Pacific Railroad; to give away nearly $2,000,000 in pensions, more than half of them undeserving; or to establish protective tariffs for the benefit of special industries; or to appropriate money for the Louisiana and Alaska purchases; or to pay bounties to sugar growers; or to pay people's money to your salary grabbers; or as it is proposed, to lend or give some hundreds of millions to finish the Nicaragua canal? In short, when you ask for a Constitutional right to extend the credit of the government to the distressed land owners of the United States . . . I am inclined to reply, "Oh, cease your fooling."

Gough then informed lawyer Vilas that section eight of the Constitution gives power to borrow money for any purpose. Small-town editor Gough ended his outburst with the observation, "You alone have a pure record in Congress, but it is only a negative one, so far as action is concerned. . . ." [61] Upon reading this outburst Senator Vilas perhaps mused for a moment over the dreadful things that would transpire if Gough's plan were put into practice. But did Vilas broach the subject for serious discussion when next he conferred with Bourbon cronies? Hardly!

Bourbon devotion to laissez-faire economics likewise remained unshaken in these dire days of chaos when Bourbons considered the problems of wage earners. Olney's handling of the Pullman strike gave emphasis to Bourbon underwriting of the concept of labor as a commodity to be bought and sold at will. The same thought process was applied by the Bourbons in connection with the long-standing wage earner demand for an eight-hour day. When confronted with this question, Vilas took the tack of saying that

[61] *Id.* to *id.*, December 6, 1895, *ibid.*

the time was not yet ripe. Answering a direct query from Samuel Gompers, president of the American Federation of Labor, the Wisconsin senator dwelt upon the necessity of bringing about other changes before labor could reap the benefits supposedly inherent in the new laborsaving devices. Apparently having in mind the need for tariff reform, Vilas informed Gompers, "Until there is a vast repair of our system of taxation, of Federal class legislation and usages in other particulars, . . . Labor must overdo." [62] Although Vilas recognized that industrialists were getting too much of the consumer's dollar, he refused to admit that the oversized melon might be cut in such a way that labor would get at least a decent slice and more people would be given jobs. And of course the consequences of an increased demand for goods—which might well derive from a spreading of work and an increase of leisure time—was outside the thinking of the Bourbon mind.

Continued Bourbon unenlightenment, along with like conservative recalcitrance in the Republican leadership, caused a continued channeling of discontented voters into new political movements. The silverite wing within the Democracy provided one outlet, the Populist party another, and incipient revolts within the Republican party still another. With the approach of the 1896 election the people's upsurge gravitated in Nebraska toward either the Populists or the Bryan Democrats, in Illinois increasingly toward Altgeld, in Iowa toward the now out-and-out silverite Boies. Discontented Minnesota voters gravitated toward Ignatius Donnelly and his Populists, although Republican Knute Nelson retained a strong following.

Political discontent in Wisconsin veered, more than elsewhere, toward a reformation of the Republican party. The deeply entrenched Bourbonism directed by Vilas caused voters to look elsewhere than to the Democracy for an out-

[62] William F. Vilas to Samuel Gompers, May 14, 1896, *ibid.*

let. An increasing number of angry citizens were hopefully watching the activities of Robert M. La Follette, who was carrying on within the Republican party an active campaign for reform. He was trying to break the corrupt political ring which dominated the state party, was fostering organizational changes that would place the control of government in the hands of the voters, and was concentrating considerable fire on the monopolistic railroads.[63] The fervent La Follette was too earnest to be a demagogue, too intelligent to place hope in the free-silver panacea. Patiently and tirelessly he stumped the state, educating the citizens in his sound ideas for reform. But not until public petulance had run its course on the free-silver question, and not until La Follette had perfected a machine capable of unseating the entrenched Republican managers, would sound reform make a break-through. After four more years La Follette captured the governorship and thereby established himself as an effective rallying point for enlightened reform. In the interim the discontented in Wisconsin and elsewhere continued to gravitate toward the shallower free-silver crusade.

Clearly the silverites were headed for domination of the national Democratic party. Throughout the West and the South state convention after state convention fell in line. Even the New York Democrats adopted, in June, a platform which impressed the gold advocates as weak and colorless.[64] By the end of June the silver men possessed far more than a majority of national-convention delegates. Wisconsin's Wall observed that the silver men "know what they want; and I think, will succeed." Wall frowned upon the last-ditch strategy of the Cleveland managers, which was to arrive at the Chicago convention "re-inforced by a large

[63] Robert M. La Follette, *La Follette's Autobiography: A Personal Narrative of Political Experience* (Madison, 1913), 89; Joseph Lincoln Steffens, *Autobiography of Lincoln Steffens* (New York, 1931), II, 452–63.

[64] Nevins, *Cleveland*, 691.

number of wealthy bankers from the East." In his opinion,
"It is too late, . . . will simply strengthen the silverites, and
permit them to cry out that this is the fight of the moneybags against the people." [65]

It was no use. At the convention the Bourbons were
strangers in their own club—or at least in what they long
had assumed to be their exclusively owned domain. All that
was left for them was to display their eloquence on the
convention floor. Massachusetts' Governor Russell spoke;
New York's David B. Hill spoke; Wisconsin's Senator Vilas
spoke. But in eloquence these redoubtable orators were out-
classed by the soaring poetic prose of Nebraska's silverite
William Jennings Bryan in his "Cross of Gold" speech.

Bryan's convention effort was great as an exhibit of masterful oratory; it was greater as a symbolic voicing of agrarian anger in particular, and of wider public restlessness in a
vaguely general way. A wiser man would have rooted his
crusade in a sounder medium than free silver as the proper
formula for restoring the nation to the people, but few wiser
men would have equaled Bryan's role as the voice of the
embittered agrarians. His convention effort was the culmina-
tion of a long and bitter fight—on his part and others'—
to restore a people's party to the people. After Bryan had
uttered his now-famous "You shall not press down upon
the brow of labor this crown of thorns—you shall not
crucify mankind upon a cross of gold," a deafening roar of
applause came from the audience. The people, or at least a
large segment of them, had spoken; and they were prepared
to act.[66]

The people's delegates succeeded in committing the party
to a free-silver platform. The platform also contained a
denunciation of the Supreme Court for invalidating the
income-tax law. The use of federal troops in the Pullman

---

[65] Wall to William F. Vilas, June 30, 1896, in Vilas MSS.
[66] Nevins, *Cleveland*, 701–703; Josephson, *Politicos*, 672–79.

strike was condemned as a violation of state rights; the practice of using the injunction in labor disputes was condemned as a violation of the people's rights. The silverite-dominated convention then turned to the selection of a standard bearer. Henry M. Teller, insurgent Republican from Colorado, was a possibility; Richard Bland of Missouri was another; and of course Bryan had many supporters. The last was nominated without serious opposition, and second place on the ticket went to Arthur N. Sewell of Maine.[67]

Many Bourbons escaped from the convention hall before Bryan's nomination, returning home to watch developments and ponder over their futures. They saw all about them an upsurge of free-silver sentiment and the closing of silverite lines, as the Populist convention also went on record for Bryan. Bourbons also witnessed some of their old and trusted henchmen debating where to turn.[68] On July 12, Wall frantically wrote Vilas, "What is my duty on the political situation? Inclined to support the nomination, but friends doing otherwise." In a few days he decided to follow his inclination to endorse Bryan.[69]

Most Bourbon leaders were certain that it was the duty of all good Democrats not to support Bryan, but they had trouble deciding upon an alternative. They wanted to retain their party identity and at the same time smash the silverites. If they offered a separate gold Democrat ticket, that might split the anti-Bryan forces and thus bring victory to the silver mob. Some finally decided to make a gesture of independence by offering a separate ticket and making it weak enough not to harm Republican candidate William McKinley.

Gold Democrats, led by such loyal followers of Cleveland as Michigan's Don Dickinson, Illinois' John M. Palmer, and

[67] Nevins, *Cleveland*, 700–701; Hicks, *Populist Revolt*, 354.
[68] Milwaukee *Journal*, July 13, 14, 15, 1896.
[69] Wall to William F. Vilas, July 12, 1896; and *id.* to *id.*, July 14, 1896, in Vilas MSS.; Milwaukee *Journal*, August 8, 1896.

Wisconsin's Vilas, brought about a "National" Democratic convention at Indianapolis. After considerable perplexity regarding whom to nominate, they placed the mantle on the not overly pleased Senator Palmer. Before becoming deeply concerned over the silver craze and entwined in the political machinations of the Grover Cleveland group, Palmer had shown conscientious respect for the wishes of the Illinois rank and file; now he was a stubborn, albeit well-meaning, goldbug. The National Democratic platform declared against free silver and the protective tariff and registered great praise for President Cleveland.[70] Lonely Cleveland was thus moved to write Vilas, "I feel grateful to those who have relieved the political atmosphere with such a delicious infusion of fresh air." [71]

The National Democratic ticket furnished a diversionary outlet for those anti-Bryan Democrats who would vote for Bryan rather than for a Republican. Cyrenus Cole, an Iowa Republican editor, later stated: "The Gold Democrats' committee in Iowa was well supplied with money for which they could find little use. When Bourke Cochran came to speak under their auspices they spent considerable money entertaining him, and I helped them do it. After the campaign the committee decided to dissipate some of the surplus funds by giving a dinner to those who assisted them. I was included in this list, for I used the *Register* to give liberal publicity to the Gold Democrats, well knowing that every vote cast for Palmer was half a vote for McKinley. . . ." [72]

The Bourbons outdid themselves in demonstrating that they were wealthy capitalists first and Democrats incidently.

[70] W. D. Bynum to William F. Vilas, August 14, 1896; *id.* to *id.*, August 24, 1896; and H. S. Robbins to *id.*, December 14, 1896, in Vilas MSS.; Nevins, *Cleveland*, 707.

[71] Cleveland to William F. Vilas, September 5, 1896, in Vilas MSS.

[72] Cole, *I Remember*, 237. See also Barnes, "Illinois and the Gold-Silver Controversy," *loc. cit.*, 58.

Reformer Tom L. Johnson later said, "It was not free silver that frightened the plutocrat leaders. What they feared, then, what they fear now, is free men." [73] Thus did Democratic plutocrats and Republican plutocrats make common cause to elect "safe" William McKinley to the presidency. H. C. Payne, Republican national executive committeeman, was one of the Republicans who felt free to enlist the cooperation of gold Democrats. During the campaign he wrote to Vilas, "You probaby know that there are two vacancies in the United States District Courts for Northern and Southern Dakota. I have no doubt it would be of incalculable benefit to the sound money cause to hold up these appointments until after the election, and a word from you to the proper parties in Washington will go far to secure that result." [74]

The campaign in its entirety aroused the citizenry to a pitch reminiscent of the 1860 contest. The McKinley managers utilized all possible tricks in the political handbook and spared no money in their application. Aware of the essential conservatism of the populace, the McKinley forces emphasized the supposed ruination that would come in the wake of applied Bryanism. Specific threats of being fired from their jobs were leveled at workers. Colonel Knight, after remarking that it was too bad that Palmer could not be elected and that Democrats were forced to take McKinley, then added that railroad employees should vote for Bryan, "but . . . will get frightened before election comes and vote for McKinley." [75] The Bryan forces, with Bryan himself setting an example through an extraordinary speechmaking tour, made a fervent appeal to the people to assert themselves for a restoration of Jeffersonian, Jacksonian democracy. The Democratic party, declared Bryan, represented

[73] Tom Loftin Johnson, *My Story*, ed. Elizabeth J. Hauser (New York, 1911), 109.
[74] Payne to William F. Vilas, no date except 1896, in Vilas MSS.
[75] Knight to *id.*, September 15, 1896, *ibid.*

"the masses of the people, the great industrial and producing masses of the people . . . the men who plow and plant, who fatten herds, who toil in shops, who fell forests, and delve in mines . . . who produce the wealth of the republic, who bear the heaviest burdens in time of peace; who are ready always to give their lifeblood for their country's flag." [76]

Conservatism carried the day. The majority was frightened more by the prospects of change than by the presence of hardship. Nature lent a hand, too, by making the present less sordid, for in August the price of wheat rose. Short crops abroad and abundant crops at home caused this sudden change. The majority of voters were as yet not sufficiently educated in the fundamentals of big-business exploitation. They were still prone to ride joyfully the superficial waves of chance prosperity one day and to grasp desperately at panaceas on less fortunate days. Not until they became more desperate, learned the true nature of the practices of unrestrained capitalism, and were instructed in basically sound reform proposals would they cease to scamper for the historic shelter of conservatism when the chips were laid down on election day.

The 1896 effort was, nevertheless, not a total loss for the common man. After many decades of protest the masses finally demonstrated in 1896 that they could actually capture control of a major political party and with it gather millions of votes. After all, Bryan polled about a million more votes than had Cleveland four years previously. Neither party, Democratic or Republican, completely forgot the potential strength of the masses when in future years it shaped political programs. For when the conservative leaders miscalculated, they found people at hand prepared to profit by the example of Bryanism. In the Progressive

[76] Charles A. and Mary R. Beard, *A Basic History of the United States* (Philadelphia, 1944), 335.

movement, the New Freedom, and the New Deal, liberal leaders utilized the experience of 1896 as an invaluable guide.

The political demise of the Bourbon clan, which had dominated the Democracy for the preceding three post–Civil War decades, was an immediate accomplishment of the people's upsurge of 1896. The Bourbons continued to add dollars to their private fortunes, but for an avocation they now preferred trout fishing to fishing for public office and party management. In 1898 a *Harper's* editor lamented that no one of the Cleveland administration would consent to write an article on the Philippine question and remarked that Cleveland himself was "too busy catching fish, and feels convinced that his countrymen would not heed him if he made any attempt to lead them in the right way." [77] The old Bourbons were leaving the chore of "leading in the right way" to their Republican friends. Perhaps former Senator Vilas aided his friend Republican Senator John S. Spooner in directing affairs at Washington. In any case these two Wisconsin conservatives went on fishing trips together. A Milwaukee newspaper, on the occasion of one of these forays, pointed out that there was nothing remarkable about their enjoying a vacation together, adding that "both are lawyers of prominence, in fact of national reputation. Both served in . . . the United States Senate. Colonel Spooner courteously retired to give Colonel Vilas an experience of six years, at the end of which time Vilas courteously stood aside while his old friend Spooner stepped in and resumed his former position." [78]

The attitude of editor John P. Irish, who had long been active in Iowa Bourbon politics, was typical of his clan. In 1900 he wrote to a fellow Cleveland worshiper: "As far as I am concerned, this year I will do what I can to add to

[77] H. L. Nelson to William F. Vilas, September 9, 1898, in Vilas MSS.
[78] Statement by Colonel Watrous in the Milwaukee *Telegraph*, undated clipping in "Vilas Scrapbook."

the defeat of Bryan. As far as principle goes the Republican party has adopted Mr. Cleveland's financial ideas and has more than half swallowed his tariff views, so that it represents more of my original Democracy than any other existing party. . . . Mr. Cleveland stands higher than ever. His fame is secure and his countrymen hail him as they greet no other private citizen." [79] A few years later Irish added Woodrow Wilson to his black list of unworthy Democrats, reporting in March, 1913, "For the most part the President's utterances are cryptic, and when otherwise they run in line with magazine literature of the last few years, which has taught that if anybody has to work somebody is to blame for it, and should be punished." [80]

Indeed, after 1896 the post–Civil War Bourbons were not happy with the party of Jefferson, Jackson, Johnson, Altgeld, Bryan, and Wilson. With the advent of New Dealer Roosevelt, their political descendants also found some cause to bemoan. The people were learning.

[79] Irish to Parker, February 14, 1900, in "Letters Written by John P. Irish," *loc. cit.,* 454.
[80] *Id.* to *id.,* March 11, 1913, *ibid.,* 492.

Bibliography

Manuscript Collections

William Allison MSS., in Iowa Department of History and Archives.

Wendall Anderson MSS., in Library of the State Historical Society of Wisconsin.

Grover Cleveland MSS., in Library of Congress.

Ignatius Donnelly MSS., including his diary, in Library of the State Historical Society of Minnesota.

James R. Doolittle MSS., in Library of the State Historical Society of Wisconsin.

Lucius Fairchild MSS., in Library of the State Historical Society of Wisconsin.

W. W. Folwell MSS., in Library of the State Historical Society of Minnesota.

Andrew Johnson MSS., in Library of Congress.

E. W. Keyes MSS., in Library of the State Historical Society of Wisconsin.

Daniel Lamont MSS., in Library of Congress.

Henry Demarest Lloyd MSS., in Library of the State Historical Society of Wisconsin.

George H. Paul MSS., in Library of the State Historical Society of Wisconsin.

Jeremiah M. Rusk MSS., in Library of the State Historical Society of Wisconsin.

H. H. Sibley MSS., in Library of the State Historical Society of Minnesota.

George B. Smith MSS., in Library of the State Historical Society of Wisconsin.

John C. Spooner MSS., in Library of Congress.

E. B. Usher MSS., in Library of the State Historical Society of Wisconsin.

William F. Vilas MSS., including his diary, in Library of the State Historical Society of Wisconsin.

Cyrus Woodman MSS., in Library of the State Historical Society of Wisconsin.

Unpublished Dissertations and Theses

Deutsch, Herman J. "Political Forces in Wisconsin, 1871–1881." Unpublished doctoral dissertation, University of Wisconsin, 1926.

Ganfield, Dorothy. "Peculiar Contribution of Wisconsin to National Politics." Unpublished doctoral dissertation, University of Wisconsin, 1930.

Jones, Virginia Bowen. "The Influence of the Railroads on Nebraska State Politics." Unpublished master's thesis, University of Nebraska, 1927.

Merrill, Horace S. "An Early History of the Black River Falls Region." Unpublished master's thesis, University of Wisconsin, 1933.

Smith, Paul Sydney. "Party Politics in Minnesota, 1865–1871." Unpublished master's thesis, University of Minnesota, 1918.

Wilcox, Benton H. "A Reconsideration of the Character and Economic Basis of Northwest Radicalism." Unpublished doctoral dissertation, University of Wisconsin, 1933.

Government Publications

Annual Report, Secretary of Interior. Washington, 1889–1892.

Congressional Globe. 46 vols. Washington, 1865–1873.

Congressional Record. Washington, 1873–1896.

Official Records of the Union and Confederate Armies in the War of the Rebellion. 31 vols. Washington, 1903–1927.

Select Committee on Indian Traders. (50 Congress, 2 Session, Senate Report No. 2710.) Washington, 1889.

Switzler, William F. *Special Report on Wool and Manufactures of Wool.* (Bureau of Statistics, Treasury Department, Document No. 1025.) Washington, 1888.

Newspapers

Various newspapers of the area covering the period 1865–1896 were used, as were two collections of newspaper clippings, the scrapbooks of William F. Vilas, and James G. Jenkins, located in the Library of the State Historical Society of Wisconsin. Detailed bibliographical information about these sources is to be found in the footnotes.

Articles in Periodicals and Other Publications

Anderson, W. A. "The Granger Movement in the Middle West with Special Reference to Iowa," *Iowa Journal of History and Politics*, XXII (January, 1924), 3–51.

Barnes, James A. "Illinois and the Gold-Silver Controversy, 1890–1896," *Transactions of the Illinois State Historical Society*, 1931 (Springfield, 1931), 35–59.

Beale, Howard K. "Reconstruction," *Encyclopedia of Social Sciences*, ed. Edwin R. A. Seligman (15 vols., New York, 1930–1935), XIII, 168–73.

———. "The Tariff and Reconstruction," *American Historical Review*, XXXV (January, 1930), 276–94.

Calkins, E. A. "General Harrison Carroll Hobart," *Proceedings of the State Historical Society of Wisconsin*, 1902 (Madison, 1902), 148–60.

Cooper, Vernon. "William Boyd Allison," *University of Iowa Studies*, New Series 240, X (1932), 133–45.

Culp, Dorothy. "The Radical Labor Movement, 1873–1895," *Papers in Illinois History*, 1937 (Springfield, 1938), 92–99.

Destler, Chester McA. "The Origin and Character of the Pendleton Plan," *Mississippi Valley Historical Review*, XXIV (September, 1937), 171–84.

Dunning, William A. "More Light on Andrew Johnson," *American Historical Review*, XI (April, 1906), 574–94.

Ellis, Lewis Ethan. "A History of the Chicago Delegation in Congress, 1843–1925," *Transactions of the Illinois State Historical Society*, 1930 (Springfield, 1930), 52–156.

Frankfurter, Felix. "Justice Holmes Defines the Constitution," *Atlantic Monthly*, CLXII (October, 1938), 484–95.

Glazer, Sidney. "Patrons of Industry in Michigan," *Mississippi Valley Historical Review*, XXIV (September, 1937), 185–94.

Greene, Evarts Boutell. "Some Aspects of Politics in the Middle West, 1860–1872," *Proceedings of the State Historical Society of Wisconsin*, 1911 (Madison, 1912), 60–76.

Harmer, Marie U., and Sellers, James L. "Charles H. Van Wyck—Soldier and Statesman," *Nebraska History Magazine*, XII (April–December, 1929), 81–128, 190–246, 322–73.

Hayes, Clara L. "William Penn Lyon," *Wisconsin Magazine of History*, IX (September, 1925–July, 1926), 2–26, 157–71, 251–84.

Hesseltine, William B. "Regions, Classes, and Sections in American History," *Journal of Land and Public Utility Economics*, XX (February, 1944), 35–44.

Hicks, John D. "The Political Career of Ignatius Donnelly," *Mississippi Valley Historical Review*, VIII (June–September, 1921), 80–132.

Hubbart, Henry C. "Pro-Southern Influences in the Free West, 1840–1865," *Mississippi Valley Historical Review*, XX (June, 1933), 45–62.

Jones, Burr W. "William Freeman Vilas," *Proceedings of the State Historical Society of Wisconsin*, 1909 (Madison, 1909), 155–64.

Jordan, H. D. "Daniel Wolsey Vorhees," *Mississippi Valley Historical Review*, VI (March, 1920), 532–55.

[Irish, John P.] "Letters Written by John P. Irish to George F. Parker," *Iowa Journal of History and Politics*, XXXI (July, 1933), 421–512.

Kern, Jean B. "The Political Career of Horace Boies," *Iowa Journal of History*, XLVII (July, 1949), 215–46.

Lloyd, Henry Demarest. "The Story of a Great Monopoly," *Atlantic Monthly*, XLVII (March, 1881), 317–34.

McGrane, Reginald C, "Ohio and the Greenback Movement," *Mississippi Valley Historical Review*, XI (December, 1924), 527–28.

Miller, Samuel F. Letter by Justice Miller, in Frankfurter, Felix, "Justice Holmes Defines the Constitution," *Atlantic Monthly*, CLXII (October, 1938), 468.

Nixon, Herman Clarence. "The Economic Basis of the Populist Movement in Iowa," *Iowa Journal of History and Politics*, XXI (July, 1923), 373–96.

———. "The Populist Movement in Iowa," *Iowa Journal of History and Politics*, XXIV (January, 1926), 3–107.

Pratt, Harry Edward. "David Davis, 1815–1886," *Transactions of the Illinois State Historical Society*, 1930 (Springfield, 1930), 157–83.

Scott, Franklin D. "The Political Career of William R. Morrison," *Transactions of the Illinois State Historical Society*, 1926 (Springfield, 1926), 134–71.

Sellers, James L. "James R. Doolittle," *Wisconsin Magazine of History*, XVII (December, 1933–June, 1934), 168–78, 277–306, 392–401, and XVIII (September–December, 1934), 20–41, 178–87.

Sheldon, Addison E. "Nebraskans I Have Known: 1. William V. Allen," *Nebraska History Magazine*, XIX (July–September, 1938), 191–206.

Shipley, Max L. "The Background and Legal Aspects of the Pendleton Plan," *Mississippi Valley Historical Review*, XXIV (December, 1937), 329–40.

Vilas, William F. "The 'Bennett Law' in Wisconsin," *Forum*, XII (October, 1891), 196–207.

———. "The State of Wisconsin," *Harper's Magazine*, LXXXII (April, 1891), 677–96.

———. "The Threat of the Present Coinage Law," *Forum*, XIII (May, 1892), 285–94.

Whyte, William F. "The Bennett Law Campaign in Wisconsin," *Wisconsin Magazine of History*, X (June, 1927), 363–90.

Wiltse, Herbert. "The Temperance Movement, 1848–1871," *Papers in Illinois History*, 1937 (Springfield, 1938), 82–92.

Wish, Harvey. "John P. Altgeld and the Background of the Campaign of 1896," *Mississippi Valley Historical Review*, XXIV (March, 1938), 503–18.

Pamphlets

Address of the Democrats in Congress to People of the United States, Platform of Wisconsin Democracy, Speeches of James R. Doolittle. (Pamphlet in Library of the State Historical Society of Wisconsin.) N.p., n.d.

Jones, Burr W. "Colonel Vilas and the Law School," pp. 16–18 of *Memorial Services of William Freeman Vilas, October 20, 1908.* Madison, 1908.

Lotham, Henry. *Address at State Fair of Nebraska at Lincoln, September, 1872.* (Nebraska State Board of Agriculture publication, in Library of the State Historical Society of Wisconsin.) Lincoln, 1872.

Morton, J. Sterling. *A Speech Delivered at Nebraska State Fair at Lincoln, September 2, 1873.* (Nebraska State Board of Agriculture publication, in Library of the State Historical Society of Wisconsin.) Lincoln, 1873.

Morton, Oliver P. *Speech . . . at Richmond, Indiana, September 29, 1865.* (Pamphlet in Library of State Historical Society of Wisconsin.) N.p., n.d.

Official Proceedings of the National Democratic Convention, held at New York, July 4–9, 1868. Boston, 1868.

Official Proceedings of the National Democratic Convention, held in Cincinnati, June 22ᵈ, 23ᵈ, 24ᵗʰ, 1880. Dayton, 1882.

White, Horace. *George Smith's Money.* (An address to the American Bankers Association, Chicago, 1893.) New York, 1893.

Books

Adler, Cyrus. *Jacob H. Schiff: His Life and Letters.* 2 vols. New York, 1928.

Appletons' Annual Cyclopaedia and Register of Important Events. 42 vols. New York, 1862–1903.

Arnett, A. M. *The Populist Movement in Georgia.* (*Columbia University Studies in History, Economics and Public Law*, No. 104.) New York, 1922.

Barnard, Harry. *"Eagle Forgotten," The Life of John Peter Altgeld.* New York, 1938.

Barnes, James A. *John G. Carlisle, Financial Statesman.* New York, 1931.

Beale, Howard K. *The Critical Year, A Study of Andrew Johnson and Reconstruction.* New York, 1930.

Beard, Charles A. and Mary R. *A Basic History of the United States.* Philadelphia, 1944.

———. *The Rise of American Civilization.* 2 vols. New York, 1927.

Belmont, Perry. *An American Democrat.* New York, 1940.

Beveridge, Albert J. *Abraham Lincoln, 1809–1858.* 2 vols. Cambridge, 1928.

Binkley, Wilfred E. *American Political Parties, Their Natural History.* New York, 1943.

Blaine, James G. *Twenty Years of Congress.* 2 vols. Norwich, Conn., 1884–1886.

Bogart, E. L., and Mathews, J. M. *The Modern Commonwealth, 1893–1918.* (*Centennial History of Illinois*, ed. Clarence W. Alvord, Vol. V.) Springfield, 1920.

Bogart, E. L., and Thompson, C. M. *The Industrial State,*

1870–1893. (*Centennial History of Illinois*, ed. Clarence W. Alvord, Vol. IV.) Springfield, 1920.

Bowers, Claude G. *The Tragic Era: The Revolution after Lincoln*. New York, 1929.

Brinkerhoff, Roeliff. *Recollections of a Lifetime*. Cincinnati, 1900.

Bryan, William Jennings. *The First Battle: Story of the Campaign of 1896*. Chicago, 1896.

Buck, Solon J. *The Agrarian Crusade*. (*Chronicles of America*, ed. Allen Johnson, Vol. VL.) New Haven, 1921.

———. *The Granger Movement*. Cambridge, 1913.

Clark, Champ. *My Quarter Century of American Politics*. 2 vols. New York, 1920.

Clark, Dan Elbert. *History of Senatorial Elections in Iowa*. Iowa City, 1912.

Clendenin, Henry W. *Autobiography of Henry W. Clendenin*. Springfield, 1926.

Cole, Arthur C. *The Era of the Civil War, 1848–1870*. (*Centennial History of Illinois*, ed. Clarence W. Alvord, Vol. III.) Springfield, 1919.

Cole, Cyrenus. *I Remember, I Remember, A Book of Recollections*. Iowa City, 1936.

Coleman, Charles H. *The Election of 1868*. (*Columbia University Studies in History, Economics and Public Law*, No. 392.) New York, 1933.

Commons, J. R., and others. *History of Labour in the United States*. 4 vols. New York, 1918–1935.

Cullom, Shelby M. *Fifty Years of Public Service*. Chicago, 1911.

Curti, Merle. *The Growth of American Thought*. New York, 1943.

Dean, Henry Clay. *Crimes of the Civil War, and Curse of the Funding System*. Baltimore, 1869.

Depew, Chauncey M. *My Memories of Eighty Years*. New York, 1922.

Destler, Chester McA. *American Radicalism, 1865–1901, Essays and Documents*. (Connecticut College Monograph, No. 3.) New London, 1946.

Dilla, Harriet M. *Politics of Michigan, 1865–1878*. (*Columbia University Studies in History, Economics and Public Law*, No. 118.) New York, 1912.

Durrie, Daniel S. *History of Madison*. Madison, 1874.

Evarts, William Maxwell. *Arguments and Speeches*. New York, 1919.

Flick, Alexander C. *Samuel Jones Tilden, A Study in Political Sagacity*. New York, 1939.

Folwell, W. W. *A History of Minnesota*. 4 vols. St. Paul, 1921–1930.

Ford, Worthington C. (ed.). *The Letters of Henry Adams, 1858–1891*. Boston, 1930.

Foulke, W. D. *Life of Oliver P. Morton*. 2 vols. Indianapolis, 1899.

Gompers, Samuel. *Seventy Years of Life and Labor*. 2 vols. New York, 1925.

Gresham, Mathilda. *Life of Walter Quinton Gresham*. 2 vols. Chicago, 1919.

Hall, Harlan Page. *Observations . . . of Political Contests in Minnesota*. St. Paul, 1904.

Harris, Wilmer C. *The Public Life of Zachariah Chandler, 1851–1875*. Chicago, 1917.

Harrison, Carter Henry. *Stormy Years, The Autobiography of Carter H. Harrison, Five Times Mayor of Chicago*. New York, 1935.

Hayes, Rutherford B. *Diary and Letters of Rutherford Birchard Hayes*, ed. Charles R. Williams. 5 vols. Columbus, 1922–1926.

Haynes, Frederick E. *James Baird Weaver*. Iowa City, 1919.

————. *Third Party Movements Since the Civil War, with Special Reference to Iowa, A Study in Social Politics*. Iowa City, 1916.

Hesseltine, William B. *Ulysses S. Grant, Politician*. New York, 1935.

Hibben, Paxton. *The Peerless Leader, William Jennings Bryan*. New York, 1929.

Hicks, John D. *The Populist Revolt*. Minneapolis, 1931.

Horn, Stanley F. *The Army of Tennessee: A Military History*. New York, 1941.

Hubbart, Henry C. *The Older Middle West, 1840–1880*. New York, 1936.

Hudson, William C. *Random Recollections of an Old Political Reporter*. New York, 1911.

Hutchinson, William T. *Cyrus Hall McCormick*. 2 vols. New York, 1935.

James, Henry. *Richard Olney*. New York, 1923.

Johnson, Allen, and Malone, Dumas (eds.). *Dictionary of American Biography*. 22 vols. New York, 1928–1946.

Johnson, Clarence C. *Giants of Hoosierdom*. Evanston, Ill., 1911.

Johnson, Tom Loftin. *My Story*, ed. Elizabeth J. Hauser. New York, 1911.

Josephson, Matthew. *The Politicos, 1865–1896*. New York, 1938.

La Follette, Robert M. *La Follette's Autobiography: A Personal Narrative of Political Experience*. Madison, 1913.

Lewis, Edwin R. *A History of American Political Thought, From the Civil War to the World War*. New York, 1937.

Locke, David R. (Petroleum V. Nasby, pseud.). *The Impendin Crisis uv the Dimocracy*. Toledo, 1868.

McCormick, Thomas J. (ed.). *Memoirs of Gustave Koerner, 1809–1896*. 2 vols. Cedar Rapids, Iowa, 1909.

McElroy, Robert. *Grover Cleveland, The Man and The Statesman*. 2 vols. New York, 1923.

McGrane, Reginald C. *William Allen, A Study in Western Democracy*. Columbus, 1925.

McPherson, Edward. *Political History of the United States During the Period of Reconstruction*. Washington, 1871.

Milton, George Fort. *The Age of Hate*. New York, 1930.

Minnesota Biographies. (*Collections of Minnesota Historical Society*, Vol. XIV.) St. Paul, 1912.

Mitchell, Stewart. *Horatio Seymour of New York*. Cambridge, 1938.

Moore, Frank. *Life and Speeches of Andrew Johnson*. Boston, 1865.

National Cyclopaedia of American Biography. 34 vols. New York, 1898–1945.

Nevins, Allan. *Abram S. Hewitt*. New York, 1935.

———. *Grover Cleveland, A Study in Courage*. New York, 1934.

———. *Letters of Grover Cleveland, 1850–1908*. New York, 1933.

Noyes, Alexander D. *Thirty Years of American Finance*. New York, 1898.

Oberholtzer, Ellis P. *Jay Cooke, Financier of the Civil War*. 2 vols. Philadelphia, 1907.

Odland, Martin W. *The Life of Knute Nelson.* Minneapolis, 1926.

Olson, James C. *J. Sterling Morton.* Lincoln, 1942.

Oval, Charles J. *Governors of Indiana.* Indianapolis, 1916.

Parker, George Frederick. *Recollections of Grover Cleveland.* New York, 1909.

Parrington, Vernon L. *Main Currents in American Thought.* 3 vols. New York, 1927–1930.

Payne, Charles E. *Joshiah Bushnell Grinnell.* Iowa City, 1938.

Perlman, Selig. *A History of Trade Unionism in the United States.* New York, 1922.

Plumb, Ralph Gordon. *Badger Politics, 1836–1930.* Manitowoc, Wis., 1930.

Pyle, Joseph G. *The Life of James J. Hill.* 2 vols. Garden City, 1917.

Pyre, J. F. A. *Wisconsin.* New York, 1920.

Randall, James G. *The Civil War and Reconstruction.* Boston, 1937.

Randall, John Herman. *The Making of the Modern Mind.* Boston, 1940.

Richardson, James D. *A Compilation of the Messages and Papers of the Presidents, 1789–1897.* 8 vols. Washington, 1897.

Roseboom, Eugene H. *The Civil War Era, 1850–1873.* (*The State of Ohio*, ed. Carl Wittke, Vol. IV.) Columbus, 1944.

Shannon, Fred A. *The Farmer's Last Frontier, Agriculture, 1860–1897.* (*Economic History of the United States,* Vol. V.) New York, 1945.

Smalley, Eugene V. *A History of the Republican Party . . . of Minnesota.* St. Paul, 1896.

Smith, Theodore C. *Life and Letters of James A. Garfield.* 2 vols. New Haven, 1925.

Stealey, O. O. *Twenty Years in the Press Gallery.* New York, 1906.

Steffens, Joseph Lincoln. *Autobiography of Lincoln Steffens.* 2 vols. New York, 1931.

Stephenson, George M. *John Lind of Minnesota.* Minneapolis, 1935.

Stephenson, Nathaniel Wright. *Nelson W. Aldrich—A Leader in American Politics.* New York, 1930.

Thomas, Harrison Cook. *The Return of the Democratic Party to Power in 1884.* (*Columbia University Studies in His-*

tory, Economics and Public Law, No. 203.) New York, 1919.

Thomson, Alexander M. *A Political History of Wisconsin*. Milwaukee, 1902.

Vilas, William F. *Selected Addresses and Orations of William F. Vilas*. Madison, 1912.

Watterson, Henry. *"Marse Henry," An Autobiography*. 2 vols. New York, 1919.

Welles, Gideon. *Diary of Gideon Welles*. 2 vols. Boston, 1911.

Wesley, Edgar Bruce. *Owatonna, The Social Development of a Minnesota Community*. Minneapolis, 1938.

Wheeler, Everett P. *Sixty Years of American Life*. New York, 1917.

White, Horace. *Money and Banking, Illustrated by American History*. Boston, 1896.

Wight, William W. *Henry Clay Payne, A Life*, Milwaukee, 1907.

Williams, Charles R. *The Life of Rutherford Birchard Hayes, Nineteenth President of the United States*. 2 vols. Boston, 1914.

Zink, Harold. *City Bosses in the United States, A Study of Twenty Municipal Bosses*. Durham, 1930.

Index